The *Revels*
History of Drama
in English

GENERAL EDITOR

T. W. Craik

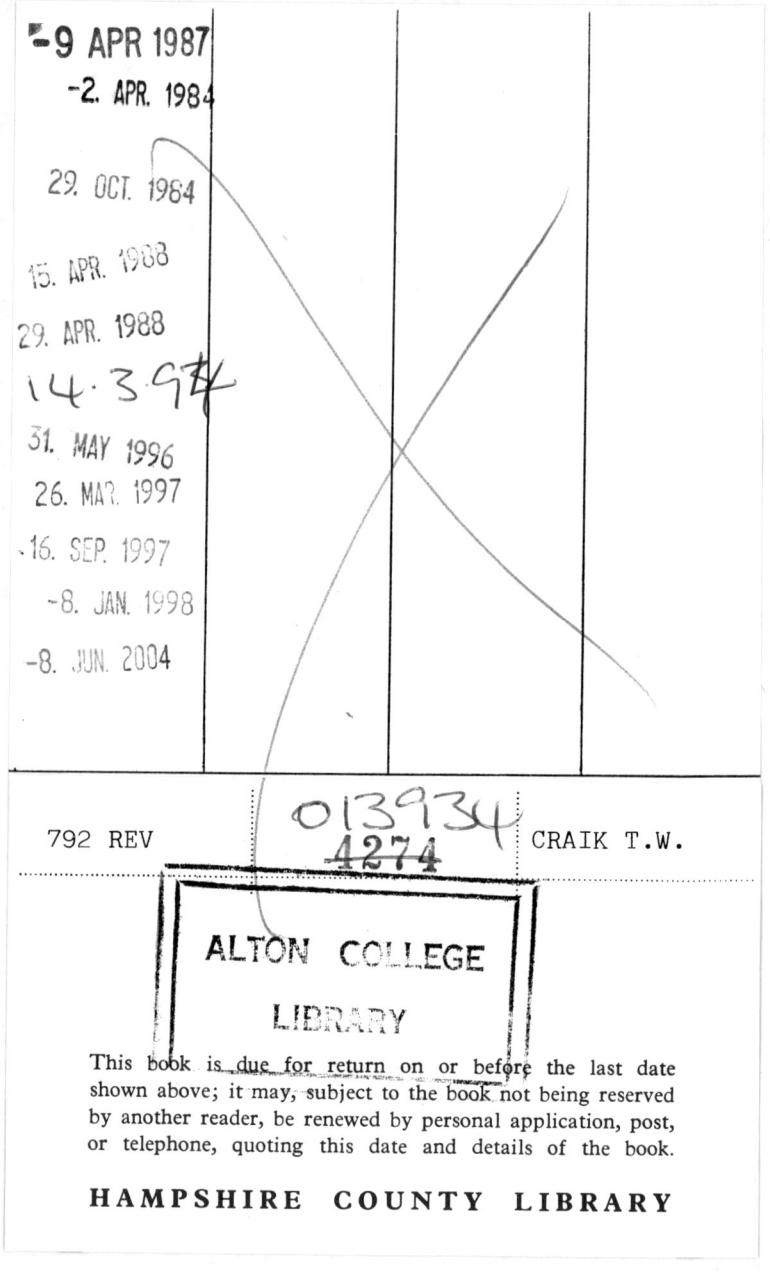

HAMPSHIRE COUNTY LIBRARY

The *Revels* History of Drama in English

VOLUME II   1500–1576

Norman Sanders,
Richard Southern,
T. W. Craik
& Lois Potter

Methuen
London and New York

First published in 1980 by
Methuen & Co. Ltd
11 New Fetter Lane, London EC4P 4EE
Published in the USA by
Methuen & Co.
in association with Methuen, Inc.
733 Third Avenue, New York, NY 10017

© *1980 Norman Sanders, Richard Southern,*
T. W. Craik, Lois Potter

Filmset by
Northumberland Press Ltd
Gateshead, Tyne and Wear
Printed in Great Britain by
Fletcher & Son Ltd, Norwich

British Library Cataloguing in Publication Data
The Revels history of drama in English.
  Vol. 2: 1500–1576
  1. English drama – History and criticism
  2. Theater – England – History
  I. Sanders, Norman
  822'.009   PR625   75–321425
  ISBN 0–416–13030–5

Contents

List of Illustrations

Acknowledgements

The authors and publishers would like to thank the following for permission to reproduce the illustrations appearing in this book:

Museum Boymans-van Beuningen, Rotterdam for No. 7
The British Library for Nos 3, 8, 10, 11, 12, 15, 16a, 16b and 17
The Syndics of Cambridge University Library for No. 9
His Grace the Archbishop of Canterbury and the Trustees of the Lambeth Palace Library for Nos 5 and 14
Faber and Faber Limited for No. 2 (from *The Staging of Plays before Shakespeare* by Richard Southern)
The Fitzwilliam Museum, Cambridge for No. 6
The Controller of Her Majesty's Stationery Office for No. 1 (Crown Copyright)
The National Portrait Gallery for No. 13
The Master and Fellows of Trinity College Cambridge for No. 4

Preface

The devoting of a volume of *The Revels History of Drama in English* to the period from 1500 to 1576 may require some explanation – though, I am sure, less than would have been required at the beginning of this century. This period forms a transition between the heyday of the miracle cycles and the early moralities on the one hand and, on the other hand, the beginnings of the dramatic age which is usually called Elizabethan. The drama of this transitional period has received much attention in the present century, and is now seen to have exercised a complex and important influence on that of the more famous period which followed. Volume II of the *Revels History* is an attempt to draw together as many aspects of that influence as possible, to show how the plays are related to the circumstances in which they arose, and to convey the quality of the plays themselves, many of which have during the past few years had their first stage performances since their own time: Medwall, Skelton, Heywood, Redford, Bale, Lindsay, Udall, Sackville and Norton, Preston, the Wagers, besides the anonymous authors of *Jack Juggler*, *Nice Wanton*, *Gammer Gurton's Needle* and several other plays, have all been brought back to dramatic life in this way.

The pattern of the volume follows that of those already published in the *Revels History* series. Sections on the social and political context of the drama and on the staging and the actors lead up to the longest section, a critical survey of the plays. I am particularly grateful to Dr Lois Potter for undertaking this section after the contributor originally commissioned to write it had withdrawn. I must also thank our fellow contributors for fulfilling their contracts and for patiently enduring the unavoidable delay in bringing out the volume. Dr Southern's section, in its original form, preceded by some five years his full-length treatment of the same topic in *The Staging of Plays Before Shakespeare*; he has revised and enlarged it since his book appeared. For helping me compile the Chronological Table and assemble the illustrations I am grateful to the contributors, to Dr O. Durrani, Dr D. M. Loades and Dr Ann Moss (all of the University of Durham), and to Jane Armstrong of Methuen. Linden Stafford has been, as always, a vigilant and acute copy-editor. The index compiled by Edwina Welham, has been checked in proof by me.

With this volume I end my part in the general editing of the *Revels History*, which I undertook at the request of the late Professor Clifford Leech in 1972. The remaining two volumes I leave, with gratitude and every confidence, to Dr Potter.

T. W. Craik

Chronological table

This table draws freely on those in the relevant volumes in *The Oxford History of English Literature* and on Samuel Schoenbaum's revision of Alfred Harbage's *Annals of English Drama 975–1700* (London, 1964). For plays, the Harbage–Schoenbaum date is given, with one or two exceptions, even when the present general editor feels dubious.

Non-dramatic writings are listed under the date of publication, unless otherwise indicated, and plays under the date of first performance (or, in the case of plays not performed, the date of composition).

A question mark after an entry indicates a doubt about the date; a question mark before an author's name indicates a doubt about the authorship.

Date	Historical events	Theatrical events	Non-dramatic literary events
1495			
1496			
1497	Vasco da Gama rounds Cape of Good Hope		
1498	Cabot discovers Labrador; Vasco da Gama reaches India; Columbus reaches South America; Savonarola burned		
1499	Perkin Warbeck and Earl of Warwick executed		
1500			Erasmus, *Adagia*; Skelton, *Bowge of Court*; De Rojas, *Celestina*?
1501	Prince Arthur m. Katherine of Aragon		Sannazaro, *Arcadia*
1502	Prince Arthur d.		
1503	Alexander VI d.; Pius III succeeds and d.; Julius II succeeds; James IV of Scotland m. Princess Margaret; Prince Henry betróthed to Katherine of Aragon		Erasmus, *Enchiridion*
1504	Colet becomes Dean of St Paul's		
1505			
1506	Treaty with Burgundy		Erasmus and More (trans.), Lucian's *Dialogues* (Latin)
1507			

Birth and death dates of non-dramatic writers	Dates of notable plays	Birth and death dates of playwrights	Continental theatrical events
Rabelais b.?	Anon., *Everyman?*; Medwall, *Nature?*	Bale b.	Anon., *Elckerlijk?*
Marot b.	Medwall, *Fulgens and Lucrece?*	Heywood b. (d. 1578)	
			Cammelli, *Filostrato e Panfila*
Henryson d.?			
Wyatt b.			
Cinthio b.; Parker b.			
Knox b.		Udall b.?	
Leland b.?		Buchanan b.	Erasmus, *Hecuba, Iphigenia in Aulis* (Latin trans. of Euripides, printed in Paris)
			N. de La Chesnaye, *La Condamnation des bancquets*

Date	Historical events	Theatrical events	Non-dramatic literary events
1508			Dunbar, *Poems*
1509	Henry VII d.; Henry VIII succeeds, m. Katherine of Aragon	Cornish becomes master of Chapel Children	Barclay, *Ship of Fools*; Hawes, *Pastime of Pleasure*; Erasmus, *Moriae Encomium* (*Praise of Folly*)
1510	Colet founds St Paul's School		Anon., *Cock Lorell's Boat*
1511	Henry VIII joins Holy League; Erasmus becomes Reader in Greek at Cambridge (till 1514)		
1512			
1513	Julius II d.; Leo X succeeds; Henry VIII invades France; Battle of Flodden, James IV d., James V succeeds		Anon., *Flowers of Ovid* (trans. *Ars Amatoria*); Lydgate (d. 1450?), *Troy Book*; Skelton, *Ballad of the Scottish King*; Machiavelli, *Il Principe* (written)
1514	Wolsey becomes Archbishop of York; Richard Hunne 'affair'		
1515	Wolsey becomes Cardinal; Act against Enclosures; Battle of Marignano		*Epistolae Obscurorum Virorum*; Barclay, *Eclogues*, I–III
1516			Fabyan, *Chronicle*; Ariosto, *Orlando furioso*; Erasmus, *Novum Instrumentum*; More, *Utopia*

Birth and death dates of non-dramatic writers	Dates of notable plays	Birth and death dates of playwrights	Continental theatrical events
	Anon., *Mundus et Infans* (*The World and the Child*)?		Ariosto, *La Cassaria*; Dolce b.
Calvin b.			Ariosto, *I Suppositi*; Macropedius, *Asotus* (written)
			Guild performances at Paris of Gringore, *Saint Louis* and *Jeu du prince des sots*; Gringore, *Sottie contre le Pape Jules II*
Mantuan d.	Anon., *Hickscorner*?		Bibbiena, *La Calandria*
Cheke b.; Poynet b.			
Ascham b.; Ramus b.	Skelton, *Magnificence*?	Watson b.?	First of many edicts from the Paris Parlement during the reign of François I aimed at restricting satirical plays, particularly the *sotties* of the Basoche (students and associates of the law schools)

Date	Historical events	Theatrical events	Non-dramatic literary events
1517	Luther publishes Wittenberg theses		
1518	Wolsey becomes *legatus a latere*; Treaty of London		Erasmus, *Colloquia*
1519	Cortes invades Mexico; Magellan begins voyage round the world (till 1520); Emperor Maximilian dies; Charles I of Spain becomes Emperor Charles V		
1520	Field of the Cloth of Gold; Leo X grants title of *Fidei Defensor* to Henry VIII, commands burning of Luther's books; Luther's three 'reformation treatises'		Henry VIII, *Assertio VII Sacramentorum*; Luther, *Von der Freiheit*
1521	Diet of Worms; Luther placed under papal ban		Barclay, *Eclogues*, IV–V; Skelton, *Speak, Parrot* (written)
1522	Leo X d.; Adrian VI succeeds; Charles V visits England	'Friendship, Prudence and Might (The Triumph of Amity)' acted before Charles V at court	Luther (trans.) *New Testament*; Vives, edn of St Augustine's *De Civitate Dei*
1523	Adrian VI d.; Clement VII succeeds		Barclay, *Mirror of Good Manners*; Berners (trans.), Froissart's *Chronicles*, I; Skelton, *Garland of Laurel*
1524			Anon. (trans.), *Gesta Romanorum*; Sachs, *Prose dialogues*
1525	Battle of Pavia		Berners (trans.), Froissart's *Chronicles*, II; Tyndale (trans.), *New Testament*

Birth and death dates of non-dramatic writers	Dates of notable plays	Birth and death dates of playwrights	Continental theatrical events
Cooper b.?; Foxe b.; Surrey b.	Rastell, *The Four Elements?*		
Crowley b.			
Colet d.; Beza b.	Heywood, *The Pardoner and the Friar?*	Grimald b.?	
Churchyard b.	Heywood, *Johan Johan?*, *The Four PP?*; anon., *John the Evangelist?*; anon., *Youth?*		Machiavelli, *Mandragola*
Brant d.; Dunbar d.?			
Douglas d.; Reuchlin d.; Du Bellay b.; Jewel b.			
Hawes d.? Ulrich von Hutten d.		Cornish d.	
Linacre d.; Ronsard b.; Camoens b.; Tusser b.?		Edwards b.	
Stow b.?; T. Wilson b.?			Machiavelli, *Clizia*

Date	Historical events	Theatrical events	Non-dramatic literary events
1526	Pizarro conquers Peru; English New Testaments prohibited and burned; English Protestants persecuted (till 1527)	'Lord Governance and Lady Public Weal' at Gray's Inn angers Wolsey	Anon., *Hundred Merry Tales*; Tyndale, *Prologue to Romans*; Boece, *Historia Scotorum*
1527	Sack of Rome	'The Heretic Luther (The Deliverance of the Pope)' acted in Latin before French ambassadors at court (by St Paul's Grammar School?)	Colet, *Aeditio;* Vida, *De Arte Poetica*
1528	Execution of Patrick Hamilton and beginning of Reformation in Scotland; Wolsey suppresses some smaller religious houses	'Religion, Peace and Justice' acted at Wolsey's house	Fisher, *Sermon at Paul's Concerning Certain Heretics*; Roy, *Read Me and Be Not Wroth*; Tyndale, *Wicked Mammon, Obedience of a Christian Man*; Castiglione, *Il Cortegiano*
1529	Fall of Wolsey; rise of Thomas Cromwell; More becomes Chancellor; Colloquy of Marburg; Luther and Zwingli disagree		Fish, *Supplication for the Beggars*; More, *Supplication of Souls*; Rastell, *Pastime of People*
1530	Wolsey d.; Diet of Augsburg	Henry VIII and gentlemen go as masquers to banquet at Wolsey's house	Colet, *Sermon made to the Convocation at Paul's*; Rastell, *New Book of Purgatory*
1531	Zwingli d.; Formation of the Schmalkaldic League	Redford becomes master of Paul's Boys	Elyot, *Governor*; Tyndale, *Answer to More*
1532	Henry VIII divorces Katherine of Aragon; More resigns chancellorship; Cromwell becomes Principal Secretary		Thynne (ed.), Chaucer's *Works* (incl. Henryson's *Testament of Cresseid*, etc.); Rabelais, *Pantagruel*, I; Machiavelli, *Il Principe*

Birth and death dates of non-dramatic writers	Dates of notable plays	Birth and death dates of playwrights	Continental theatrical events
Machiavelli d.	?Rastell, *Calisto and Melebea*?, ?Rastell, *Gentleness and Nobility*?; anon., *Godly Queen Hester*?		Sachs, *Lucretia*; Machiavelli d.
	Heywood, *The Play of the Weather*?		Ariosto, *La Lena*; Ariosto, *Negromante*
Castiglione d.; Skelton d.		Skelton d.	Gnaphaeus, *Acolastus*
Fish d.; Sannazaro d.; Hoby b.; Mulcaster b.?		Farrant b.?	Textor, *Dialogi*; Marguerite de Navarre, *La Nativité de Jésus-Christ*, *L'Adoration des trois rois*, *Les Innocents*, *Le Désert*
Zwingli d.			Intronati (Sienese society of noble amateur author-actors), *Gl'Ingannati*
Allen b.		Norton b.	Monologue of *Le Franc-Archier de Bagnolet*

Date	Historical events	Theatrical events	Non-dramatic literary events
1533	Cranmer becomes Archbishop of Canterbury; Henry VIII excommunicated, m. Ann Boleyn; Frith burned		More, *Apology*; Tyndale, *Treatise of the Sacraments*; Udall, *Flowers for Latin Speaking*
1534	Clement VII d.; Paul III succeeds; Acts of Succession and Supremacy; John Leland's antiquarian tour of England begins (to 1543)	Udall headmaster of Eton	Starkey, *Dialogue between Pole and Lupset* (written); Whytington (trans.), *Three Books of Tully's Offices*; Polydore Vergil, *Historia Anglica*
1535	Henry VIII assumes title of 'Supreme Head' of Church in England; Cromwell's visitation of the monasteries; More and Fisher executed	Lord Mayor's Show becomes customary in London	Berners (trans.), *Golden Book of Marcus Aurelius*; Coverdale (trans.), *Bible*; Abrabanel (Leone Ebreo), *Dialoghi di Amore*
1536	Ann Boleyn executed; Henry VIII m. Jane Seymour; suppression of monasteries begins (to 1539); Pilgrimage of Grace; Calvin's *Institutio* published; Tyndale executed in Netherlands; Calvin detained by Farel in Geneva; Erasmus d.		?Cheke, *Remedy for Sedition*; Calvin, *Institutio*
1537	Confession de la Foi de Genève; Jane Seymour d.	Udall's Eton boys act before Cromwell	Cranmer, *Institution of a Christian Man*
1538	James V of Scotland m. Marie de Guise; English Bible ordered to be placed in all English churches; Anabaptists persecuted; Calvin expelled from Geneva	Ralph Radcliffe begins plays at Hitchin School	Elyot, *Latin–English Dictionary*; Lindsay, *Complaint of the Papyngo*

Birth and death dates of non-dramatic writers	Dates of notable plays	Birth and death dates of playwrights	Continental theatrical events
Ariosto d.; Berners d.; Frith d.; Montaigne b.	Heywood, *Love?*, *Witty and Witless?*		Malingre, *Moralité de la maladie de Chrestienté*; Ariosto d.
Cornelius Agrippa d.; Cartwright b.; North b.	Anon., *Temperance and Humility?*	Legge b.	Marguerite de Navarre, *Le Malade*
Erasmus d.; Rastell d.; Tyndale d.; Golding b.; Sackville b.		Rastell d.; Sackville b.	Marguerite de Navarre, *L'Inquisiteur*; Macropedius, *Rebelles*; Rebhun, *Susanna*
Murner d.	Anon., *Albion Knight?*; anon., *Thersites*	Preston b.?	Kirchmayer, *Pammachius*; Macropedius, *Asotus* printed
Starkey d.; Guarini b.; Reginald Scot b.?	Bale, *God's Promises*, *John the Baptist's Preaching in the Wilderness*, *The Temptation of Our Lord*, *Three Laws*, *King John*		First permanent theatre established at Lyon

Date	Historical events	Theatrical events	Non-dramatic literary events
1539	Six Articles Act against heresy	Bale's *King John* at Cranmer's house in Canterbury	*The Great Bible* ('Cranmer's Bible'); Taverner (trans.), *Bible*
1540	Jesuit Order founded; fall and execution of Cromwell; Henry VIII m. Ann of Cleves (marriage annulled); m. Katherine Howard	Original version of Lindsay's *Satire of the Three Estates* acted before Scottish court at Linlithgow; Wedderburn's Protestant plays acted at Dundee	Douglas, *Palace of Honour*?; Palsgrave (trans.), Gnaphaeus's *Acolastus*
1541	Colloquy of Ratisbon; Calvin recalled to Geneva		
1542	War with Scotland (to 1560); Katherine Howard executed; James V d., Mary Queen of Scots b. and succeeds; founding of the Roman Inquisition		Lyly, *Introduction to the VIII Parts of Speech* ('Lyly's Latin Grammar'); Hall, *Union of the Families of Lancaster and York*?; Udall (trans.), Erasmus's *Apophthegms*
1543	Mary Queen of Scots betrothed to the Dauphin, taken to France; Henry VIII m. Katherine Parr; Act 'for the Advancement of True Religion' against unauthorized translations of Bible; Copernicus's *De Revolutionibus* explains solar system	Act of Parliament forbids plays meddling with religious doctrine	Harding, *Chronicle* (includes More's *History of Richard III*); Copernicus, *De Revolutionibus*
1544	Henry VIII at war with France; Boulogne captured		Bale, *Brief Chronicle concerning Sir John Oldcastle*; Leland, *Assertio ... Arturii Regis Britanniae*

Birth and death dates of non-dramatic writers	Dates of notable plays	Birth and death dates of playwrights	Continental theatrical events
Fenton b.?; Gascoigne b.?	Redford, *Wit and Science?*	Gascoigne b.?	School performances at Bordeaux of Buchanan, *Baptistes, Jephthes* and *Alcestis* (Latin trans. of Euripides) (to 1544)
Vives d.; Googe b.; Painter b.; Turberville b.?	Grimald, *Christus Redivivus* (Latin)?; Watson, *Absalon* (Latin)?		Wickram, *Der verlorene Sohn*; various neoclassical authors, *Comoediae et Tragoediae* (printed by Brylinger)
			Performance of *Actes des apôtres* by the Confrères de la Passion (amateur, guild actors) at Paris at the Hôtel de Flandres; Cinthio, *Orbecche*; Kirchmayer, *Pammachius*, Part 2
Wyatt d.; Bellarmine b.; Rich b.?	Anon., *The Four Cardinal Virtues?*		Marguerite de Navarre, *Comédie des quatre femmes*, performed by ladies of the court for the king
Copernicus d.; Deloney b.?; Du Bartas b.; Baptista Porta b.			
Marot d.; Tasso b.; Whetstone b.?			Marguerite de Navarre, *Trop, Prou, Peu, Moins*

Date	Historical events	Theatrical events	Non-dramatic literary events
1545	Council of Trent meets	Kirchmayer's *Pamachius*, acted at Christ's College, Cambridge, causes Gardiner to complain to Vice-Chancellor; first permanent Master of Revels appointed	Ascham, *Toxophilus*; *The King's Primer* (includes Cranmer's *Litany*); Skelton, *Philip Sparrow*, etc.
1546	Cardinal Beaton murdered at St Andrews; end of French War; Luther d.		Bale, *Acts of English Votaries*; Heywood, *Dialogue of Proverbs*, I
1547	Henry VIII d.; Edward VI succeeds; Surrey executed; Somerset becomes Protector; chantries suppressed; Battle of Mühlberg; Council of Trent breaks up	Anti-Catholic plays mark Edward VI's coronation festivities; Act of 1543 repealed; Westcott becomes master of Paul's Boys	Cranmer and others, *Certain Sermons or Homilies*; Sternhold and Hopkins, *Psalms*, I; Dedekind, *Grobianus*
1548			Bale, *Illustrium Majoris Britanniae Scriptorum Summarium* (= *Catalogus*, = *Scriptores*); Latimer, '*Plough*' Sermon
1549	Paul III d.; war with France (to 1550); Kett's rebellion; Act of Uniformity; *Consensus Tigurinus*; First *Book of Common Prayer*	Kett's rebellion solicits support from audience gathered to see annual play at Wymondham near Norwich; all English plays banned for two months	*Book of Common Prayer*; Challoner (trans.), Erasmus's *Praise of Folly*; Cheke, *Hurt of Sedition*; Leland, *Journey and Search for England's Antiquities*; Wyatt, *Psalms*; Du Bellay, *Défense de la langue française*
1550	Julius III succeeds; Catholic bishops removed in England		Crowley, *One and Thirty Epigrams*; Ronsard, *Odes*, I–IV; Vasari, *Lives of the Painters* (to 1578)
1551	Council of Trent meets again	Royal Proclamation requires all professional acting companies to be licensed	Robinson (trans.), More's *Utopia*

Birth and death dates of non-dramatic writers	Dates of notable plays	Birth and death dates of playwrights	Continental theatrical events
Harvey b.?	Anon., *The Resurrection of Our Lord*?		School performance of Muret, *Julius Caesar*, at Bordeaux
Brinkelow d.; Elyot d.; Fischart d.; Luther d.; Desportes b.			
Bembo d.; Copland d.; E. Hall d.; Cervantes b.; Stanyhurst b.	Grimald, *Archipropheta* (Latin)?; anon., *Impatient Poverty*?	Redford d.	Dolce, *Didone*; various neoclassical authors, *Comoediae et Tragoediae* (printed by Oporinus)
Bruno b.; Pettie b.			The Confrères de la Passion erect a theatre at the Hôtel de Bourgogne
Giles Fletcher, Sr, b.?			Dolce, *Giocasta*
Trissino d.	Wever, *Lusty Juventus*?; anon., *Love Feigned and Unfeigned*?; anon., *Nice Wanton*?; anon., *Somebody, Avarice and Minister*?	Woodes b.?	De Bèze, *Abraham sacrifiant*
Bucer d.; Breton b.?; Camden b.			

Date	Historical events	Theatrical events	Non-dramatic literary events
1552	Somerset executed; Second Act of Uniformity; Second *Book of Common Prayer*	*Troas*, first of Seneca's plays acted in England, at Trinty College, Cambridge	Second *Book of Common Prayer*
1553	Forty-Two Articles; Edward VI d.; Mary succeeds	Bale's anti-Catholic trilogy (*Gods Promises, John the Baptist's Preaching, Temptation of Our Lord*) acted at Kilkenny; *Anglia Deformata et Anglia Restituta* acted at Trinity College, Cambridge; renewal of ban on doctrinal plays	More (d. 1535), *Dialogue of Comfort*; Wilson, *Art of Rhetoric*; ?Mendoza, *Lazarillo de Tormes*
1554	Sir Thomas Wyatt's rebellion; Lady Jane Grey executed; Mary m. Philip of Spain; England reconciled with Rome; Knox meets Calvin at Geneva; Reginald Pole becomes Cardinal Legate in England	Lindsay's *Satire of the Three Estates*, final version, acted at Calton Hill, Edinburgh, before Marie de Guise, nobles and public	Lindsay, *Dialogue betwixt Experience and ane Courtier*; Lydgate (d. 1450), *Dance of Death*; Bandello, *Novelle*, I–III
1555	Julius III d.; Paul IV succeeds; Latimer and Ridley burned; religious peace of Augsburg	Udall headmaster of Westminster School	Baldwin (ed.), *Mirror for Magistrates* (suppressed); Heywood, *Two Hundred Epigrams*; Wickram, *Rollwagen-Büchlein*
1556	Cranmer burned; war between Philip and the Pope	Seditious plays against Philip and Mary performed by Sir Francis Leke's company	Heywood, *Spider and the Fly*
1557	War with France (to 1559); victory of St Quentin; Pole's legatine commission withdrawn	Seditious plays in Kent	Bale, *Catalogus* (enlarged); More, *English Works*; North (trans.), Guevara's *Dial of Princes*; Surrey (trans.), Virgil's *Aeneid*, II, IV; Tottel (ed.), *Songs and Sonnets* ('Tottel's Miscellany'); Tusser, *Hundred Good Points of Husbandry*

Birth and death dates of non-dramatic writers	Dates of notable plays	Birth and death dates of playwrights	Continental theatrical events
Barclay d.; Holland b.; Ralegh b.?; Spenser b.	Lindsay, *Satire of the Three Estates*; Udall, *Ralph Roister Doister*?		
Rabelais d.; Hakluyt b.; Munday b.	'Mr S.', *Gammer Gurton's Needle*?; anon., *Respublica*	Munday b.	
Gosson b.; Greville b.; Hooker b.; Lyly b.?; Sidney b.	Anon., *Jacob and Esau*?; anon., *Wealth and Health*?	Lyly b.?	Jodelle, *Cléopâtre captive* and *La Rencontre*, performed at Paris, at the court and at the Collège de Boncourt (the parts were taken by Jodelle's poet friends); Sachs, *Die ungleichen Kinder Evae, Tristrant und Isalden*
Lindsay d.; Polydore Vergil d.; Andrewes b.; Malherbe b.	Anon., *Jack Juggler*?	Gager b.; Lindsay d.	
Aretino d.; Poynet d.; Udall d.		Udall d.; Peele b.	
T. Watson b.		Kyd b.?	Sachs, *Der hürnen Sewfried*

Date	Historical events	Theatrical events	Non-dramatic literary events
1558	Loss of Calais; Mary d.; Elizabeth I succeeds		Knox, *First Blast of the Trumpet against the Monstrous Regiment of Women*; Phaer (trans.), Virgil's *Aeneid*, I–IV
1559	Paul IV d.; Pius IV succeeds; Knox returns to Scotland, where revolution begins; Third Act of Uniformity and Act of Supremacy; Parker becomes Archbishop of Canterbury; Peace of Cateau-Cambrésis	Renewed governmental prohibition of plays of religious controversy	Third *Book of Common Prayer*; Bullein, *Government of Health*; Baldwin (ed.), *Mirror for Magistrates*; Du Bellay, *Regrets*; Marguerite de Navarre, *Heptaméron*
1560	Treaty of Edinburgh; French expelled from Scotland	Westcott begins regular court performances with Paul's Boys	Whittingham and others, *Geneva Bible*
1561	O'Neill's rebellion in Ireland	Thomas Ashton becomes headmaster of Shrewsbury School, begins annual open-air religious plays there	Hoby (trans.), Castiglione's *The Courtier*; Norton (trans.), Calvin's *Institution of Christian Religion*; Scaliger, *Poetice*
1562	Council of Trent meets again; civil war in France	*Gorboduc* first performed at Inner Temple, then acted at court before Elizabeth I	Brooke, *Romeus and Juliet*; Heywood, *Works* (Proverbs and Epigrams); Jewel, *Apologia pro Ecclesia Anglicana*; Sternhold and Hopkins, *Whole Book of Psalms*
1563	Thirty-Nine Articles of Religion; first Poor Law; *Index Librorum Prohibitorum* instituted		Foxe, *Acts and Monuments* (= Foxe's Book of Martyrs); Googe, *Eclogues, Epitaphs and Sonnets*

Birth and death dates of non-dramatic writers	Dates of notable plays	Birth and death dates of playwrights	Continental theatrical events
Scaliger d.; Perkins b.; Warner b.?	Bale, *King John* (revised version)?; L. Wager, *The Life and Repentance of Mary Magdalene?*	Greene b.; Lodge b.	Performance of Roze, *Antonius et Cleopatra*, at the Collège de Navarre
	Jasper Heywood (trans.), Seneca's *Troas*; W. Wager, *The Longer Thou Livest the More Fool Thou Art?*	Chapman b.?	
Melanchthon d.	Jasper Heywood (trans.), Seneca's *Thyestes*; Ingelend, *The Disobedient Child?*; W. Wager, *Enough is as Good as a Feast?*; anon., *The Pedlar's Prophecy?*; anon., *Tom Tyler and his Wife?*	Chettle b.?	
Bacon b.; Harington b.?; Sandys b.; Southwell b.	Jasper Heywood (trans.), Seneca's *Hercules furens*; Preston, *Cambises?*		Badius, *Comédie du pape malade*; Grazzini, *La Spiritata*
Bandello d.; Montemayor d.; Wickram d.?; Constable b.	Norton and Sackville, *Gorboduc*	Grimald d.	Lope de Vega b.
Brooke d.; Daniel b.?; Drayton b.; Sylvester b.	Nevyle (trans.), Seneca's *Oedipus*	Bale d.	

Date	Historical events	Theatrical events	Non-dramatic literary events
1564	Calvin d.	Elizabeth I visits Cambridge, sees Plautus' *Aulularia*, Haliwell's *Dido* (Latin), Udall's *Ezechias*, in King's College Chapel	*Scots Psalter*; Bullein, *Dialogue against the Fever Pestilence*
1565			Allen, *Defence and Declaration*; Cooper, *Thesaurus* (English–Latin dictionary); Golding (trans.), Ovid's *Metamorphoses*, I–IV; Stow, *Summary of English Chronicles*; Cinthio, *Hecatommithi*
1566	Pius IV d.; Pius V succeeds; Gowrie conspiracy; revolt in the Netherlands	Elizabeth I visits Oxford, sees *Marcus Geminus* (Latin), Calfhill's *Progne* (Latin), Edwards's *Palamon and Arcite*, in Christ Church hall; Richard Farrant begins annual court play with Windsor Chapel Children	Adlington (trans.), Apuleius's *The Golden Ass*; Painter, *Palace of Pleasure*, I; Luther, *Tischreden*
1567	Duke of Alva in the Netherlands; the 'Council of Blood'		Drant (trans.), Horace's *Art of Poetry, Epistles, Satires*; Fenton (trans.), Bandello's *Tragical Discourses*; Painter, *Palace of Pleasure*, II; Paynell (trans.), anon., *Amadis of France*; Turberville, *Epitaphs, Epigrams, Songs and Sonnets*; Wedderburns, *Gude and Godlie Ballatis*
1568	English College, Douai, founded; flight of Mary Queen of Scots to England		Parker and others, *Bishops' Bible*; Lindsay, *Works*; Skelton, *Works*
1569	Rising in the North against Elizabeth	Last performance of York miracle cycle	Newton (trans.), Cicero's *De Senectute*; Underdowne (trans.), Heliodorus' *Ethiopian History*

Birth and death dates of non-dramatic writers	Dates of notable plays	Birth and death dates of playwrights	Continental theatrical events
Calvin d.	'R.B.', *Apius and Virginia*?; Jeffere, *The Bugbears*?	Marlowe b.; Shakespeare b.	
	Edwards, *Damon and Pithias*; W. or L. Wager, *The Cruel Debtor*?; anon., *King Darius*		
Hoby d.; Vida d.	Gascoigne and Kinwelmershe, *Jocasta*; Gascoigne, *The Supposes*; Nuce (trans.), Seneca's *Octavia*; Studley (trans.), Seneca's *Agamemnon* and *Medea*; Wilmot, *Gismond of Salerne*?	Edwards d.	Dolce, *Tragedie* (published)
Campion b.	Pickering, *Horestes*?; W. Wager, *The Trial of Treasure*?; anon., *Liberality and Prodigality*?	Nashe b.	
Ascham d.; Coverdale d.; Markham b.?; Wotton b.	Fulwell, *Like Will to Like*?; anon., *The Marriage of Wit and Science*		Bienvenu, *Comédie du monde malade et mal pansé*; Garnier, *Porcie*; Dolce d.
Barnes b.?; Davies b.; Góngora b.; Marini b.	Garter, *Susanna*?		

Date	Historical events	Theatrical events	Non-dramatic literary events
1570	Elizabeth excommunicated by Pius V		Ascham, *The Schoolmaster*; Googe (trans.), Kirchmayer's *Popish Kingdom*; Henryson, *Moral Fables*
1571	Battle of Lepanto; Ridolfi Plot; Elizabeth breaks off diplomatic relations with Spain		
1572	Pius V d.; Gregory XIII succeeds; Massacre of St Bartholomew; Knox d.; Sea Beggars seize Brill	Act for the punishment of vagabonds (includes unlicensed travelling players); Richard Mulcaster begins annual court play with Merchant Taylors' boys	R. H. (trans.), Lavater's *Of Ghosts and Spirits walking by Night*; Wilson, *Discourse upon Usury*; Camoens, *Lusiadas*; Ronsard, *Franciade*, I–IV
1573	Diplomatic relations with Spain resumed	Italian players (including women) allowed to act in London by command of Privy Council	Gascoigne, *A Hundred Sundry Flowers*; Tyndale, Frith and Barnes, *Works*; Tasso, *Aminta*
1574	Persecution of papists in England	Elizabeth I grants patent to Earl of Leicester's company	Higgins (ed.), *Mirror for Magistrates* (4th authorized edn)
1575	New Poor Law; Anabaptists burned in England	Elizabeth I visits Kenilworth, is entertained by Earl of Leicester with shows; Mayor of Chester summoned for permitting performance of miracle cycle; Westcott using part of St Paul's school property for 'private theatre' performances	Churchyard, *Churchyard's Chips*, I; Tasso, *Gerusalemme Liberata*
1576	Sack of Antwerp; Grindal Archbishop of Canterbury; Frobisher's voyage begins; priests from Douai arrive in England	James Burbage builds The Theatre, in Shoreditch, first public playhouse in London; Richard Farrant takes over Chapel Royal plays, sets up Blackfriars 'private' theatre	Gascoigne, *The Steel Glass*; Pettie, *The Petite Palace of Pettie his Pleasure*; *The Paradise of Dainty Devices*

Birth and death dates of non-dramatic writers	Dates of notable plays	Birth and death dates of playwrights	Continental theatrical events
Rowlands b.?	Anon., *Sir Clyomon and Sir Clamydes?*; anon., *July and Julian?*; anon., *Misogonus?*		The Confrères de la Passion begin to let their theatre at the Hôtel de Bourgogne to professional troupes on a regular basis; they cease to act themselves *c.* 1600
Jewel d.	Anon., *New Custom?*		Establishment of first Italian troupes and *commedia dell'arte* in France; forbidden by the Paris Parlement, but protected by the court
Knox d.; Ramus d.; Donne b.; Jonson b.	Woodes, *The Conflict of Conscience?*	Jonson b.	
Cinthio d.; Laud b.			Garnier, *Hippolyte*
Barnfield b.; J. Hall b.	Anon. (trans. Niclaes), *An Interlude of Minds?*		Garnier, *Cornélie*
Parker d.; Purchas b.	Gascoigne, *The Princely Pleasures at Kenilworth Castle*, *The Glass of Government*; anon., *Processus Satanae?*	T. Heywood b.?; Tourneur b.	
Bullein d.	Lupton, *All for Money?*; Wapull, *The Tide Tarrieth No Man*; anon., *Common Conditions?*	Marston b.?	

I The social and historical context

Norman Sanders

1 Drama and society

During the first three-quarters of the sixteenth century England experienced great upheavals in almost every aspect of its national life. The
reigns of the five rulers spanning this period were characterized not by
any continuity of policy but rather by each monarch's attempts to handle
pressing problems of government caused by shifts in religious belief and
the pressures of intellectual change.

At the beginning of the century the victor of Bosworth Field still had
nine years to reign. He had, between 1485 and 1500, managed to lay the
basis for a strong government which effectively negated any doubts about
the legality of his claim to the throne. His suppression of rebellion, his
handling of the pretenders Simnel and Warbeck, and his maintaining of
peace with Scotland all succeeded in creating a greater sense of security
and prosperity than had seemed possible at the beginning of his reign. His
younger son, Henry VIII, thus inherited from his father in 1509 an orderly
and economically sound country in which there was a large acceptance of
strong central royal authority. However, the son's aims were different from
those of the father: the exaltation of royal supremacy was intensified specifically at the expense of papal influence; and the well-stocked treasury
was squandered in efforts to compete with the spectacular courts of Europe

and in costly military adventures directed against France, Scotland and the Emperor Maximilian. By 1525 extra taxation was necessary to replenish the royal coffers, with consequent bad relations between king and parliament. With the latter part of his reign came his marital difficulties, the dissolution of the monasteries, the break with Rome, and the establishment of the Church of England.

The eleven years covering the reigns of Edward VI and Mary pointed the nation in opposite religious and therefore political directions. The aims of the Reformation were pursued with great vigour by the boy king and his protectors; while Mary's accession in 1553 heralded a sometimes savagely enforced attempt to return England to the Roman fold. The first sixteen years of the rule of Elizabeth saw an initial exuberance at Protestant reascendancy and the formulation of her religious settlement, which maintained a tension between opposing religious positions by leaving as much as was practicable to the individual conscience provided private spiritual concerns did not grow to be a matter of public faction.

Such religious and political changes had their implications for economic life, social structures, legal and educational institutions – for the whole fabric of life of every citizen. Day-to-day realities were also being influenced by that movement of thought to which we give the name 'the Renaissance'. Like most useful words, this has come to mean many different things. At its simplest level it describes one intellectual activity that Englishmen were involved in at this period: namely, the recovery of Greek and the refining of medieval Latin in the light of the classical usage of that language. But it is also used in a more rag-bag fashion to embrace the restoration of learning after a dark night of ignorance, the dawn of a new civilization, the rediscovery of the physical world, the beginning of the physical sciences, the breaking with a primitive past, the growth of sophisticated art, the establishment of a humanistic world to replace a rigidly theocentric existence. Use of the term in this way tends to oversimplify what was a very complex business.[1] All of these attitudes were certainly prevalent. Sixteenth-century humanists were selfconsciously aware of being part of a *renascentia*; and revolutions in ideas that we so label were rife between 1500 and 1576 – running parallel with the changes in belief that we call 'the Reformation'. However, the ways these two forces influenced the national life did not have the coherence they assume in the pattern making

[1] For example, C. S. Lewis, *English Literature in the Sixteenth Century Excluding Drama* (Oxford, 1954), pp. 1–65, and G. Wickham, *Early English Stages 1300–1660*, Vol. II, Pt 1 (London, 1963), pp. 13–53.

of some historians; rather they were intertwined in a complex manner. As one recent writer has put it,[1]

> It is a mistake ... to think of the Reformation as simply a rather distant event in ecclesiastical history; for immediately the sovereign takes into his own hands authority for the interpretation of religious doctrine on his subjects' behalf, doctrine and politics become inextricably mixed. Similarly, it is a mistake to equate the Renaissance with academic reaction towards classical learning and artistic precept. A reaction in this direction undoubtedly occurred, but being Italian-inspired it could not escape association in England with Rome, the Papacy and Catholicism. If the English Reformation ... was greeted on the continent by a Counter-Reformation, it could well be said that the Italian Renaissance, after an initial friendly welcome into England, was subsequently challenged by a Counter-Renaissance.

With radical changes in the nation's spiritual and intellectual life and their effects in the social and political spheres, it was inevitable that so public an art form as the drama should have been affected. In 1500 the medieval theatre was a flourishing popular form of entertainment, staffed by amateurs as an integral part of their social and professional lives and keyed to the calendar of the universal church. By 1575, Sir John Savage, Mayor of Chester, was being summoned to London, imprisoned in the Tower and called to account for his actions in allowing the city's mystery cycle to be performed in defiance of a banning order issued by the Diocesan Court of the High Commission for the North. At the beginning of the century the Corpus Christi play was buttressed by a variety of other amateur dramatic activities. The choir schools in and around London were good enough to be called frequently to court by Henry VII and Henry VIII to perform both Latin plays and imitation classical dramas written by their schoolmasters. Professional minstrels competed with these singing boys at court and travelled round the provincial towns practising their art. The spectacular masquings and disguisings were a favourite pastime of the court itself, and the humbler holiday games of May Day, Robin Hood and St George played a part in both the courtly and popular mimetic life. However, by 1575 professional actors were no longer simply a part of this richly varied tapestry of national entertainment; they were beginning to emerge as the specially favoured practitioners of the leading

[1] Wickham, op. cit. Vol. II, p. 53.

Elizabethan art form. For, about the same time as Sir John Savage's indictment, Queen Elizabeth was granting a patent to the Earl of Leicester's Company to permit them to perform regularly in the City of London, and James Burbage was making plans to build his theatre at Shoreditch.

The movement of England during the sixteenth century from participation as a segment of Catholic Europe to religious and political independence in a continent of critically balanced antagonisms was paralleled by a change in the nation's dramatic life from a vital, largely amateur activity which threaded every level of society to a mainly metropolitan professional business, favoured by the court, patronized by the nobility, and arousing anger and disapproval in a powerful segment of the middle classes. This change may be attributed largely to three factors: (1) the governmental drive to eliminate religious drama from the national life because of its connection with the Roman Church; (2) the drama's association with religious and social issues, and its employment by the authorities and others for propaganda purposes, from which emerged the need for legal instruments of control; (3) the persistence of royal patronage of dramatic activity as an integral part of court life.

2 The suppression of the mystery cycles

The reign of Henry VIII witnessed the first steps taken by government to control religious drama. The immediate reasons for them were political and doctrinal; but in practice they were only another move in a long history of official attempts to regulate all popular activities. Pre-Reformation efforts had been based upon the realization that any event which entails a crowd will require policing to avoid personal violence, breach of the peace and damage to property. For example, during the fifteenth century strong measures were adopted to regulate tournaments, which were thus transformed from bloody battle schools into stylized displays of skill and horsemanship that retained their popularity well into the seventeenth century. This reformation was effected by placing these shows officially in the hands of the monarch, whose executives were the King of Arms and the heralds, under the authority of the Earl Marshal. Legislative action had the same effect on the practice of mummings, so that a traditional folk activity, which contained the seeds of possible civic disturbance, became the sophisticated disguising and ultimately the masque. The Feast of Fools was repeatedly subjected to ecclesiastical inhibition; and the drama, while it was still in the hands of the clergy and within the confines of the church architecturally as well as administratively, could be disciplined whenever necessary, as a 1348 edict of the Bishop of Hereford illustrates:

> Whereas many of the plays performed in churches contain evil jesting forbidden by the Apostle at any time, and especially unbecoming in the house of the Lord, and further, the devotions of the faithful are disturbed by these exhibitions, the bishop desires to root them out of the diocese, and formally forbids them in the church of L [i.e. Ludlow or Ledbury], where they have been frequent, under penalty of excommunication.[1]

When religious plays moved out of the church precincts and thus became subject to secular as well as ecclesiastical authority, the responsibility for their orderly proceeding was apparently divided equally between the Mayor's Court and the Ecclesiastical Court, an amicable arrangement reflected in the records of Lincoln, Beverley and Coventry and echoed in the banns and proclamations for the Chester Cycle:

> Wherefore Maister mair in the kynges name straitly chargeth and commaundeth that euery person and persons of what astate degre or condicion so euer he or they be resortyng to the said plaiez do use themselues pecible without makyng eny assault affrey or other disturbans wherby the same playes shalbe disturbed and that no maner person or persons who so euer he or they be do use or weyre unlaufulf wepons within the precynct of the said Citie during the tyme of the said playes not only upon payn of cursyng by thauctoritie of the said Pope Clement bulles but also opon payne of enprisonment of their bodiez and makyng fyne to the kyng at maister mairs pleasure.[2]

However, once Henry VIII began to disagree with the Pope, any sharing of the responsibility for policing religious drama was no longer possible. Even before Henry's divorce from Katherine of Aragon and the actual break with Rome, we find evidence of governmental pressures being felt by the producers of the Corpus Christi plays. The playlet of the Assumption of the Virgin was suppressed at Chester, perhaps as early as 1515; all the plays at Ipswich were 'laid aside' in 1518, 1519 and 1521; at New Romney in 1517–18 the Sergeant of the Warden of the Cinque Ports brought a mandate to the barons of the town indicating they ought not to permit the playing of the Passion of Christ until they had the king's leave; and the plays at Beverley are not mentioned after 1520. These records bear witness

---

[1] Register of John de Trillek, Bishop of Hereford (1344–61), as quoted in Wickham, op. cit. Vol. II, p. 55.

[2] Wickham, op. cit., Vol. I, p. 343.

not only to the government's reformist attitudes but also to the continuing centralizing tendency of Henry's reign. By 1531 Henry had substituted his own authority for that of the Pope and so automatically assumed complete rather than merely secular control of the cycles. He was excommunicated on 11 July 1533, and his leadership of the English church was confirmed by Act of Parliament in January 1534–5. Between 1535 and 1539 he dissolved the monasteries, an action which had incalculable consequences for provincial social life, for education and scholarship, and for English religious drama.

The results of these events were immediate for the Corpus Christi plays. For example, in 1532 William Newhall, town clerk of Chester, deleted from the banns and proclamations all reference to papal control of the audience; and at Ipswich the city play was 'laide aside for ever by order'. Such steps certainly reflect the religious tenor of the time; but they are also evidence of a genuine fear of civil disorder developing from people congregating for a religious festival in a period of theological turmoil. It is this note that is struck in one of the king's letters dating from this time:

> Whereas we understand by certain report of the late evil and seditious rising in our ancient city of York, at the acting of a religious interlude of St Thomas the Apostle, made in the same city on the 23rd of August now last past; and whereas we have been credibly informed that the said rising was owing to the seditious conduct of certain papists who took a part in preparing for the said interlude, we will and require you that from henceforward ye do your utmost to prevent and hinder any such commotion in future, and for this ye have my warrant for apprehending and putting in prison any papists who shall, in performing interludes which are founded on any portion of the Old or New Testament, say or make use of any language which may tend to excite those who are beholding the same to any breach of the peace.[1]

The letter also gives us a clue to the nature of the early means used to suppress the old religious drama – not the decree or public legislation, but rather royal pressure exerted through local ecclesiastical and secular authorities who were acutely aware of the religious uncertainties in the nation created by Henry's actions after his divorce from Katherine.

In the reign of Edward VI the movement of separation from Rome became full-scale Protestantism. His first act which touched the stage was the repealing in 1547 of Henry VIII's statute of 1543, which had allowed

[1] J. O. Halliwell-Phillipps (ed.), *Letters of the Kings of England* (London, 1848), Vol. I, p. 354.

'songs, plays, and interludes … for the rebuking and reproaching of vices and the setting forth of virtue' provided they did not meddle with the interpretation of Scripture. This action effectively restored the advantage to Protestant propagandist playwrights. Two years later the Act of 6 August proclaimed prohibition of all plays until the Feast of All Saints next, on the grounds that for the most part the interludes being performed 'contained matter tending to sedition and to the contemning of sundry good orders and laws, whereupon were grown such disquiet … and uproars in the realm.'[1] While these edicts were clearly aimed at interlude playing and did not directly affect the performance of the great cycles, it is apparent that the atmosphere they created caused provincial authorities to view the Corpus Christi dramas with something less than the enthusiasm shown in their heyday; particularly as in 1548 the feast of Corpus Christi itself was officially cancelled as a feast of the English church. The York playlets on the Death, Assumption and Coronation of the Blessed Virgin were excised; and in the Towneley manuscript some doctrinal passages regarding the Seven Sacraments and Transubstantiation were marked for omission in performance. At Hereford, theological doubts permitted economic changes as the city determined in 1548 to use the contributions collected for the staging of the pageants 'which are now omitted and surceased, upon the ruinous and decayed causeys, pavements, streets, and walls, cleansing the town ditch or such like reparations'.[2] That official disapproval of the cycles was severely felt by local authorities in England between 1547 and 1553 is indicated by the records at York, which suggest a renewed eagerness among the townspeople in the year of Mary's accession for an extensive remounting of its 'Corpuschristy play'; and by the church-wardens' accounts at Ashburton in Devon, where the plays were resumed after their non-occurrence for the whole of Edward's reign.

Elizabeth made no more systematic efforts to root out the Corpus Christi pageants than had her father and half-brother; but during her reign their gradual suppression at the hands of local bodies continued. Playing at York and Norwich was suspended for a time in 1559 and later resumed; and other districts persisted with performances of Passion plays and mysteries only in defiance of authority. What is clear is that between 1569 and 1580 the four major English cycles were put down by the intervention of some power or other. At York, Dean Hutton, a member of the Royal Commission for Ecclesiastical Causes in the North, intervened to criticize the religious

[1] H. C. Gardiner, *Mysteries' End* (New Haven, Conn., 1946), p. 60.
[2] Ibid. p. 61 note.

content of the Creed Play which was proposed for performance in 1568; and his 'advise' prevented all dramatic activity for that year. A result of this experience was that only an 'amended and corrected' version of the cycle was played at fourteen stations in 1569; which was to be the last performance in this first city of the north – significantly in the year of the defeat of the Northern Rebellion. The Wakefield Cycle would appear to have run into similar censorship trouble with the Diocesan Court of the High Commission of the North in May 1576. In Chester the mayor, John Hankey, fell foul of the ecclesiastical authorities for not staying the annual performance in 1571 although commanded to do so; and his successor, Sir John Savage, in 1574 allowed the plays to be held, despite 'an inhibition and the primate's letters from York and from the Earl of Huntingdon',[1] and suffered the consequences. Though less clearly discernible, a like pattern of suppression is evidenced in the records at Coventry, where the plays lasted until 1580; and there are scattered indications that the demise of the cycles took place about the same time in cities such as Newcastle, Lincoln and Doncaster.

These events in no way marked the end of all pageant plays in England: the actings of cycle dramas by local companies apparently continued in the extreme north-western counties as late as 1612. But by the end of the third quarter of the sixteenth century the Corpus Christi play was no longer the centrepiece of the nation's theatrical activity.

---

[1] G. Ormerod, *The History of the County Palatine and the City of Chester* (London, 1882), Vol. I, p. 236.

3 Drama and propaganda

While the demise of the mystery plays is the record of a vital social and religious dramatic activity succumbing to variously exercised central authority, the spread of the moralities and interludes is the story of a strong medieval theatrical growth affecting and being affected by the political and religious fluctuations of the time. The enormous importance that drama assumed during these years of national turmoil is well attested by the extent to which its management and control occupied the attentions of the most powerful men in the land. This can be understood only in the light of certain aspects of the Tudor age. First, it was a far more oral than literary culture, which meant that a kind of communication like the theatre relying on the spoken word had far greater immediate impact among the bulk of the people than did any literary text. In fact, most of the changes in official doctrinal attitudes would have reached the nation by way of the pulpit rather than the printing press. Second, as we have already seen, for centuries the central national experience of drama was religious in content. Third, the national mind was thoroughly trained in the 'interpretation' of plays; the feigning aspect of dramatic art was more readily admitted than it now is. The idea that a play is an emblem or a masking of a truth which is to be divined by the audience was an established fact of theatre; and one which may be detected later in the response demanded by the courtly allegories of John Lyly, by the Elizabethan history play and by the Jonsonian masques. Nothing brings this feature of the theatre of the time more vividly to the modern mind than to see someone like R. Willis picking his way with obvious ease through the meaning of the interlude *The Cradle of Security*.[1] Fourth, within the medieval tradition of acting there had developed most of the stage conventions which the Elizabethan stage was to use for establishing intimate rapport between actor and audience: the aside, the soliloquy, the rhetorical question and direct address. Finally, there was that other legacy from the medieval drama – the audience's expectation that eternal religious verities would be projected by means of recognizable contemporary localization in the manner of Noah's wife and her gossips, or Mak and Gill. With these habits of viewing drama prevailing and in a time of violent religious upheaval and divided loyalties, it was almost inevitable that the popular professional drama should have been drawn into the great debates of the age.

Drama as social comment appeared early in Henry VIII's reign. The aristocratic council, which had effectively governed England during his first five years on the throne, began to be shouldered aside by the new rising administrative caste headed by Wolsey. And it is the influence of these low-born royal advisers that we find John Skelton limning in his humanist morality *Magnificence* (1515–23). Even without making simplistic equations between Magnificence and Henry, any of Magnificence's counsellors and Wolsey, Sad Circumspection and Norfolk, it is readily discernible that the court poet is voicing baronial fears about royal extravagance and fiscal responsibility.

Even closer to the throne than Skelton was Sir Thomas More's circle. Liberal humanists like More also experienced dismay at Henry's imperialistic military ambitions. Certainly they were reformers and were vocal on the subjects of ecclesiastical abuses and social injustice; but they found it impossible to side enthusiastically either with the remnants of the old feudalism or with the declared policies of Wolsey and the new men. It is from this group that the most striking of the early interludes derive. In no obvious sense are these pieces propagandist; but they all touch on issues that were of great contemporary interest and were surely topics of conversation in the More household. For example, John Heywood's *The*

[1] In *Mount Tabor* (1639), quoted in E. K. Chambers, *The Mediaeval Stage* (Oxford, 1903), Vol. II, p. 189 note.

Play of the Weather (1525–33) is a discussion in comic form of the necessity
for reconciling those who would change and those who would preserve the
status quo;[1] and his *Four PP* (1520–2) is a farcical treatment of the idea
of social harmony between the secular and religious factions in the realm.[2]

The most committed reformer of the group was Heywood's son-in-law,
John Rastell, the lawyer and printer, who may have held heretical views
as early as 1507 during his Coventry years. His *Gentleness and Nobility*
(1527–30) portrays the oldest of economic rivalries – between the knight
and the ploughman – in a dialogue which explicitly sets out to determine
'who is a very gentleman and who is a nobleman, and how men should
come to authority'. The same subject is handled in more starkly dramatic
fashion in *Calisto and Melebea* (1527–30), where Calisto's aristocratic idleness and lasciviousness, encouraged by the bawd Celestina, are contrasted
with the virtuous poverty of Melebea and the servant Parmeno. Confirm-
ing the social theories of these two plays but setting them in a far wider
intellectual context is *The Nature of the Four Elements* (1517–18). In this
the didactic programme is scarcely concealed; it is a dramatic manifesto
of the new humanism and a plea for the necessity for learned governors:

> Then hedys, rulers, and governours all
> Shuld come therto be cause of their vertue,
> And in auctoritie they ought not continue
> Except they be good men, discret and wise.

Other plays of the same period touch specific issues more directly. For
example, *Albion Knight* (1537) plainly grew out of the Pilgrimage of Grace,
and depicts Principality and Commons dangerously at loggerheads on the
subjects of disloyalty, the use of taxes, royal favouritism and low-born
counsellors.[3] *Godly Queen Hester* (1525–9) is equally outspoken in its
biblical treatment of Katherine of Aragon's marital troubles and Wolsey's
anti-monastic views.[4]

[1] See K. W. Cameron, *John Heywood's 'Play of the Wther'*, *A study in Early Tudor Drama* (Raleigh, NC, 1941); P. Hogrefe, *The Sir Thomas More Circle* (Urbana, Ill., 1959), pp. 305–9; D. M. Bevington, *Tudor Drama and Politics* (Cambridge, Mass., 1968), pp. 64–70.

[2] See A. W. Reed, *Early Tudor Drama* (London, 1926), pp. 139–44; D. M. Bevington, op. cit. pp. 71–3.

[3] See M. H. Dodds, 'The Date of *Albion Knight*', *The Library*, IV (1913), pp. 157–70; G. A. Jones, 'The Political Significance of the Play of *Albion Knight*', *Journal of English and Germanic Philology*, XVII (1918), pp. 267–80.

[4] See B. Spivack, *Shakespeare and the Allegory of Evil* (New York, 1958), pp. 256–9; W. W. Greg's introduction to his edition of *Godley Queen Hester* (Louvain, 1904).

There is sufficient evidence that such plays as these did indeed possess a perceived topicality for their Tudor audiences. Edward Hall in his *Chronicle* describes a series of events which illustrates the instinctive response to the drama of social comment at the highest level of government. At Christmas 1526–7 a play was performed at Gray's Inn, the author of which was Master John Roo, a serjeant-at-law:

> ... the effecte of the plaie was, that lord gouernance was ruled by dissipacion and negligence, by whose misgouernance and euill order, lady Publike wele was put from gouernance: which caused Rumor Populi, Inward grudge, and disdain of wanton souereignetie to rise with a greate multitude, to expell negligence and dissipacion and to restore Publik welth again to her estate, which was so done.

This legal entertainment 'was highly praised of all menne' except one member of the audience – Cardinal Wolsey, who

> ... imagined that the plaie had been diuised of hym [i.e. was about him], and in a greate furie sent for the said master Roo, and toke from hym his Coyfe [i.e. insignia of office] and sent hym to the Flete, and after he sent for the yong gentlemen, that plaied in the plaie, and them highly rebuked and thretened, and sent one of them called Thomas Moyle of Kent to the Flete.[1]

It is not surprising that, once eager episcopal reformers under Cranmer and ambitious politicians like Cromwell prevailed in government and the break with Rome became inevitable, the power of drama as religious propaganda should have been realized. The king himself had experience of being its object when a dissident play was performed in Suffolk on May Day 1537, which showed 'a king, how he should rule his realm' and contained an improvising actor who 'played Husbandry and said many things against gentlemen, more than was in the book of the play'.[2] He had also enormously enjoyed dramatic representations of his defiance of the Pope. The Spanish Ambassador Chappuys relates how Henry in June 1535 walked a distance of ten miles at two o'clock in the morning in order to be present at a show based upon a chapter of the Apocalypse. Once there, the king concealed himself in a house so that he could witness the per-

[1] Edward Hall, *The Union of the Two Noble and Illustre Famelies of Lancaster and Yorke* (1548; London, 1809), p. 719.
[2] *Letters and Papers of Henry VIII*, Vol. XII, Pt 1 (1537), pp. 557, 585.

formance unseen; but he was so delighted with seeing 'himself represented as cutting off the heads of the clergy, that in order to laugh at his ease, and encourage the people he disclosed himself.' Furthermore, he 'sent to tell his lady [i.e. Ann Boleyn] that she ought to see the representation of it repeated on the eve of St Peter.'[1] It was presumably incidents such as this that occasioned the report to the Pope that Henry 'feist jouer ou permist estre jouées des farces dedans Londres fort ignominieuses'.[2]

Henry's ministers saw in the drama more than its capacity to tickle the royal sense of humour with topical fare. Cranmer's interest in Protestant drama is evidenced by his being the dedicatee in 1538 of the most remarkable propagandist play, Thomas Kirchmayer's *Pammachius*; and it was for Cromwell that Thomas Wylley, vicar of Yoxford, wrote a lost play, directed against the Pope's counsellors and Virgin worship, that earned him prohibition from preaching by his fellow Suffolk clerics. However, it was Cromwell's employment of John Bale that brought into being the full-scale, government-directed theatrical attack on papistry. Bale had a long career of heretical activity even while he was still in holy orders. When a Catholic prior he had openly mocked the idea of transubstantiation, he left his order and married; and his own congregation in Thorndon, Suffolk, had indicted him for his radical beliefs. He was perhaps the most intransigent and famous of those 'sundry and divers fresh and quick wits ... by whose industry and ingenious labours divers excellent ballads and books were contrived and set abroad, concerning the suppression of the Pope and all popish idolatry', who, John Foxe assures us, always surrounded Henry's chief minister.[3]

Bale was the English translator of *Pammachius*, and it was probably under its influence that he wrote his own *King John*, which was performed at Cranmer's house at Christmas 1538–9 at a cost of 70s. Clearly this play had the effect intended by Cromwell, at least among some Englishmen. In an account of a trial occasioned by troubles growing out of one of its performances, John Alforde was so persuaded by it that he said, 'It was a pity that the bishop of Rome should reign any longer, for he would do with our King as he did with King John'; and Thomas Brown opined, 'King John was as noble a prince as ever was in England, and thereby we might perceive that he was the beginner of the putting

[1] *Letters and Papers of Henry VIII*, Vol. VIII (1535), p. 373.
[2] A. Hamy, *Entrevue de François Premier avec Henry VIII* (Paris, 1898), Doc. ccclxxviii.
[3] John Foxe, *The Acts and Monuments* (London, 1838), Vol. V, p. 403.

down of the bishop of Rome, and thereof we might all be glad.'[1]

Such government-commissioned plays were obviously more systematically planned (and certainly acted by Bale's company) to reflect as accurately as possible the official view of the Catholic Church and the Reformation programme) than were the popular interludes, which by and large simply echo aspects of current religious ideas. For example, *Three Laws* (1538) not only levels the commonplace Protestant charges against the papists but also deals with the Catholic Church's organization, ritual and doctrine: relics, the Virgin cult, confession, pardons, purgatory, images, clerical celibacy and the stress on good works as a means to salvation. Just how great were Bale's ambitions for the drama's role in the English Reformation may be gauged from the indications that he planned a Protestant mystery cycle designed to replace its Catholic counterparts. The extant fragments of it – *God's Promises*, *John the Baptist* and *The Temptation of Our Lord* – suggest that the main emphasis was to be on the personal virtue of Christ and salvation through faith.

Official sanction of propagandist drama came to an end with Henry's reversal of his religious policy in 1540; and the execution of Cromwell resulted in the disbanding of Bale's troupe and the playwright's own exile. Evidence that the king no longer encouraged theatrical propaganda is slight; but it does point to very changed playing conditions during the last years of his reign. The only two extant moralities dating from the years 1540–6, *The Four Cardinal Virtues* (a fragment) and Grimald's *Christus Redivivus*, are noticeably uncontroversial; and the court records suggest that the sumptuous masque was more to the taste of the ageing and diseased monarch than plays about decapitating cardinals. In 1545 the students of Christ's College, Cambridge, performed *Pammachius*;[2] but by this date a piece associated with Cromwell and Bale had become, in the words of Bishop Gardiner to Vice-Chancellor Parker, 'so pestiferous as were intollerable'. It seems clear that during these years efforts were made by ecclesiastical and secular authorities to curtail the acting of all 'lewd plays', whatever their persuasion, that meddled with religious doctrine as it was defined by the new head of the Church of England.

[1] J. S. Brewer (ed.), *Letters and Papers, Foreign and Domestic, of the Reign of Henry VIII* (London, 1862–1918), Vol. XIV, Pt 1, pp. 22–3.

[2] For the correct dating of this performance, see W. J. Griffin, *Modern Language Notes*, LVIII (1943), pp. 50–1, where he discusses the erroneous presentation of the evidence by E. K. Chambers, *Medieval Stage*, Vol. II, p. 220, and by V. G. Gildersleeve, *Government Regulation of the Elizabethan Drama* (New York, 1908), p. 6.

With the accession of Edward VI, Protestant reformers fully expected from the Protector Somerset a new freedom to pursue polemic. At the beginning of the reign all the signs were propitious for renewed propagandist activity in the theatre and out of it. Henry's Act of 1543 regulating 'interpretation of scripture' was repealed in 1547; Henrician exiles of the Cromwellian breed returned to England; and Bale characteristically refurbished his *King John* to hail the coming of the young royal prophet who would restore God's laws to the realm. The Revels Accounts also indicate that the coronation festivities were strongly anti-papal, with their payments for friars' garments, cardinals' hats, a crown and cross for the Pope, and a priest's white gown to be worn by the king himself. Indeed there is ample proof that at this time 'with God's word was every man's mouth occupied; of that were all songs, interludes and plays made', as one nostalgic Protestant exile of Mary's reign puts it.[1]

The moralities dating from this period are all heavily polemical. Plays such as the lost *Old Custom* (1520–50)[2] and Grimald's *Archipropheta* (1547) are thinly veiled attacks on papist practices; the fragmentary *Somebody, Avarice and Minister* (1547–50) anatomizes Henry's errors in backing off from the full implementation of Protestant ideals; and R. Wever's *Lusty Juventus* (1547–53) is a relatively temperate consideration of papist error and the need for reforming responsibility. Even in some of the plays written for the boys' companies, such as *Jacob and Esau* (1550–7) and *Nice Wanton* (1547–53), we find a Calvinist slant being given to the educational materials and treatment traditional in the school entertainments. But it is a nameless court interlude of the Seven Deadly Sins that reminds us that Protestant vehemence was as virulent as it had ever been: this apparently had a dramatis personae of 'pride, a Pope; wrathe, a bisshopp; envie, a fryer, couetous, a person; glotonye, a Sole preste; lecherye, a Muncke; Slothe, a hermett'.[3]

However, when Edward's reign was only two years old, the fact that polemical drama could be a two-edged weapon was brought home to the government in spectacular fashion. In 1549 Robert Kett led 16,000 men to

---

[1] Preface to *A Confutation of Unwritten Verities made by Thomas Cranmer, late Archbishop of Canterbury and set forth by E.P.* (n.d.); published under Mary.

[2] This play with an indication of its subject matter is mentioned in an inventory of the effects of John Dudley, Earl of Warwick (1547); see A. Feuillerat, 'An Unknown Protestant Morality Play', *Modern Language Review*, IX (1914), pp. 94–6; C. R. Baskervill, 'On Two Old Plays', *Modern Philology*, XIV (1916), p. 16.

[3] Gardiner, op. cit. p. 57 note.

blockade Norwich, during which uprising, according to Holinshed's *Chronicle*, Kett knew that

> ... there should be a publike plaie kept at Wimondham, a towne distant from Norwich six miles, which plaie had beene accustomed yearelie to be kept in that towne, continuing for the space of one night and one daie at the least. Wherevpon the wicked contriuers of this vnhappie rebellion, tooke occasion by the assembling of such numbers of people as resorted thither to see that plaie, to enter further into their wicked enterprise.[1]

This connection between drama and revolution produced immediate government action. On 6 August there was a royal proclamation prohibiting all English plays for two months; and two years later the proclamation of April 28 required the licensing of all professional acting companies and provided severe controls to prevent the performance of anything smacking of sedition. That these decrees were enforced with some scrupulousness is evident from the Privy Council's permission, granted in June 1551 to the Marquis of Dorset, for his players to act 'only in his lordship's presence'; and in the following summer its committing to the Tower one 'cowper for the making of plays'.[2]

After Edward's increasingly active enforcement of Protestant doctrine, it was to be expected that Mary's coming to the throne would result not only in a more equal religious division but in a propaganda war in which plays would naturally figure. As has been noted above,[3] the lovers of the mystery cycles experienced a renewed enthusiasm for their staging under a Catholic government; but the Protestant interludes apparently continued to be played, causing a warning to be issued on 18 August 1553 against 'playinge of Interludes and pryntynge false bookes, ballettes, rymes, and other lewde treatises in the englyshe tonge, concernynge doctryne in matters now in question and controuersye, touchinge the hyghe poyntes and misteries of christen religion.'[4] This edict was strictly enforced for about two years; but after 1555, probably in reaction to Mary's marriage with Philip of Spain, some Protestant playwrights became more specific in their

[1] Raphael Holinshed, *The Chronicles of England, Scotland, and Ireland* (London, 1558–87), Vol. III, pp. 963–4.
[2] J. R. Dasent (ed.), *Acts of the Privy Council of England 1542–1604* (London, 1890–1907), Vol. III, p. 307, and Vol. IV, p. 73.
[3] See p. 10.
[4] W. C. Hazlitt, *The English Drama and Stage under the Tudor and Stuart Princes 1543–1642* (London, 1869), pp. 15–18.

criticism. Letters from the Privy Council to the Mayor of Canterbury concern seditious plays being performed in Kent in 1557; and a year earlier a touring company under the patronage of Sir Francis Leke was guilty of acting 'very naughty and seditious matter touching the King and Queen's Majesties'.[1]

Unlike her brother and father, Mary made no attempt to use the stage as a means of promulgating her religious policies. Certainly there were pro-Catholic plays performed during her reign, such as the lost *Anglia Deformata et Anglia Restituta* at Trinity College, Cambridge, and *Genus Humanum* at court in 1553 or 1554; and the popular morality *Impatient Poverty* (1547–58), while not being generally pro-Catholic, also deals in a general way with the value of penance and the ecclesiastical courts. Only *Respublica*, intended for production at court during the Christmas festivities of 1553 by a boys' company, closely touches a live religious question of Mary's reign: namely, the restitution of the church lands, which the queen found in practice to be politically and financially impossible, despite her personal desire to restore the church to its pre-Henrician splendour.

Mary's death marked the end of the theatre of religious propaganda, of the period when central national issues and dramatic content were one and the same. There was, of course, a certain amount of anti-papal theatrical activity at the commencement of Elizabeth's reign: the new queen is reported to have witnessed in 1558 a mumming of 'crows in the habits of Cardinals, of asses habited as Bishops, and of wolves representing Abbots'.[2] Moreover, there is some evidence that Secretary Cecil, like Cromwell before him, flirted with the idea of using the stage for political purposes; for the Spanish Ambassador reported home in 1559:

> She [i.e. Elizabeth] was emphatic in saying that she wished to punish certain persons who had represented some comedies in which your Majesty was taken off ... I knew that a member of her Council had given the arguments to construct these comedies, which is true, for Cecil gave them, as indeed she partly admitted to me.[3]

A dispatch of Paulo Tiepolo, the Venetian Ambassador with King Philip, gives us an idea of what such comedies were about:

---

[1] The letter is quoted in E. Rickert, 'Political Propaganda and Satire in *A Midsummer Night's Dream*', *Modern Philology*, XXI (1923), p. 137.
[2] Quoted by Bevington, op. cit. p. 127, from a letter of Il Schifanoya to Castellan of Mantua.
[3] Letter of Il Schifanoya to Castellan of Mantua, *Calendar of State Papers, Spanish*, N.S., I (1558–67), p. 62. Cited by Bevington, op. cit. p. 127.

These plays were so ... vituperative and abominable that it was mar-
vellous that they should have been so long tolerated, for they brought
upon the stage all personages whom they wished to revile, however
exalted their station, and among the rest, in one play King Philip, the
late Queen of England and Cardinal Pole, reasoning together about
such things as they imagined might have been said by them in the
matter of religion, so that they did not spare any living person, saying
whatever they fancied about them.[1]

About the same time too some of the earlier propagandist moralities of
the previous reigns began to appear in print: *Lusty Juventus* and *Nice
Wanton* were entered in the Stationers' Register in 1560; Bale's *Three Laws*
in 1562–3; and *The Cruel Debtor* appeared before the end of the decade.

Yet despite Elizabeth's tolerance of 'farces prejudicial to other princes',[2]
she was never wholehearted in her support of them. All indications are
that the queen was intent on not having her religious settlement disturbed
by the drama or anything else. A degree of internal religious tension was
manageable; but it must not be allowed to influence unduly the delicate
path she was treading to ensure that the two Catholic powers of France
and Spain did not unite against her realm. In April and May 1559, steps
were taken by proclamation to strengthen the controls instigated by Edward
and Mary; and so successful was her effort to remove the old theological
controversies from the public domain that by 1565 she was able to cut off
the Dean of St Paul's when he digressed on the subject of images with the
brusque 'Leave that, it has nothing to do with your subject, the matter is
now threadbare.'[3]

Thus we find the moralities of the 1560s concerning themselves more
with topics such as the implications of the Marian restoration of Catholicism: Protestant anxieties clearly lie behind *King Darius* (c. 1565), *New
Custom* (c. 1571) and William Wager's *The Longer Thou Livest the More
Fool Thou Art* (1559–68) and *Enough is as Good as a Feast* (1559–70). In
fact, with the exception of Nathaniel Woodes's *The Conflict of Conscience*
(1570–81), the bitter anti-Catholicism of which may have been prompted
by the dangers posed by Mary Stuart and the Northern Rebellion, there
is a general shift in play content away from religious doctrine and towards

---

[1] *Calendar of State Papers, Venetian*, VII (1558–80), pp. 80–1.
[2] See Bishop Quadra's dispatch to Spain in 1562 where he complains that 'notwithstanding
her promises no attempt was made to put a stop to it', *Calendar of State Papers, Spanish*,
N.S., I (1558–67), p. 247.
[3] *Calendar of State Papers, Spanish*, N.S., I (1558–67), p. 405.

problems arising from the economic and social changes of the first twelve years of Elizabeth's reign.[1]

Only one play catches something of the sense of immediacy found in the old propagandist moralities in its consciousness of dealing with pressing national issues. This is *Gorboduc*, which was performed before the queen in 1562 and was the product of a collaboration between two gentlemen-lawyers, Thomas Norton, a former tutor of Edward Seymour, and Edward Sackville, later the Earl of Dorset. The play, distinguished only by Sir Philip Sidney's praise and bearing its neoclassicism like a pall, belaboured Elizabeth with its twin messages of parliament's desire to determine the nation's political future and Protestant fears about the royal succession. With modern historical hindsight her reaction to unsolicited dramatic advice seems predictable; but the play may have taught her a lesson it little aimed at. After parliament had met in October 1566 to face the same problems as those raised in the play, and presented its demands to the queen, backed by the threatened stoppage of public moneys, she answered: 'I have as good a courage answerable to my place as ever my father had. I am your anointed Queen. I will never be by violence constrained to do anything.'[2] *Gorboduc* was the last play of its type; and by 1581 even discussion of the rights of any heir to the throne carried the penalty of execution.

This is not to say that the drama of social comment was to disappear from the English stage after 1563. Later Elizabethan audiences obviously bore into the theatre some remnant of the long-developed response that had impelled the Prologue of *Jack Juggler* to claim his play was

> such a trifling matter as when it shal be done
> Ye may report and saye ye haue hearde nothing at all
> Therfore I tell you all, before it be begone
> That no man looke to heare of matters substancyall
> Nor mattiers of any grauitee either great or small.

In the romances, comedies, histories and tragedies that held the stages of Burbage's Theatre and its rivals after 1576, 'matters substantial and of any gravity' were handled distantly: under the cloak of Lylian mythologizing, through the possible applicability of recent history, by the contemporary relevance of eternal verities. There were, of course, notable exceptions

---

[1] See D. M. Bevington's discussion of the religious and social content of the plays of this period, op. cit. pp. 127–40.
[2] J. E. Neale, *Queen Elizabeth I* (New York, 1957), pp. 148–50.

which called forth strong action by the authorities; but the miscalculation of the Earl of Essex at the end of Elizabeth's reign in making a performance of *Richard II* coincide with his rebellion is perhaps a measure of the distance drama had travelled in this as in so many other respects between the royal performance of *Gorboduc* and the year of *Hamlet*.

4 The growth of control

The intimate connection between national events and the drama during the years 1500 and 1575 inevitably produced the legal instruments for a system of control which led to the particular locations of the great Elizabethan playhouses and the mode of operation of the companies that occupied them. Although mention has already been made of some of the steps taken by the authorities in response to theatrical provocation of various kinds, a clearer picture of the main movement to place control of the drama in the hands of the central government can be gained by tracing the way in which legislation expanded its scope as the years passed.

Prior to the Reformation, secular and ecclesiastical authorities controlled those amateur entertainments that came within their natural purview: tournaments, mummings, the Feast of Fools, the Corpus Christi cycles. The early professional troupes were sometimes servants of the royal household attached to the retinue of the king himself or to members of his family. Henry VII had a four-man troupe; Prince Arthur had his own company by 1498 and Prince Henry by 1506. Other companies were patronized by the great nobles of the realm, such as the Earls of Oxford, Northumberland, Derby, Arundel and Shrewsbury, all of whom had their own players by 1500. Still other acting groups belonged to local civic authorities. All of these not only performed for their masters but also travelled extensively, competing during the first half of the century with minstrels, bearwards, rope-walkers, hoop-jumpers, sword-players, jugglers and tumblers. These itinerant groups and individual performers apparently experienced no difficulty in practising their various skills: after presentation of their credentials to the highest local officers and often an initial paid command-performance before the local council, they were then free to play publicly in the district.[1]

However, conditions changed drastically after Henry VIII's break with Rome in 1531. As we have seen, early stage-originated disturbances could be handled by the reprimand of a cleric like Bishop Gardiner, or by the intervention of the town clerk of Chester or Ipswich, or by a decision of a York Justice of the Peace. The first important royal public step is to be found in the Act of 1543. This does not require any licensing in its provision that

> ... it shalbe lawfull to all and everye persone and persones, to sette foorth songes, plaies and enterludes, to be used and exercysed within this Realme and other the kinges Domynions, for the rebuking and reproching of vices and the setting foorth of vertue.

Nevertheless, the decree was made for 'the advancement of true religion and for the abolishment of the contrary', and so provides 'allwaies the saide songes, playes or enterludes meddle not with the interpretacions of Scripture, contrarye to the doctryne set foorth or to be sett foorth by the Kinges Majestie'.[2]

Two years later the City of London's 'Proclamation for the Abolishment of Interludes' is clearly making specific application of the Act of 1543 as well as adding some pressing city problems as reasons for further control:

> ... fforasmoche as by reason and Occasyon of the manyfold and sundrye Enterludes and commen Playes that nowe of late dayes have been by dyvers and sondrye persones more commonly and besylye set foorthe and played than heretofore hathe bene accustomed.... And that namelye and cheiffelye upon the Sondaye and other hallydayes in the tyme of Evensonge and other devyne service Celebrate and said in the said citie to whiche places greate parte of the youthe of the

[1] See G. Dawson, 'Records of Plays and Players in Kent 1450–1642', Malone Society Collections, VII (1965), pp. xvi–xxii.
[2] Statutes of the Realm (London, 1810–28), Vol. III, p. 894.

same Citie and manye other light Idle and evyll disposed persones daylye and Contynuallye frequentynge hauntynge and followyinge the same playes have not onelye bene the Rather moved and provoked therebye to all proclyvytye and Redynes of dyvers and sondrye kyndes of vyce and synne. And the said youthe by that Occasyon not onely provoked to the unjuste wastynge and Consumynge of theire maisters goodes and the neglectinge and Omyssyon of theyre faithefull service and due Obedyence ... to the great decaye and hurt of the common welthe of the said Citie as of Archerye and other laufull and laudable exercyses. ... his highnes therfore straitlye Chargethe and commaundethe that no maner of person or persones from hensforthe of what soever estate degree or Condition he or they be of presume or take upon hym or them at any tyme hereafter to playe or set foorthe or cause to be played any maner of Enterlude or commen playe within any maner of place or places of this his graces said Citie. Onles it be in the houses of noble men or of the lorde Maire Shryves or aldermen of the same his highnes Citie for the tyme beinge Orels in the houses of gentlemen or of the substancyall and sad Comminers or hed parissheners of the same Citie or in the open stretes of the said citie as in tyme paste it hath bene used and accustomed or in the commen halles of the Companyes felowshipps or brotherheddes of the same Citie.[1]

Thus do the complaints against public performance, which were to be used to justify suppression for the next hundred years, make their appearance: conflict with the times of divine service, inducement to vice and idleness, corruption of youth, competition with traditional and useful pursuits, the threat to an orderly commonwealth.

Edward VI's policy followed his father's. There is the proclamation of 6 August 1549 outlawing performances of all plays for two months. Section III of the Act of Uniformity of the same year provides penalties specifically for interludes which 'speake anye thinge in derogacion depravinge or dyspisinge' of *The Book of Common Prayer*; and a second proclamation of 28 April 1551 requires that plays be submitted for licensing 'in writing vnder his maiesties signe, or signed by vi of his highnes priuie counsaill'. As had happened in Henry's reign, this action of the central government was followed by the City of London's applications of its provisions: a minute from the Aldermanic Court inhibiting John Wylkynson's theatrical

[1] For the full text of the proclamation, see Wickham, op. cit. Vol. II, Pt 1, pp. 327–8.

activities; a plea to the Lord Chancellor for his help in controlling playing in the suburbs; a determination that all interludes acted in the City must be perused by two Secondaries of the Compters; a listing of certain actors who must give their recognizances not to perform without official allowance.[1]

In the first year of her reign, Mary reaffirmed the controls of her predecessors; but naturally she had in mind inhibition of the now strongly developed anti-papal dramatic activity. Her 1553 proclamation restates the requirements for licensing and makes explicit the reason for suppressing Protestant interludes:

> ... forasmuche also as it is well knowen, that sedition and false rumours haue bene nouryshed and maynteyned in this realme .... by playinge of Interludes ... concernynge doctryne in matters now in question and controuersye, touchinge the hyghe poyntes and misteries of christen religion.[2]

As a result of this legislation at least one patron, Sir Francis Leke, was ordered by the Lord President to examine his company of actors about their practices while travelling and to be answerable for them himself. That such examinations were in effect a censoring of play texts is made clear by the actions of the Privy Council in 1557. The Lord Mayor of London in June of that year is directed to arrest an itinerant troupe and ban its performances unless its productions were '*first* seen and allowed'. The same month a company in Canterbury is examined by the mayor who had received its 'lewd play-book' from the Privy Council; and in September the Mayor of London seizes another company and sends its play, *The Sackful of News*, to the Privy Council for examination.[3]

Elizabeth stiffened even further these regulations for stage control early in her reign. On 16 May 1559 her proclamation detailed the administration of the licensing procedure:

> The Quenes Maiestie doth straightly forbyd al maner Interludes to be playde, eyther openly or priuately, except the same be noticed before hande, and licenced within any Citie or towne corporate by the Maior or other chiefe officers of the same, and within any shyre, by suche

---

[1] For the documentation of these and other similar actions, see E. K. Chambers, *The Elizabethan Stage* (Oxford, 1923), Vol. IV, pp. 261–2.

[2] See p. 19, n. 4 above.

[3] See Gildersleeve, op. cit. p. 12.

as shalbe Lieuetenauntes for the Quenes Maiestie in the same shyre, or by two of the Justices of peax inhabyting within that part of the shire where any shalbe played.[1]

The document continues by laying out for these censors the standards by which they are to judge the plays' contents; and proceeds to spell out the 1553 Marian emphasis on the patrons' responsibilities for their servants:

And further her maiestie gyueth speciall charge to her nobilitie and gentilmen, as they professe to obey and regarde her maiestie, to take good order in thys behalfe wyth their seruauntes being players, that this her maiesties commaundement may be dulye kepte and obeyed.

The extent to which this directive was 'dulye kepte and obeyed' may be illustrated by the action of no less a nobleman than Sir Robert Dudley himself, who in the following June wrote on behalf of his players to the Earl of Shrewsbury (then Lord President of the North) to ask permission for them to tour in Yorkshire, because they are 'honest men ... and suche as shall plaie none other matter, I trust, but tollerable and convenient'.[2]

One further piece of legislation, which applied to a far broader class of people than interlude players, also had the effect of narrowing the responsibility for the actors. This was the famous Statute 14 of 1572: 'An Acte for the Punishment of Vacabondes, and for the Relief of the Poore and Impotent' which was aimed at regulating the apparently large migrant population of England at this time: pedlars, tinkers, chapmen, begging-scholars from the universities, as well as travelling entertainers of all kinds. The only actors exempted from its provisions were 'servants of any Baron of this Realm or ... any other honorable Personage of greater Degree'. When Robert Dudley's Men were granted a royal patent in 1574, we find set down for a single company the implications of the 1572 statute:

Knowe ye that we of oure especiall grace, certen knowledge, and mere mocion haue licenced and auctorised, and by these presentes do licence and auctorise, our lovinge Subiectes ... seruauntes to oure trustie and welbeloued Cosen and Counseyllor the Earle of Leycester, to vse, exercise, and occupie the arte and facultye of playenge ... Comedies, Tragedies, Enterludes, and stage playes, to gether with their musicke,

---

[1] See Hazlitt, op. cit. pp. 19–20; and E. K. Chambers, *The Elizabethan Stage*, Vol. IV, pp. 263–4.
[2] See Gildersleeve, op. cit. p. 15.

to shewe, publishe, exercise, and occupie to their best commoditie
during all the terme aforesaide, aswell within oure Citie of London
and liberties of the same, as also within the liberties and fredomes of
anye oure Cities, townes, Bouroughes et cetera whatsoeuer as without
the same, thoroughte our Realme of England.... Prouyded that the
said Commedies, Tragedies, enterludes, and stage playes be by the
master of oure Revells for the tyme beynge before sene and allowed,
and that the same be not published or shewen in the tyme of common
prayer, or in the tyme of greate and common plague in oure said Citye
of London.[1]

While effective control of the acting profession was thus moving into
the hands of legal officers and noblemen directly answerable to the queen,
a hint of the new battle over the drama, which was to be fought out in
the 1580s and 1590s between the court and the City, shows its head. The
Bishop of London, Edmund Grindall, wrote to the Privy Council on 23
February 1564:

> Mr. Calfhill this mornynge shewed me your letter to him, wherin ye
> wishe some politike orders to be devised agaynste Infection. I thinke
> it verie necessarie, and wille doo myne endevour bothe by exhortation,
> and otherwise. I was readye to crave your helpe for that purpose
> afore, as one nott vnmyndefulle of the parishe.
>
> By searche I doo perceive, thatt ther is no one thinge off late is more
> lyke to have renewed this contagion, then the practise off an idle sorte
> off people, which have ben infamouse in all goode common weales: I
> meane these Histriones, common playours; who now daylye, butt
> speciallye on holydayes, sett vp bylles, whervnto the youthe resorteth
> excessively, and ther taketh infection: besydes that goddes worde by
> theyr impure mowthes is prophaned, and turned into scoffes; for
> remedie wheroff in my iugement ye shulde do verie well to be a meane,
> that a proclamation wer sett furthe to inhibitte all playes for one whole
> yeare (*and iff itt wer for ever, it wer nott amisse*) within the Cittie, or 3.
> myles compasse, vpon paynes aswell to the playours, as to the owners
> off the howses, wher they playe theyr lewde enterludes.[2]

Here are the same causes for concern as in the Proclamation of 1545,
to which is added the danger of the plague; but the tone is different, as are

[1] E. K. Chambers, *The Elizabethan Stage*, Vol. II, pp. 87–8.
[2] Ibid. Vol. IV, pp. 266–7.

the social circumstances. The Puritan note is struck in the parenthesis (italicized here): playing is the work of the devil, so that any reasons moral, social, political, religious or medical will serve to persuade a too tolerant court that the theatre is no part of a truly Protestant commonwealth. As we have seen, the queen's response was to give Leicester's company royal approval and support.

The conflict over the theatres was joined; as Wickham puts it:

> If the State was in the process of taking over from the Church the responsibility for deciding what subject matter should or should not be presented on the stage, and who should perform it, municipal authorities remained as keen under the new regime as they had been under the old to preserve their time-honoured right to control the physical conditions of performance.[1]

In the same year as Leicester's Men received their patent, an exchange occurred which indicates the shape of events to come. The Privy Council wished to appoint a Mr Holmes to have 'the appointment of places for playes and enterludes within this citie'; its request was turned down by the City mayor and aldermen because it violated rights of control 'extending to the hart of our liberties'.[2] By the end of 1574 the Common Council of London, during the mayoralty of Sir James Hawes, had issued its vividly worded complaint against the theatres in the Act of 6 December, specifying 'that from henceforthe no playe, Commodye, Tragidye, enterlude nor publycke shewe shalbe openlye played or shewed within the liberties of the Cittie … which shall not be firste pervsed and Allowed in suche order and fourme and by suche persons as by the Lorde Maior and Courte of Aldermen for the tyme beinge shalbe appoynted.'[3] And by 1576 the Burbages had built their Theatre outside the 'liberties of the Cittie' in the northern suburb of Shoreditch.

[1] Wickham, op. cit. Vol. II, Pt 1, p. 81.
[2] E. K. Chambers, *The Elizabethan Stage*, Vol. IV, p. 271.
[3] Ibid., p. 274.

5 Private playing and the court

While the public theatre was making its way between 1500 and 1575 through the maelstrom of political and religious change, coterie drama of one sort or another continued to flourish, sometimes touched by national events, but more often pursuing an independent life.

At both universities there was a tradition of revelling. Records indicate that liturgical plays were acted in some colleges during the fifteenth century; and Boy Bishops, Lords of Misrule and Christmas Princes resisted all efforts – such as those of Edward VI's visitors in 1549 – to put them down. Mummings, moralities and allegories in the medieval manner all appear in the accounts of various important colleges during the first half of the sixteenth century.[1] However, unlike the popular drama, the growth of academic theatrical activity was a by-product of the revival of classical learning and was influenced by the expansion and secularization of the universities during this period. Many important foundations date from this time – Christ Church (1546) and St John's (1555) at Oxford; Christ's (1505), St John's (1511) and Trinity (1546) at Cambridge – and the admission of gentlemen-commoners at the end of the fifteenth century had led to a modification of the semi-monastic rule of life. More important,

[1] See Malone Society Collections, V (1959–60).

English academics, following the lead set in Italy and Germany, became enthusiastic about the use of classical drama as an educational tool. By the mid-century the acting of classical plays seems to have been a feature of college festivities. For example, the Christ Church Lord of Misrule's pastime in 1554 was to include not more than two comedies and two tragedies 'of the which fower playes there shall be a Comedy in Lattin and a Comedy in Greek and a Tragedie in Lattin and a Tragedy in Greek'.[1]

Performances of Plautus, Terence and Aristophanes were supplemented by native and continental productions. At both universities biblical plays were written by college fellows for their students. Nicholas Grimald's *Christus Redivivus* was performed at Brasenose in 1540 and his *Archipropheta* at Christ Church or Exeter in 1547; while at Cambridge John Christopherson's *Jephthas* may have been presented at Trinity in 1554. It was at Cambridge too that the importations, Willem de Volder's (Gnaphaeus's) *Acolastus* and George Macropedius's *Asotus*, were staged. Just how seriously the role of drama was taken in the universities at this time may be illustrated by the writing of *Absolom* by Thomas Watson, who was a strong advocate of the new learning and who was responsible (with Sir John Cheke and Sir Thomas Smith) for the vitalizing of the study of Aristotle at Cambridge. Even more striking is the effort of the Regius Professor of Divinity, Martin Bucer, in his 1550 New Year gift to Edward VI, *De Regno Christi*, to set out the principles which should govern the form and content of tragedies and comedies intended to be acted by young scholars.[2]

There is some evidence that colleges had contact with the professional stage and sometimes employed travelling actors in their revels during the first part of the century. However, by 1575 itinerant companies visiting university towns were beginning to create a problem of discipline. In October of that year the Vice-Chancellor of Cambridge wrote to the Privy Council

> ... touchinge the misdemeanour of diuers badd persons, which wandringe aboute the Countrye vnder the colour of licenses for the makeinge of shewes, and playeinge of Enterludes and settinge furth of other vaine games and pastimes, ... thereby allure manie of our Scholers

[1] F. S. Boas, *University Drama in the Tudor Age* (Oxford, 1914), p. 17.
[2] *De Regno Christi*, Bk II, ch. 54, 'De honestis ludis', where are listed scriptural episodes appropriate for comedies and tragedies; see Boas, op. cit. pp. 65–8.

from the good course of theire studies and vsual exercises for the increase of learninge.[1]

This letter brought an order from the Council which prohibited performances 'within that Vniuersity and Towne, or within fyue miles compasse, but such as by the lawes of the Realme are vsuall'. We know that at least one fellow profited from seeing popular drama – Mr S. of Christ's College, Cambridge; for he managed to produce the best play to come from the universities, *Gammer Gurton's Needle*, which blended professional vitality with classical form. Only once did college theatre feel the repercussions of the religious controversy which plagued the popular stage. This was the result of the 1545 Lenten performance of *Pammachius* also at Christ's College,[2] so scandalous an affair that it provoked a correspondence between Bishop Gardiner and Vice-Chancellor Matthew Parker, which brings the whole subject of selecting, editing and mounting academic plays under review.

It was in Elizabeth's reign that the universities were able to display their histrionic abilities before the most sophisticated of audiences. The court visited Cambridge in August 1564 and Oxford in August–September 1566. With help from Sir Thomas Benger's Office of the Revels, both institutions produced elaborate programmes of dramatic entertainment for their royal visitor, which accurately reflect the nature of academic theatre at this time. On a great stage specially erected in King's College Chapel were presented Plautus' *Aulularia*, Edward Haliwell's Senecan tragedy *Dido* and Nicholas Udall's *Ezechias*, a scriptural play in English. At Oxford the performances took place in the great hall of Christ Church, which was equipped with newly constructed balconies and an elaborate system of lighting. The plays were a Latin prose comedy, *Marcus Geminus*; Part 1 of Richard Edwards's *Palamon and Arcite*, based on Chaucer's *Knight's Tale*, and James Calfhill's *Progne*, the source for which was probably the earlier Latin play of Gregorio Corraro.

The Inns of Court also had a tradition of entertainment dating from the beginning of the fifteenth century. By 1500 the various colleges had established a regular pattern of revels, which, in addition to the 'grand Christmasings', fell on such feast days as St Erkenwold, Candlemas, All Saints, St Thomas and Midsummer Day. Most of the Inns elected a Master of Revels for each festival, and there was a custom of inviting

---

[1] Malone Society Collections, I (1908), pp. 192–3.
[2] See above pp. 16–17.

professional troupes either to supplement or replace the amateur activity. Occasionally the young lawyers produced a noteworthy entertainment, such as that at the Middle Temple in 1561 when Robert Dudley was the Constable-Marshal. The importance attached to these activities may be judged by the admission of Arthur Brooke (the author of *Romeus and Juliet*) to membership of the Inner Temple without a fee in 1562 'in consideration of certain plays and shows at Christmas last set forth by him'.

In some respects the lawyers' entertainments were influenced by continental models more strongly than were their Oxbridge counterparts. It was at Gray's Inn that anglicized Italian comedy made its appearance with Gascoigne's *Supposes* (Ariosto's *I Suppositi*), Jeffere's *Bugbears* (Grazzini's *La Spiritata*) and the anonymous *Two Italian Gentlemen* (Pasqualigo's *Il Fidele*); and the Inner Temple offered court audiences *Gorboduc*, *Jocasta* and *Gismond of Salerne*. These legal dramatics were largely untouched by public events and were not affected by the instruments of control forged for managing the popular stage. The odd incidents such as John Roo's play at Gray's Inn that Wolsey took amiss in 1526[1] and the Masters' ban on all plays in 1550 appear to have been unusual. In general, acting at the Inns of Court seems to have been covered by the 1574 Act of Common Council's exemptions:

> ... anie plaies, Enterludes, Comodies, Tragidies, or shewes to be played or shewed in the pryvate hous, dwellinge, or lodginge of anie nobleman, Citizen, or gentleman ... withowte publique or Commen Collection of money of the Auditorie or behoulders theareof.[2]

As in the universities, acting in the public schools was a product of the revival of classical learning; although there was a long history of entertainment of various kinds. The statutes of Eton provide for a Boy Bishop as early as 1444, Christmas plays were customary by 1559, and there are numerous expenditures for theatricals recorded in the audit books between 1525 and 1573. Under the mastership of Nicholas Udall there seems to have been additional emphasis on acting, as the school performed before Cromwell in 1538; and *Ralph Roister Doister* may have been a product of his tenure. The only record of a court performance by the school is 6 January 1573. Westminster School also used drama as a teaching technique. Udall became headmaster there in 1555; and Strype claims that Udall's predecessor Alexander Nowell 'brought in the reading of Terence for the

---

[1] See above pp. 14–15.
[2] E. K. Chambers, *The Elizabethan Stage*, Vol. IV, p. 276.

better learning of the pure Roman style'. The Sub-Almoner's payment of 'xvi^d for wryting of a play for the chyldren' in 1521 indicates an acting tradition similar to that of Eton. However, it was not until Elizabeth's reign that the school began a series of court performances of Terentian dramas. Mulcaster's school, Merchant Taylors', started acting soon after its foundation in 1561 and by the early 1570s was performing not only before its parent company but also at court. Here again a distinguished alumnus, the seventeenth-century judge Sir James Whitelocke, attests in later life to the educational value of playing in teaching the boys 'good behaviour and audacitye'.[1]

It was, of course, the boys' companies of St Paul's, the Chapel Royal and Windsor Chapel that were the most celebrated child performers of the period. These twelfth-century foundations had a much more venerable performing history than the universities, the Inns of Court and the public schools. St Paul's Boys were playing Old Testament dramatizations as early as 1378 and by Henry VII's reign were regular participants in court festivities. The Chapel Royal Company appeared once or twice a year at court between 1506 and 1512; and St Paul's Boys acted an anti-Lutheran piece in Latin and French before the king and the ambassadors of François I in 1527, as well as *Phormio* and *Dido* before Wolsey the following year. By the latter half of the century the children's companies were regular visitors to court under such men as Sebastian Westcott, William Hunnis and Richard Edwards.

The court was the patron of the most lavish form of private dramatic entertainment of the period. Before Henry VII's reign, impromptu disguisings took place occasionally at court and in the houses of the nobility. The king himself was not especially fond of revels and was observed to be 'rather a princely and gentle spectator than seem[ing] much to be delighted'; but his queen was very attached to festivity of all kinds.[2] It is recorded as an unusual event when one Christmas, owing to illness, there were 'no disgysynges and but right few plays'.[3] Every year during this austere king's reign there was an Abbot or Lord of Misrule to direct the Christmas festival, in which the king's own company of players and the Gentlemen and Children of the Chapel Royal played a main part, as well as the occasional civic troupe and French players.

At Henry VIII's accession revelling experienced a new vitality. The first

[1] Ibid. Vol. II, pp. 69–76.
[2] See E. Welsford, *The Court Masque* (Cambridge, 1927), p. 116.
[3] Ibid. p. 116.

part of his reign was, according to the chroniclers, a feast of mummings, disguisings, elaborately equipped joustings and tournaments of chivalry. Both his coronation in 1509 and the queen's churching in 1510 were occasions for sumptuous entertainments, as was the celebration of the marriage agreement between Princess Mary and the Dauphin in 1518. The appointment of Sir Thomas Cawarden as permanent Master of Revels in 1545 is but one indication of the new prominence court entertainment had attained.

By the time of Edward VI and Mary the pattern of court revels had assumed a form that was to persist through Elizabeth's reign. Under the supervision of the 'Magister Jocorum' there were regular performances of masques and interludes by the royal companies, other adult players and the Gentlemen and Children of the Chapel at Shrovetide and Christmas seasons, with extra holidays, such as St Andrew's, St Mark's, Hallowmas and Easter, sometimes being the occasion for plays. Candlemas (the feast of the Purification of the Virgin) was celebrated regularly during Mary's reign but only once in Edward's. By the time of Elizabeth the calendar of court playing had become fixed at St Stephen's (26 December), St John the Evangelist (27 December), Innocents (28 December), New Year (1 January), Twelfth Night (6 January), Shrove Sunday, Shrove Monday and Shrove Tuesday, with additional feasts at other times of the year sometimes being celebrated with dramatic entertainments.[1] The boys' companies provided a good deal of the theatrical fare for these festivities, with the burgeoning adult troupes – such as Leicester's, Lincoln's, Warwick's, Sussex's and Howard's Men – becoming more prominent as the years passed.

The Office of the Master of the Revels was a position of Tudor origin, the first mention of which occurs at Christmas 1494 under Henry VII. At this time it was a temporary post quite distinct from that of the Lord of Misrule whose duties were quasi-dramatic. The most distinguished temporary Master during the early years of Henry VIII's reign was Sir Henry Guildford, sometime Comptroller of the Royal Household. All the temporary Masters worked with a permanent official, the Porter and Yeoman of the Wardrobe, a role filled for a long period by Richard Gibson, a former King's player. At Cawarden's permanent appointment in 1545, John Bridges was named Yeoman, and a clerk to keep the accounts was added to the staff. In 1547 the office was housed in the Old Priory at Blackfriars, and

[1] See J. Leeds Barroll, *The Revels History of Drama in English*, Vol. III, pp. 49–52.

it was here that most of the administrative duties were performed by Thomas Blagrave from 1551 to 1559. After Cawarden's death, a patent issued on 18 January 1560 gave the mastership to Sir Thomas Benger, under whom the premises were moved from Blackfriars to the Hospital of St John of Jerusalem at Clerkenwell. During the tenure of Benger the office was still effectively in the hands of Blagrave, who also acted as temporary Master between Benger's retirement in November 1573 and Christmas 1579.

Benger's retirement coincided with Burghley's becoming Lord Treasurer, under whom it was proposed that the administration of the Revels should be thoroughly investigated and reformed. In the absence of any patented Master, the oversight of the office was placed in the hands of John Fortescue, Master of the Wardrobe, and Henry Sackford, Master of the Tents – these being the two departments of the royal household with which the Revels post had been linked since its inception. There is some evidence of immediate attempts at economy at this time, probably in reaction to the increased expenditures occasioned by the entertainment provided for the French embassy of the Duc de Montmorency; and the office produced a number of memoranda which give some insight into the range of its duties at this period: the buying, storing and upkeep of costumes; the planning of 'devices'; the hiring and supervision of workmen; the anticipation of the monarch's desires for a particular event; the methods of accounting; and the handling of the complicated system of payment by imprests.[1]

From other sources we know that the Master of the Revels during this time had emerged as a censor of plays as well as a producer of them. For example, in 1571 the Revels Accounts list six plays 'being chosen owte of many, and founde to be the best that were to be had, the same also being often perused and necessarely corrected and amended by all thafforeseide officers'.[2] This is the function that was referred to in the patent granted to Leicester's Men in 1574; and in subsequent years the Revels Accounts are frequently to record payments for the 'perusing and reforming of plays'. It is also the function which gave the next two Masters, Sir Edmund Tilney and Sir George Buc, such enormous influence over the acting and printing of plays in the years after 1579.

---

[1] See E. K. Chambers, *The Elizabethan Stage*, Vol. I, pp. 80–6, and Barroll, op. cit.
[2] Gildersleeve, op. cit. p. 49.

Table: a calendar of plays
1495–1575

This calendar gives a general picture of the dramatic activity of the period. It includes not only those plays which were printed but also those which are referred to in various documents of the time and which no longer exist. When a play survives in printed form, in a manuscript or in handwritten or printed fragment, the title is italicized. Wherever we have only a title as proof of a play's existence, this is enclosed in single quotation marks.

PERFORMANCES. The listing of royal performances, taken from the court account books, includes only those plays, masques and entertainments whose titles we know. There was, of course, some court entertainment in the years where the entry 'Not known' appears.

PRINTINGS and REPRINTINGS. Very few plays got into print during the first fifty years of the century; but with the spread of the printing trade and increased theatrical activity, more play texts were published. It is difficult to date publications with any accuracy, and so printings and reprintings are listed in the earliest year of the limits between which they must have appeared. Once plays begin to be entered in the Stationers' Register and to bear dates in their imprints and colophons, more accurate dating becomes possible. Stationers' Register entry dates are given wherever they exist; when exact dating is not possible, each entry is followed by the dates between which the play was probably printed.

PLAYS WRITTEN. Plays believed to have been composed during a particular year are listed under the year heading. Exact dating is rarely possible and so *termini ad quem* and *a quo* are given in brackets after each title. The plays so listed are additional to those performed and written and printed in any given year.

When plays are translations or adaptations of classical or Continental dramas, the original author is given, and the original author and title wherever the English title differs from that of the source play.

1495   PERFORMANCES
Not known

PRINTINGS
None known

REPRINTINGS
None known

PLAYS WRITTEN
Nature (*c.* 1490–*c.* 1501)
'Comoediolae' (*c.* 1491–9)
The Summoning of Everyman (adapt. Dorlandus's *Elckerlijc*) (*c.* 1495–1500)

1496   None known

1497   PERFORMANCES
Not known

PRINTINGS
None known

REPRINTINGS
None known

PLAYS WRITTEN
Fulgens and Lucrece (*c.* 1490–*c.* 1501)

1498   None known

1499   None known

1500   None known

1501   PERFORMANCES
     At court: Not known
     Elsewhere: 'The Marriage of Prince Arthur' (19 November): Westminster and Richmond

PRINTINGS
None known

REPRINTINGS
None known

PLAYS WRITTEN
None known

1502   PERFORMANCES
　　　　At court: Not known
　　　　Elsewhere: 'The Welcome of Katherine of Aragon' (12 November):
　　　　　　　　　London

PRINTINGS
None known

REPRINTINGS
None known

PLAYS WRITTEN
None known

1503   PERFORMANCES
　　　　At court: Not known
　　　　Elsewhere: The Droichis [*Dwarf's*] *Part of the Play* (*The Manner of the
　　　　　　　　　Crying of a Play*) (1 May): Edinburgh
　　　　　　　　　'The Welcome for Princess Margaret' (7 August): Edin-
　　　　　　　　　burgh

PRINTINGS
None known

REPRINTINGS
None known

PLAYS WRITTEN
None known

1504   PERFORMANCES
　　　　At court: Not known
　　　　Elsewhere: *The Life of St Meriasek, Bishop and Confessor*: Camborne,
　　　　　　　　　Cornwall

PRINTINGS
None known

REPRINTINGS
None known

PLAYS WRITTEN
None known

1505 None known

1506 None known

1507 PERFORMANCES
    At court: 'The Jousts of the Months of May and June' (May and
             June)
    Elsewhere: 'The Joust of the Wild Knight and the Black Lady' (June):
             Scottish court

PRINTINGS
None known

REPRINTINGS
None known

PLAYS WRITTEN
None known

1508 PERFORMANCES
Not known

PRINTINGS
None known

REPRINTINGS
None known

PLAYS WRITTEN
The World and the Child (*Mundus et Infans*) (1500–22)

1509 PERFORMANCES
    At court: 'The Scholars of Dame Pallas and Knights of Diana' (June)
    Elsewhere: 'The Coronation Triumph of Henry VIII' (24 June):
             London and Westminster

PRINTINGS
None known

REPRINTINGS
None known

PLAYS WRITTEN
None known

1510 PERFORMANCES
   At court: 'The Entertainment of the Ambassadors' (10 February)
       'Almains and Spaniards' (14 November)
       'Robin Hood's Men'
   Elsewhere: 'The Nine Hierarchies of Angels': Coventry

   PRINTINGS
   The Summoning of Everyman (1510–25)

   REPRINTINGS
   None known

   PLAYS WRITTEN
   None known

1511 PERFORMANCES
   At court: 'A Pageant of a Mountain' (6 January)
       'The Four Chevaliers of the Forest Salvigny' (13 February)
       'The Garden of Pleasure' (14 February)
       'The Ship of Fame' (1 May)
   Elsewhere: 'The Welcome for Queen Margaret' (May): Aberdeen
       'St George' (20 July): Bassingborne, Cambridge

   PRINTINGS
   None known

   REPRINTINGS
   None known

   PLAYS WRITTEN
   None known

1512 PERFORMANCES
   At court: 'The Castle Dangerous' (1 January)
       'An Epiphany Masque' (6 January)
       'The Dolorous Castle' (June)
   Elsewhere: Not known

   PRINTINGS
   Fulgens and Lucrece (1512–16)

   REPRINTINGS
   None known

   PLAYS WRITTEN
   None known

1513 PERFORMANCES
At court: 'The Rich Mount' (6 January)
'Beauty and Venus'
'The Masque at Tournay' (18 October): Tournay
Elsewhere: Not known

PRINTINGS
None known

REPRINTINGS
None known

PLAYS WRITTEN
Hickscorner (*c.* 1513–16)

1514 PERFORMANCES
At court: 'The Triumph of Love and Beauty' (6 January)
Elsewhere: Not known

PRINTINGS
None known

REPRINTINGS
None known

PLAYS WRITTEN
None known

1515 PERFORMANCES
At court: 'The Place Perilous (Wild Men)' (6 January)
'Robin Hood's Feast' (1 May)
Elsewhere: Not known

PRINTINGS
Hickscorner (1515–16)

REPRINTINGS
None known

PLAYS WRITTEN
'Achademios' (*c.* 1504–23)
'Virtue' (*c.* 1504–23)
'Good Order' (*c.* 1504–29)
Magnificence (1515–23)

1516   PERFORMANCES
> *At court:*   'The Eltham Pageant of a Castle' (6 January)
> 'Troilus and Pandar' (6 January)
> *Elsewhere:* Not known

PRINTINGS
Andria (trans. Terence) (1516–33)

REPRINTINGS
None known

PLAYS WRITTEN
None known

1517   PERFORMANCES
> *At court:*   'The Garden of Esperance' (6 January)
> *Elsewhere:* Not known

PRINTINGS
None known

REPRINTINGS
None known

PLAYS WRITTEN
The Nature of the Four Elements (1517–18)

1518   PERFORMANCES
> *At court:*   'The Rock of Amity' (8 October)
> 'A Masque of Palmers'
> *Elsewhere:* 'The Entertainment of the French Ambassadors' (October): Wolsey's House
> 'St Erasmus': Aberdeen

PRINTINGS
None known

REPRINTINGS
None known

PLAYS WRITTEN
None known

1519   PERFORMANCES
> *At court:*   'The Entertainment of the Hostages' (7 March)
> 'Revels called a Maskalyn'
> *Elsewhere:* Not known

PRINTINGS
None known

REPRINTINGS
None known

PLAYS WRITTEN
The Pardoner and the Friar (1513–21)

1520 PERFORMANCES
　　　　At court: 'A Pageant of a Wagon' (1 February)
　　　　　　　　　　'Summer and Lust'
　　　　　　　　　　'The Field of the Cloth of Gold' (9–24 June): Guisnes
　　　　Elsewhere: Not known

PRINTINGS
None known

REPRINTINGS
None known

PLAYS WRITTEN
Youth (1513–29)
Andria (trans. Terence) (1516–33)
The Four PP (1520–2)
Johan Johan the Husband, Tib His Wife and Sir Johan the Priest (adapt.
Farce du pâté) (1520–33)
John the Evangelist (*c.* 1520–*c.* 1557)

1521 PERFORMANCES
　　　　At court: 'The Entertainment of the Emperor's Ambassadors'
　　　　Elsewhere: Not known

PRINTINGS
None known

REPRINTINGS
None known

PLAYS WRITTEN
None known

1522 PERFORMANCES
　　　　At court: 'Friendship, Prudence and Might (The Triumph of
　　　　　　　　　　Amity)' (15 June)

Elsewhere: 'The Conquest of Lady Scorn' (4 March): Wolsey's House
'The Welcome for Emperor Charles V' (6 June): London

PRINTINGS
The World and the Child (*Mundus et Infans*) (17 July)

REPRINTINGS
None known

PLAYS WRITTEN
None known

1523   None known

1524   PERFORMANCES
At court: 'The Entertainment of the Scottish Ambassadors' (28 December)
Elsewhere: Not known

PRINTINGS
None known

REPRINTINGS
None known

PLAYS WRITTEN
None known

1525   PERFORMANCES
At court: Not known
Elsewhere: 'The Golden Fleece' (2 February): Canterbury
'Ite in Vineam (The Parable of the Vineyard)': Calais

PRINTINGS
None known

REPRINTINGS
The Summoning of Everyman (1525–30)

PLAYS WRITTEN
'Microcosmus' (1520–32)
'Mundus Plumbeus' (1520–32)

1526   PERFORMANCES
At court: Not known

Elsewhere: 'Lord Governance and Lady Public Weal' (Christmas): Gray's Inn

PRINTINGS
The Nature of the Four Elements (1526–30)

REPRINTINGS
None known

PLAYS WRITTEN
None known

1527 PERFORMANCES
  At court: 'Love and Riches (The Father of Heaven)' (5 May)
  'Heretic Luther (The Deliverance of the Pope)' (10 November)
  'The Masque for the French Ambassadors' (10 November): at Greenwich
  Elsewhere: 'A Masque of Venus, Cupid, Six Damsels, and Six Old Men' (3 January): Wolsey's House
  'The Visit of Henry VIII to Wolsey' (5 May): Wolsey's House

PRINTINGS
Calisto and Melebea (adapt. de Rojas's *Celestina*) (*c.* 1527–30)

REPRINTINGS
None known

PLAYS WRITTEN
Godly Queen Hester (1525–9)
Gentleness and Nobility (*c.* 1527–30)

1528 PERFORMANCES
  At court: Not known
  Elsewhere: 'Religion, Peace and Justice' (7 January): Wolsey's House
  A Play of Love (Christmas): Inns of Court
  'Adam and Eve'; 'Bacchus'; 'Crispin and Crispinianus'; 'The Deaths of the Apostles'; 'Joseph and Mary'; 'The Passion of the Saviour'; 'Vulcan': Dublin

PRINTINGS
None known

REPRINTINGS
The Summoning of Everyman (1528–9?)

PLAYS WRITTEN
The Play of the Weather (1525–33)

1529   PERFORMANCES
Not known

PRINTINGS
Gentleness and Nobility

REPRINTINGS
None known

PLAYS WRITTEN
None known

1530   PERFORMANCES
Not known

PRINTINGS
Magnificence (1530?)
Nature (1530–4)
Pater, Filius et Uxor (*The Prodigal Son*) (adapt. Textor's *Juvenis, Pater, Uxor*) (*c.* 1530–4)
Youth (1530–5)

REPRINTINGS
The Summoning of Everyman (1530–5)

PLAYS WRITTEN
None known

1531   None known

1532   PERFORMANCES
       At court: 'The Triumph at Calais and Boulogne' (11–29 October):
              France
       Elsewhere: Not known

PRINTINGS
None known

REPRINTINGS
None known

PLAYS WRITTEN
None known

1533 PERFORMANCES
At court: 'Against the Cardinals'
Elsewhere: 'The Coronation Triumph of Ann Boleyn' (31 May): London

PRINTINGS
Johan Johan, Tib His Wife and Sir Johan the Priest (12 February)
The Pardoner and the Friar (5 April)
Old Christmas (*Good Order*)
The Play of the Weather
A Play of Love (1533–4). SR *c.* April–May 1563.

REPRINTINGS
None known

PLAYS WRITTEN
Witty and Witless (*c.* 1520–*c.* 1533)
'Old Custom' (*c.* 1520–50)

1534 PERFORMANCES
At court: Not known
Elsewhere: 'Placidas, alias Sir Eustace': Braintree, Essex

PRINTINGS
None known

REPRINTINGS
None known

PLAYS WRITTEN
None known

1535 PERFORMANCES
At court: Not known
Elsewhere: 'The Lord Mayor's Show' (29 October): London

PRINTINGS
Temperance and Humility (*c.* 1521–35)

REPRINTINGS
None known

PLAYS WRITTEN
None known

1536 PERFORMANCES
Not known

PRINTINGS
None known

REPRINTINGS
None known

PLAYS WRITTEN
'The Life of John the Baptist' (c. 1530–9)
'Christ and the Doctors' (c. 1530–9)
'Baptism and Temptation', Parts 1 and 2 (c. 1530–9)
'The Raising of Lazarus' (c. 1530–9)
'The Council of Bishops' (c. 1530–9)
'Simon the Leper' (c. 1530–9)
'The Lord's Supper' (c. 1530–9)
'The Passion of Christ' (c. 1530–9)
'The Burial and Resurrection' (c. 1530–9)
'On the Seven Sins' (c. 1530–9)
'Pater Noster Play' (c. 1530–9)

1537   PERFORMANCES
       At court: Not known
       Elsewhere: Thersites (adapt. Textor) (12–24 October): Eton? Oxford?
             'A Reverent Receiving of the Sacrament': before Crom-
             well (?)

PRINTINGS
None known

REPRINTINGS
None known

PLAYS WRITTEN
'Upon Both Marriages of the King' (1533–9)
'Against the Pope's Councillors' (1535–c. 1537)
'Against Adulterators of the Word of God' (c. 1536–9)
'Against Momi and Zoili' (c. 1536–9)
'A Rude Commonalty'
'The Woman on the Rock'
Albion Knight (c. 1537–66)
'On Sects Among the Papists' (c. 1538–48)
'Treacheries of the Papists' (c. 1538–48)

1538   PERFORMANCES
       At court: Not known
       Elsewhere: 'The Welcome for Marie de Lorraine' (10 June; July):
             St Andrews and Edinburgh

PRINTINGS
None known

REPRINTINGS
None known

PLAYS WRITTEN
'The Knaveries of Thomas Becket' (*c.* 1536–9)
God's Promises
John the Baptist's Preaching in the Wilderness
The Temptation of Our Lord and Saviour Jesus Christ by Satan
Three Laws of Nature, Moses and Christ
'The Image of Love' (*c.* 1538–48)
'Pammachius' (adapt. Kirchmayer) (1538–48)

1539   PERFORMANCES
    At court: 'King Arthur's Knights'
    Elsewhere: King John (2 January): Cranmer's House, Canterbury

PRINTINGS
None known

REPRINTINGS
None known

PLAYS WRITTEN
Courage, Kindness, Cleanness (1531–47)
D, G and T (1531–47)
Wit and Science (1531–47)
'Piscator sive Fraus Illusa' (1535–43)
'De Papatu' (*c.* 1537–48)
'Ezekias' (1537–56)
'The Sacrament of the Altar'

1540   PERFORMANCES
    At court: Not known
    Elsewhere: Christus Redivivus: Brasenose College, Oxford
        A Satire of the Three Estates, Version 1 (6 January):
        Linlithgow
        'The Beheading of John the Baptist': Playfield, Dundee
        'Dionysius the Tyrant': Playfield, Dundee

PRINTINGS
Acolastus (trans. de Volder [Gnaphaeus])

REPRINTINGS
None known

PLAYS WRITTEN
Absolom (*c.* 1535–44)
Christus Redivivus
'Christus Nascens'

1541   PERFORMANCES
    At court: Not known
    Elsewhere: 'The Nine Worthies': Dublin

PRINTINGS
The Four Cardinal Virtues (1541–7)
The Four PP (1541–7)

REPRINTINGS
None known

PLAYS WRITTEN
Baptistes sive Calumnia (1540–5)

1542   PERFORMANCES
Not known

PRINTINGS
None known

REPRINTINGS
None known

PLAYS WRITTEN
The Four Cardinal Virtues (1537–47)
Jephthes sive Votum (1540–5)

1543   PERFORMANCES
    At court: 'A Masque of Women' (1 January)
               'A Masque of Almains'
               'A Masque of Mariners'
    Elsewhere: Not known

PRINTINGS
Christus Redivivus

REPRINTINGS
None known

PLAYS WRITTEN
Alcestis (trans. Euripides)
Medea (trans. Euripides)
'Philoctetes' (trans. Sophocles)

1544   PERFORMANCES
Not known

PRINTINGS
Medea (trans. Euripides)

REPRINTINGS
The Play of the Weather

PLAYS WRITTEN
Jephthes (c. 1539–c. 1544)

1545   PERFORMANCES
  At court: 'A Masque of Egyptian Women'
  Elsewhere: Pammachius: Cambridge

PRINTINGS
None known

REPRINTINGS
None known

PLAYS WRITTEN
The Resurrection of Our Lord (c.1530–c. 1560)

1546   PERFORMANCES
  At court: Not known
  Elsewhere: 'The Market of Mischief': Norwich

PRINTINGS
None known

REPRINTINGS
None known

PLAYS WRITTEN
'De Johannis Huss Bohemie Noti Condemnatione' (1546–56)
'De Jobi Iusti Afflictionibus' (1546–56)

'De Jona a Deo ad Ninivitas Ablegati Defectione' (1546–56)
'De Judith Bethuliensis Incredibili Fortitudine' (1546–56)
'De Lazaro a Divitas aedibus Abacto' (1546–56)
'De Sodomo et Gormorre Incendio' (1546–56)
'De Susanne per Judices Iniquos ob Lese Pudicitie Notam Divini Libera-
   tione' (1546–56)
'The Melibeus of Chaucer' (1546–56)
'The Most Firm Friendship of Titus and Gisippus' (1546–56)
'The Rare Patience of Chaucer's Griselda' (1546–56)

1547 PERFORMANCES
        At court: 'The Story of Orpheus' (9 March)
                   'A Masque of Prester John' (Christmas)
        Elsewhere: 'The Coronation Triumph of King Edward VI' (19
                   February): Westminster and London
                   Archipropheta (adapt. Schoepper's Joannes Decollatus):
                   Oxford

      PRINTINGS
      God's Promises (1547–8)
      John the Baptist's Preaching in the Wilderness (c. 1547–8)
      The Temptation of Our Lord and Saviour Jesus Christ by Satan (c. 1547–8)
      Three Laws of Nature, Moses and Christ (c. 1547–8). SR c. August 1562
      Somebody, Avarice and Minister (c. 1547–50)

      REPRINTINGS
      None known

      PLAYS WRITTEN
      'Athanasius sive Infamia' (c. 1540–c. 1547)
      'De Puerorum in Musicis Institutione' (c. 1540–c. 1547)
      'Fama' (c. 1540–c. 1547)
      'Protomartyr' (c. 1540–c. 1547)
      'Troilus, from Chaucer' (c. 1540–c. 1547)
      Impatient Poverty (c. 1547–58)

1548 PERFORMANCES
        At court: 'A Masque of Young Moors' (12 February)
                   'The Tower of Babylon' (Christmas)
                   'A Masque of Men'
                   'Two Masques of Women'
        Elsewhere: Not known

      PRINTINGS
      Archipropheta

REPRINTINGS
The Four PP (1548–68)

PLAYS WRITTEN
'De Meretrice Babylonica'

1549   PERFORMANCES
　　　　At court: 'A Masque of Almains' (Christmas)
　　　　Elsewhere: Not known

PRINTINGS
None known

REPRINTINGS
None known

PLAYS WRITTEN
'Jube the Sane' (1547–53)

1550   PERFORMANCES
Not known

PRINTINGS
John the Evangelist (*c.* 1550)

REPRINTINGS
None known

PLAYS WRITTEN
Love Feigned and Unfeigned (*c.* 1540–*c.* 1560)
'Tragedies of Euripides' (trans. Euripides) (*c.* 1540–72)
'Free Will' (trans. Bassano by Thomas Hoby)
Lusty Juventus (1547–53)
Nice Wanton (1547–53)

1551   PERFORMANCES
　　　　At court: 'A Masque of Amazons' (Christmas)
　　　　　　　　'A Masque of Argus' (Christmas)
　　　　　　　　'A Masque of Moors and Amazons' (Christmas)
　　　　Elsewhere: Not known

PRINTINGS
None known

REPRINTINGS
None known

PLAYS WRITTEN
None known

1552 PERFORMANCES
  At court: 'A Drunken Masque' (2 January)
  'A Masque of Men' (6 January)
  'Riches and Youth' (6 January)
  'Aesop's Crow' (Christmas)
  'A Masque of Babions' (Christmas)
  'A Masque of Covetous Men' (Christmas)
  'A Masque of Matrons' (Christmas)
  'A Masque of Polanders' (Christmas)
  'A Masque of Soldiers' (Christmas)
  'A Masque of Women of Diana' (Christmas)
  Elsewhere: *A Satire of the Three Estates*, Version 2 (7 June): Castle Hill, Cupar, Fifeshire

PRINTINGS
None known

REPRINTINGS
None known

PLAYS WRITTEN
Ralph Roister Doister (1545–52)
'Self-Love' (1551–3)

1553 PERFORMANCES
  At court: 'Cupid, Venus and Mars' (6 January)
  'A Masque of Bagpipes' (Easter and May Day)
  'A Masque of Cats' (Easter and May Day)
  'A Masque of Greek Worthies' (Easter and May Day)
  'A Masque of Medioxes' (Easter and May Day)
  'A Masque of Tumblers' (Easter and May Day)
  'The State of Ireland' (Easter and May Day)
  'Genus Humanum' (Christmas)
  Elsewhere: *Respublica* (Christmas): London
  'Anglia Deformata et Anglia Restituta' (Christmas): Trinity College, Cambridge
  God's Promises (20 August): Kilkenny
  John the Baptist's Preaching in the Wilderness (20 August): Kilkenny
  The Temptation of Our Lord and Saviour Jesus Christ by Satan (20 August): Kilkenny

PRINTINGS
None known

REPRINTINGS
None known

PLAYS WRITTEN
'Strylius'
Gammer Gurton's Needle (c. 1552–63)

1554 PERFORMANCES
    At court: 'A Masque of Arcules, with Mariners' (St Andrew's Tide)
    'A Masque of Mariners' (Hallowmas)
    'A Masque of Venetian Senators' (Christmas)
    'A Masque of Venuses with Cupids' (Christmas)
    Elsewhere: *A Satire of the Three Estates*, Version 3 (12 August):
    Calton Hill, Edinburgh
    'The Entertainment for Queen Mary' (December): Edinburgh

PRINTINGS
Jephthes sive Votum

REPRINTINGS
The Play of the Weather (1554–60)

PLAYS WRITTEN
Jacob and Esau (c. 1550–7)
Wealth and Health (1554–c. 1555)

1555 PERFORMANCES
    At court: 'A Masque of Goddesses, Huntresses, with Turkish
    Women' (24–6 February)
    'A Masque of Turks Magistrates with Turks Archers'
    (24–6 February)
    Elsewhere: Not known

PRINTINGS
None known

REPRINTINGS
Youth (1555–8)

PLAYS WRITTEN
'De Crumena Perdita'
Jack Juggler (adapt. Plautus's *Amphitruo*) (c. 1553–8)
Synedrii sive Concessus Animalium (1554–5)

1556   PERFORMANCES
>> *At court:*   Not known
>> *Elsewhere:* 'The Hatfield Masque for the Princess Elizabeth': Hatfield
>> (or 1554?)
>> 'Holophernes': Hatfield (or 1554?)

> PRINTINGS
> *Alcestis* (trans. Euripides)
> *Christus Triumphans*

> REPRINTINGS
> None known

> PLAYS WRITTEN
> 'The Way to Life' (1556–7)

1557   PERFORMANCES
>> *At court:*   'A Great Masque of Almains, Pilgrims and Irishmen'
>> (25 April)
>> *Elsewhere:* 'The Sackful of News' (August): London
>> 'The Six Worthies': Dublin

> PRINTINGS
> None known

> REPRINTINGS
> None known

> PLAYS WRITTEN
> None known

1558   PERFORMANCES
>> *At court:*   Not known
>> *Elsewhere:* 'The Marriage of Queen Mary' (July): Edinburgh

> PRINTINGS
> None known

> REPRINTINGS
> None known

> PLAYS WRITTEN
> *Iphigenia in Aulis* (trans. Euripides) (1549–77)
> 'Thebais' (trans. Seneca) (*c.* 1550–*c.* 1559)
> *The Life and Repentance of Mary Magdalene* (*c.* 1550–66)
> *King John* (revis. 1558–62?)

1559 PERFORMANCES

  At court: 'Papists' (6 January)
     'A Masque of Swart Rutters' (5 February)
     'A Masque of Fishermen, Fishwives and Marketwives (7 February)
     'A Masque of Astronomers' (24 May)
     'A Masque of Almains and Palmers'
     'A Masque of Conquerors' (1558–9)
     'A Masque of Hungarians' (1558–9)
     'A Masque of Mariners' (1558–9)
     'A Masque of Moors' (1558–9)
     'A Masque of Turks' (1558–9)
     'A Masque of Nusquams, with Turkish Commoners' (1559–60)
  Elsewhere: 'The Coronation Triumph of Queen Elizabeth' (14 January): London
     'A Masque of Shipmen and Country Maids' (August): West Horseley

PRINTINGS

Troas (trans. Seneca). SR 14 January, 2 editions

REPRINTINGS

The Play of the Weather (1559–75)

PLAYS WRITTEN

Patient and Meek Grissil (1558–61)
The Longer Thou Livest the More Fool Thou Art (*c.* 1559–68)

1560 PERFORMANCES

  At court: 'A Masque of Actaeons' (1559–60)
     'A Masque of Clowns' (1559–60)
     'A Masque of Barbarians' (1 January)
     'A Masque of Italian Women' (6 January)
     'A Masque of Patriarchs' (6 January)
     'A Masque of Diana and Six Nymphs Huntresses' (27 February)
  Elsewhere: Not known

PRINTINGS

Impatient Poverty. SR 10 June
Nice Wanton. SR 10 June
Robin Hood. SR 30 November (?)
Thyestes (trans. Seneca) (26 March)

REPRINTINGS
A Play of Love (1560–65)
Troas (trans. Seneca) (1560?)

PLAYS WRITTEN
Tom Tyler and His Wife (1558–63)
The Disobedient Child (*c.* 1559–70)
Enough is as Good as a Feast (*c.* 1559–70)
'Sapientia Solomonis' (adapt. Sixt Birck)
Aegio (*c.* 1560–5)

1561   PERFORMANCES
    At court: 'Huff, Suff and Ruff' (*Cambises?*) (Christmas 1560–1)
                'A Masque of Wise and Foolish Virgins' (25–8 October)
    Elsewhere: 'The Passion of Christ' (25 May): Shrewsbury
              'The Welcome for Queen Mary' (2 September): Edinburgh
              Apollo et Musae Exules (October?): Scottish court

PRINTINGS
Godly Queen Hester. SR January/February
Witty and Witless. SR January/February
Hercules Furens (trans. Seneca)
Thersites (adapt. Textor) (1561–3)

REPRINTINGS
Impatient Poverty (1561–8)

PLAYS WRITTEN
Cambises ('Huff, Suff and Ruff'?) (*c.* 1558–69)
'Romeus and Juliet' (*c.* 1560–2)
Hercules Oetaeus (trans. pseudo-Seneca) (1561–*c.* 1570)
The Pedlar's Prophecy (1561–*c.* 1563)

1562   PERFORMANCES
    At court: *Gorboduc* (18 January)
             'Julius Caesar' (?)
    Elsewhere: *Gorboduc* (6 January): Inner Temple
              'John Baptist': Cambridge
              'The Marriage Entertainment for Lord James Stuart'
              (8 February): Scottish court

PRINTINGS
Jack Juggler (adapt. Plautus' *Amphitruo*). SR *c.* November
'The Two Sins of King David'. SR *c.* June

REPRINTINGS
Three Laws of Nature, Moses and Christ
Youth (1562–9)

PLAYS WRITTEN
Devices for Nottingham Castle (projected May)

1563 PERFORMANCES
      At court: Not known
    Elsewhere: 'Aeneas and Queen Dido' (27 June): Chester
                'Six Shepherds' (11 January): Scottish court
                'Barbarous Terryne': Ipswich

PRINTINGS
Oedipus (trans. Seneca). SR *c.* March

REPRINTINGS
None known

PLAYS WRITTEN
' 'Tis Good Sleeping in a Whole Skin' (*c.* 1560–*c.* 1565)

1564 PERFORMANCES
      At court: Not known
    Elsewhere: 'Old Tobit' (6 July): Lincoln
                'Dido' (7 August): King's College, Cambridge
                'Ezekias' (8 August): King's College, Cambridge
                'Mock Mass' (10 August): Hinchinbrook, Cambridgeshire
                Cupid, Chastity and Time (13–15 February): Scottish court

PRINTINGS
None known

REPRINTINGS
None known

PLAYS WRITTEN
'Ajax Flagellifer' (trans. Sophocles) (projected 9 August)
Apius and Virginia (1559–67)
The Bugbears (adapt. Grazzini, *La Spiritata*) (1563–*c.* 1565)
'Holofernes' (*c.* 1563–5)

1565 PERFORMANCES
      At court: *Damon and Pithias* (January?)
                'A Masque of Hunters and the Nine Muses' (18 February)
                'Juno and Diana' (4–6 March)
                'A Masque of Satyrs and Tilters' (4–6 March)
                'Massinissa and Sophonisba'
    Elsewhere: 'Julian the Apostate': Shrewsbury
                Pompae Deorum in Nuptiis Mariae; Pompae Equestres (29
                July): Scottish court

PRINTINGS
Lusty Juventus. SR 14 August 1560, 3 editions (?)
Albion Knight. SR *c.* August
Gorboduc. SR *c.* September
King Darius. SR *c.* October
Aegio
Wealth and Health (1565?)
Enough is as Good as a Feast (1565–70)

REPRINTINGS
Jack Juggler (1565–70)
Nice Wanton (?)

PLAYS WRITTEN
The Cruel Debtor (*c.* 1560–5)
Damon and Pithias

1566   PERFORMANCES
At court: *Sapientia Solomonis* (trans. Sixt Birck) (17 January)
Gismond of Salerne (?)
Elsewhere: *The Southampton Wedding Masque* (24–6 February)
The Radcliffe Wedding Masque (1 July)
'Marcus Geminus' (1 September): Christ Church College, Oxford
'Palamon and Arcite', Part 1 (2 September): Christ Church College, Oxford
'Palamon and Arcite', Part 2 (4 September): Christ Church College, Oxford
'Progne' (adapt. Corraro) (5 September): Christ Church College, Oxford
Jocasta (trans. Dolce): Gray's Inn
The Supposes (trans. Ariosto): Gray's Inn
'Pompae Deorum Rusticorum' (17 December): Scottish court

PRINTINGS
Agamemnon (trans. Seneca). SR *c.* February
The Cruel Debtor. SR *c.* March
Medea (trans. Seneca). SR *c.* June
Hercules Oetaeus (trans. pseudo-Seneca). SR 22 July–20 August
Octavia (trans. Seneca). SR 22 July–20 August
Ralph Roister Doister. SR *c.* October
'Far Fetched and Dear Bought is Good for Ladies'. SR October
'A Play of Fortune'. SR *c.* November
The Life and Repentance of Mary Magdalene. SR *c.* December–January 1566–7

REPRINTINGS
Lusty Juventus (1565–8)

PLAYS WRITTEN
'Julian the Apostate' (1556–66)

1567   PERFORMANCES

      At court: *Interlude of Vice* (*Horestes*) (?)
               'As Plain as Can Be' (1567–8)
               'Jack and Jill' (1567–8)
               'The Painful Pilgrimage' (1567–8)
               Liberality and Prodigality (?)
               'Prodigality' (same as above?) (1567–8)
               'Six Fools' (1567–8)
      Elsewhere: 'Samson': Red Lion Inn, London
               'Wylie Beguylie' (3 January): Merton College, Oxford

PRINTINGS
Hippolytus (trans. Seneca). SR January
'The College of Canonical Clerks'. SR January/February 1566/7
Interlude of Vice (*Horestes*)
The Trial of Treasure

REPRINTINGS
The Life and Repentance of Mary Magdalene

PLAYS WRITTEN
None known

1568   PERFORMANCES

      At court: 'The King of Scots' (1567–8)
              The Marriage of Wit and Science (?)
              'Wit and Will' (same as above?) (1567–8)
      Elsewhere: Not known

PRINTINGS
Jacob and Esau. SR *c.* October–November 1557
Like Will To Like. SR *c.* September

REPRINTINGS
None known

PLAYS WRITTEN
Free Will (trans. Bassano by Henry Cheke) (*c.* 1565–72)

1569   PERFORMANCES
'The Passion of Christ': Shrewsbury

PRINTINGS
Patient and Meek Grissil (1566–9). SR *c*. April 1566; *c*. February 1569
The Longer Thou Livest the More Fool Thou Art. SR *c*. April
The Disobedient Child. SR *c*. August
The Marriage of Wit and Science. SR *c*. August
Cambises. SR *c*. September–October

REPRINTINGS
The Four PP (14 September)

PLAYS WRITTEN
'The Destruction of Thebes' (projected 15 May at Oxford)
The Most Virtuous and Godly Susanna (1563–9)

1570   PERFORMANCES
   At court: Not known
   Elsewhere: 'The Cradle of Security' (1565–75): Gloucester

PRINTINGS
None known

REPRINTINGS
Gorboduc (1570–1)

PLAYS WRITTEN
Sir Clyomon and Sir Clamydes (*c*. 1570–83)
July and Julian (*c*. 1570)
Misogonus (*c*. 1560–77)

1571   PERFORMANCES
   At court: 'Lady Barbara' (27 December)
              'Iphigenia' (28 December)
   Elsewhere: 'The Siege of Edinburgh Castle' (July): St Andrews

PRINTINGS
Damon and Pithias. SR 22 July (?) 1567

REPRINTINGS
None known

PLAYS WRITTEN
New Custom ('New Guise') (1570?–3)

1572   PERFORMANCES
        At court: 'Ajax and Ulysses' (1 January)
                'Narcissus' (6 January)
                'Cloridon and Radiamanta' (17 February)
                'Paris and Vienne' (19 February)
                'A Masque of Apollo, the Nine Muses and Lady Peace'
                (15 June)
                'Fortune' (Christmas 1572–3)
                'Chariclea' (1572–3)
                'A Double Masque' (1572–3)
     Elsewhere: *The Masque for Lord Montacute*: Montacute House

PRINTINGS
None known

REPRINTINGS
None known

PLAYS WRITTEN
Herodes (*c.* 1570–5)
The Conflict of Conscience (1570–81)

1573   PERFORMANCES
        At court: 'A Masque of Janus' (1 January)
                'Predor and Lucia' (26 December)
                'Alcmaeon' (27 December)
                'A Masque of Lance Knights' (27 December)
                'Mamillia' (28 December)
     Elsewhere: Not known

PRINTINGS
Free Will (trans. Bassano by Henry Cheke). SR 11 May 1561
Jocasta (trans. Dolce)
The Masque for Lord Montacute
New Custom ('New Guise')
The Supposes (trans. Ariosto)

REPRINTINGS
None known

PLAYS WRITTEN
None known

1574   PERFORMANCES
        At court: 'A Masque of Foresters or Hunters' (1 January)
                'Truth, Faithfulness and Mercy' (1 January)

'Herpetulus the Blue Knight and Perobia' (3 January)
'A Masque of Six Sages' (6 January)
'Quintus Fabius' (6 January)
'A Masque of Six Virtues' (projected 2 February)
'Timoclea at the Siege of Thebes by Alexander' (2 February)
'Philemon and Philecia' (21 February)
'A Masque of Seven Ladies' (23 February)
'A Masque of Seven Warriors' (23 February)
'Perseus and Andromeda' (23 February)
'Panecia' (Christmas 1574–5)
'Phedrastus' (projected Christmas 1574–5)
'Phigon and Lucia' (projected Christmas 1574–5)
'Pretestus' (Christmas 1574–5)
'A Masque of Six Pedlars' (1574–5)
Elsewhere: 'The Forlorn Son' (1 August): St Andrews School
The Queen's Entertainment at Bristow (13–21 August): Bristol

PRINTINGS
An Interlude of Minds (trans. Niclaes's *Ein Gedicht des Spels van Sinnen*)

REPRINTINGS
None known

PLAYS WRITTEN
None known

1575　PERFORMANCES
At court: 'King Xerxes' (6 January)
Elsewhere: The Princely Pleasures at Kenilworth Castle (9–27 July): Kenilworth
'The Entertainment at Worcester' (August): Worcester
The Queen's Entertainment at Woodstock (September): Woodstock

PRINTINGS
Gammer Gurton's Needle. SR *c.* January 1563
Apius and Virginia. SR *c.* October 1567
The Glass of Government, 3 issues
The Queen's Entertainment at Bristow

REPRINTINGS
Jocasta (trans. Dolce)
The Masque for Lord Montacute (1575?)
The Supposes (trans. Ariosto)

PLAYS WRITTEN

Abraham's Sacrifice (trans. Beza)
Processus Satanae (*c.* 1570–5)

Note: The following interludes cannot be dated save by the references to their existence; but they were apparently popular pieces during the period.

'Dives and Lazarus'
'The Dialogue of Dives'
'The Devil and Dives'
'Delphrygus and the King of Fairies'
'The Highway to Heaven'
'Man's Wit'
'The Twelve Labours of Hercules'
'Hit the Nail o' the Head'
'Craft upon Subtlety's Back'
'Joseph's Afflictions'
'Manhood and Misrule (Manhood and Wisdom)'
'Susanna's Tears'
'Nineveh's Repentance'

11 The technique of
play presentation
Richard Southern

The technique of
play presentation

(i) Technicalities of presentation

The period 1500–76 begins with what is at present reckoned the first secular
comedy in English, and ends with the erection of the first building in
modern Europe ever to be designed for the public presentation of plays.
The comedy was Henry Medwall's *Fulgens and Lucrece* (*c.* 1497), and the
playhouse was James Burbage's The Theatre put up in Shoreditch in 1576.
The question with which this chapter is concerned is: how were plays
presented between these two dates when there were no theatres in which
to present them?

Today many fringe theatres have to work in just such conditions, but now
they have the precedent of 300 years of public theatre presentation to
follow; in 1500 no public theatre building as such had ever been conceived
– at any rate, since Roman times. Yet there remain to us from this period
some seventy or more plays in manuscript or in early printed editions (to
say nothing of the many irretrievably lost), and all created by their authors
for presentation without benefit of a theatre.

How far can the conditions which the performers of these plays had to
face be reconstructed today, and what playing techniques did they develop
to suit those conditions?

(ii) Interludes and court pageants

It has become convenient to give this group of plays the generic title of
'Tudor interludes', a name not entirely above controversy but possibly
deriving from the fact that some of the earliest at least were performed as
interludes at banquets. But, however that may be, when taken in chronological order – as far as this is possible today[1] – they show a gradual
technical development which makes a significant link between the medieval
moralities on the one hand and the birth of the Elizabethan drama on the
other. Moreover, in their technique of presentation they seem to offer an
acceptable explanation of how the features of the physical Elizabethan stage
– that subject of such lengthy controversy – eventually came about in the
form they did.

The technique of presentation of the Tudor interludes has to be reconstructed from the acting directions in the scripts and from significant
features in the lines of the dialogue. For the purpose of discussing its
development it is convenient to divide the period into three roughly equal
parts – 1500–30, 1530–50 and 1550–76 – each period offering a particular
advance in technique.

Before turning to details it is to be noticed that interludes formed only a
part of the theatre picture of the times. A more spectacular part, though
one less concerned with the performances of plays, was in the private
masques or disguisings given in the court of Henry VIII. Here, as the state
papers of the time show, there were elements of astounding technical
elaboration in the way of wheeled pageants and artificial forests and castles
built on the floor of the hall. On occasion the players of interludes were
invited to assist in these princely extravagances, and the suggestion is sometimes made that they might have imported into their own technique the
immensely expensive devices of the court; but there is much to indicate
that this was not so – or only very rarely – and it seems more practical
to see the interluders as making use of means more to hand in ordinary life.

(iii) Place and doors

Two technical terms to be found in the texts of the earliest group of plays
serve to open the subject. The first is clearly a legacy from earlier times

[1] The table in A. Harbage (ed.), *Annals of English Drama 975–1700*, rev. S. Schoenbaum
(London, 1964), is here – as elsewhere in the present volume – taken as a guide.

when medieval moralities were performed in open-air rounds (for example, *The Castle of Perseverance*), and it was then in the Latinized form of *platea* or *placea*. It now becomes modernized into 'place' and is used to name the area or place where the show is given. At l. 833 in Medwall's *Fulgens and Lucrece* (*c.* 1497) appears the acting direction 'Avoyde the place A' ('A' is the title of one of the characters). Again, in Skelton's *Magnificence* (*c.* 1515) there are several directions such as 'Magnyfycence alone in the place' (f. xvii *r*). This is a link with past technique. But the other term is an innovation, and can no longer relate to outdoor performance. It concerns the use of 'doors'. For example, in Medwall's *Nature* (as early as about 1495) a character cries, 'A gentleman comes in at the doors . . . and none of these knaves [the audience (!)] . . . bids him welcome' (f. C.ii). How far can a study of the scripts explain this use of *place* and *doors*? And to what specifically can the place and doors refer?

The interludes were played by small groups of professional or semi-professional actors. Usually such groups were servants of a dignitary, who maintained them to perform on festival occasions in his own house, but who left them free to travel between times and act in local public halls and such. Medwall was 'chapelayne' to Cardinal Morton, Archbishop of Canterbury, and it is likely that his plays were performed in the Archbishop's palace at Lambeth. What apartment, with 'doors', in the palace could have served for such a performance?

There are several lines in *Fulgens* which are informative. In the first, a character remarks that he has no acquaintance in 'this hall'. In another an appeal is made to the good fellows that be 'in this hall'. And again a player apologizes for digressing from the matter he began when he 'entred the hall'. The *hall*, then, of the palace was the place of the performance. What was the character of a hall?

(iv) The Tudor great hall

A medieval great hall was the meeting place of practically all classes from nobles to retainers. It not only served as a common dining room but was the centre of the social and administrative life of an estate, and it was built to a traditional pattern.

At the upper end was a dais on which the lord's high table stood; other tables ranged along the two side walls, leaving the centre of the floor free.

At the lower end was the most significant feature of all for the history of play presentation – the screens.

The screens consisted of a row of three partitions across the end of the hall, one either side with a third in the middle, arranged to leave two openings between for the comings and goings of the servants and others. The whole trio enclosed a passageway across the end of the hall from side to side; at one end of this passage was the main entrance door to the hall from the outside world, and at the other a further door into a garden, court-yard or orchard. The far side of the passage consisted of the end wall of the hall with openings through it to the kitchens and buttery beyond. It was a comparatively narrow space, some 6–9 feet wide, and the general name for it was the 'entry'. In later times this entry might be roofed in and railed, forming a 'minstrels' gallery' above, overlooking the body of the hall.

In Tudor times this whole feature became a decorative unity, with carving and panelling, of which the two openings were an essential part since they were the only means of entry into the hall itself for the general mass of the people. (The one other access was a small door on to the high-table dais at the upper end leading from the private apartments of the house, and this was reserved for the lord and his immediate family.) Thus it was only through the two openings in the screens that the members of a troupe of players could make their entrances into the 'place' of the hall floor to play to the lord at the upper end and to the guests and retainers along the side tables and any crowd of onlookers that gathered along the screens at the lower end to watch the event.

The Great Hall at Lambeth Palace, where Medwall's plays may have been performed, originally dated from about 1440; it was demolished in the Commonwealth but rebuilt after the Restoration 'on the old model' (see the description of 'The Great Hall, now the Library' in the *Handbook to Lambeth Palace and Art in the Service of the Church Exhibition*, London, 1951). A print survives of the remodelled interior, reproduced in the *Handbook*, and – but for the unusual length of this hall – it probably offers as good an idea as may be of the appearance of the setting of an early interlude in a Tudor great hall. Lambeth Hall was 93 feet long as against, for instance, the hall at Penshurst Place which itself is pretty big and is only 68 feet long; both are 38 feet wide.

A typical hall in a country house would be on a more intimate scale: 40 feet long by 20 feet wide are not unusual dimensions. Moreover, the screens in the Lambeth Palace print are of an early type lacking the gallery above, such as was built at Haddon Hall about 1475. But drawing an

average between the two will produce a workable impression of the framework into which any company of interluders might come to play. To this
must be added to complete the picture three particular conditions: the social
occasion, the spectators and the lighting.

(v) Conditions of performance

The occasion of an interlude performance was almost always one of festive
celebration, such as a marriage or a birthday, or Christmas or Twelfth
Night. Guests were invited to the hall-feast by the master of the house.
The hall might be crowded, not only with diners at the tables but also with
their retainers and additional servants packed in a standing crowd at the
lower end before the screens.

This introduces the second factor necessary for visualizing an interlude
performance; the standing crowd of onlookers at the screens inevitably
influenced the character and the timing of players' entrances; this in turn
is reflected very noticeably in the frequency of some sort of preparatory lines
in the dialogue before a character's entrance, involving what may be termed
a delayed or 'heralded' entrance. One example may serve for many: near
the opening of *Fulgens* two characters are talking about the imminent
beginning of 'a play' which they intend to watch along with the real
audience. They break off and one says 'Peace, no more words, the players
are even now here at hand.' But the two go on talking for twelve more lines
before we reach the direction '*Intrat Fulgens*'.

This delaying of an entrance, or more accurately this calling attention
to an entrance some lines before the character has to come in, continues
right into the full Elizabethan drama. Without an understanding of the
conditions originally imposed by the hall screens it might seem meaningless,
but having realized these it is not difficult to imagine the sensation, the
turning of heads and the backing out of the way (on the part of the crowd by
the doors) that must inevitably have preceded the coming through of a new
character into the hall. It would be very difficult for the players on the
floor to ignore this distraction or to avoid a break in their atmosphere
resulting from it. No character could make a sudden dramatic appearance
with precise timing because he could not tell, by a matter of some seconds,
how long it would take him to get in. And so the players had to accept the
position and – making a virtue of necessity – they had to achieve their

'entrance effect' by some other means than its timing. And one such is the means noted here: the anticipated, or heralded-and-delayed, entrance. It is possibly to this that we may attribute the curious 'yonder-he-cometh' convention which often marks entrances in Elizabethan plays and which seems so artificial in modern revivals.

Another technicality forced upon the players by this condition and by the fact generally of performing in the centre of a crowd is the inevitable acknowledgement of the presence of the spectators. There could be no impression of 'stage illusion'; instead there was genuine realism – or, in fact, reality. And this in turn supported the custom of direct address to members of the audience which we find so general in interludes, and often with telling and humorous (and even scurrilous) effect.

The third factor in visualizing a proper picture of an interlude performance is the comparative dimness of the light in the hall where it took place. Though some performances did take place in daylight, the majority were at night and would have to be seen by torchlight. An amusing reference to this is made by the Vice in John Heywood's *The Play of the Weather* (*c.* 1528). As he makes his entrance on to the floor he calls officiously to a servant standing by – 'Brother, hold up your torch a little higher!' – so that he himself may be better lit, just as a present-day comic might call for a spotlight.

(vi) The 'differentiation of acting areas'

Having pictured the occasion, the crowd and the dimness of the light, we may now imagine the players coming through the doors in the screens and on to the open floor of the hall to play. And now a further characteristic of interlude technique can be pointed out. Because of the throng and the flickering torchlight, it could be easily accepted by the audience that two characters might quite convincingly act as though they could not see each other, or even that two groups of several characters might be present in the acting area at the same time and each develop some passage of the plot without recognition of the presence of the other. And, equally acceptably, the two groups could come together and combine in a common action at the moment the dramatic situation was ready for it.

This is an especially valuable facility in interlude conditions, since it can achieve the effect of what in a modern theatre would involve a scene change, and it is because the interluders had no scenery that this convention was of such value to them; so valuable, in fact, that it persisted, and was exploited, to the heights of Elizabethan drama and became indeed the butt of Sir Philip Sidney's gibe against the licence of a stage 'where you shall have *Asia* of the one side, and *Affrick* of the other ...' (*The Defence of Poesy*, 1595). As a convention it is, of course, still acceptable in the theatre today where a part of the stage can be reckoned as isolated from the rest for the purposes of the action, or one side used to show London and the other Paris – or, for that matter, Asia and Africa.

As a detailed instance of the above, Medwall's earlier play, *Nature* (*c.* 1495), has an opening direction in two parts, each referring to a different group of players. The first group enters and takes up positions at one end of the hall but remains completely silent; then the second group enters, remains at the opposite end of the hall and opens the action of the play proper, proceeding for no less than 406 lines of dialogue without any reaction at all from the first group. This opening action ends with the simulation of a journey as four characters from the second group break away and set out for a meeting with the hitherto silent first group. Only when that journey is accomplished does the first group begin to take part in the dialogue. The dual direction reads as follows: .

> Fyrst cometh in Mundus and syttyth down [and] sayth nothynge and wyth hym Worldly affeccyon berynge a gown and cap and a gyrdyll for Man.
> Than cometh in Nature / Man / Reason / and Innocencye / and Nature syttyth down and sayth ...

And the dialogue then begins between Nature and Man, with Reason, Innocence and Sensuality intervening according to their characters. The journey of Man up the hall to the World is eventually undertaken. World then dismisses Reason and Innocence and next makes use of another of the interluders' significant conventions – that of the changing of costume – by investing Man in the garments already brought in by Worldly Affection. But before the meeting of Man and the World has taken place these 406 lines of dialogue have to be spoken, during which World has sat silent and, ostensibly, been entirely unconscious of the preparations for the meeting. And when it comes he takes it up as a new step in the plot.

What has happened is that the interluders have made use of the facility open to them to differentiate between action in one part of the hall and action in another part – a facility that I may term the 'differentiation of acting areas'.

Presently World and his servant go out and Sensuality is left to discuss with Man the desirability of engaging some fine fellow to look after his affairs.

It is at this point that another very interesting and informative example of differentiation arises. All attention on the scene now developing between Man and Sensuality at the upper end of the hall is suspended, although the two do not exit and thus must still remain visible but silent. The plot takes a new turn upon the bursting-in of a strange figure, thrusting through the spectators by the screens at the lower end and berating everyone for not according him a welcome suited to his importance. His name is Pride, and he demands:

> Who dwelleth here [?] wyll no man speke[?]
> Is there no fole nor hody peke[!]
> Now by the bell yt were almys to breke
> Some of these knaues brows[.]
> A gentylman comys in at the dorys
> That all hys dayes hath worn gylt sperys
> And none of thys knaues nor cutted horys
> Byddys hym welcom to house.
> Wote ye not how great a lord I am[?]

He goes on in this way, boasting his own importance (and incidentally giving a most informative description of his clothes and appearance), for over 100 lines before at length he sees the others watching him and breaks off, sending his page to effect an introduction to them. So here we have an extension to the differentiation effect in that, while the one party may be completely unconscious of the other, the latter may be allowed both to see and to hear the former.

Notice that here is the important reference to doors in its context. This use of the plural form 'dorys' adds final confirmation that the entrance used by players as they came into a great hall was the entrance through the screens; the word is in the plural precisely because there was a *pair* of such doors in any normal layout of screens – and there was no comparable pair of doors anywhere else in the hall.

(vii) Some features of plays of the first period 1500–1530

All the surviving interludes up to 1530 can be presented with no more than the simple facilities offered by the open floor of the hall and the doors in the screens at the lower end, plus the use when required of one or two chairs, and of the effects possible in the players' costumes, and in changing them to symbolize a change of heart or of fortunes or of degree. Occasionally certain hand-properties are called for but they are mostly simple and likely to be available among the ordinary furniture of the hall. From the dramatic point of view, however, a fairly rich use is made of these basic facilities.

I propose now to touch briefly on some of the other interludes of this early period which have informative details about presentation, and to take one of them at somewhat greater length.

First, *The World and the Child* or *Mundus et Infans* (anon., *c.* 1508); this is notable for its exploitation of the use and changing of costume to clarify and embellish the story. The plot is very slight, consisting simply of five successive dialogues. In each of them Man discusses a phase of his life with a second character, a different one in each dialogue: first with the World himself; second, with Conscience; third, with Folly; then briefly with Conscience again; and lastly with Perseverance. At the beginning of each period of his life, from childhood to age, he is invested by the World with a new garment. He begins as an infant, playing with a peg-top:

I am a chylde as you may se ...
I am not worthely wrapped nor went [i.e. wound]

He craves from World 'Mete and clothe my lyfe to saue'; World replies 'These garmentes gaye I gyue to the[e]'. When the Child becomes a youth he says he is 'proudely apparelde in garmentes gaye'. When he grows to manhood the World arrays him anew 'In robes ryall ryght of good hewe' and adds 'And here I dubbe the a knyght'. Later Manhode says:

I am proudely aparelde in purpure and byse
As golde I glyster in gere ...

Towards the end Manhode coughs and staggers and groans in age and may well have put on wig, beard and old man's gear.

The next interlude in the provisional chronological order deserves treatment apart; not only is it a work of notably outstanding stature poetically, but dramatically it exemplifies most instructively all the technicalities of this early group of plays. It is John Skelton's *Magnificence* (*c.* 1515).

(viii) *Magnificence*, an interlude considered in detail

The plot of the play concerns the scheming of five rogues to oust Measure (who represents moderation) from Magnificence's household so that they may plunder Magnificence's estate without restraint.

The play is what is called 'undivided'. In passing it is worth remarking that no playscript of this early date is divided into acts and scenes. So far as I know the first example of such division among Tudor interludes appears in the anonymous *Respublica* which is dated as late as 1553. Even there the method of division generally is to treat the entrance of any new character as beginning a new scene, which is different from our present-day method. Today we give the name 'scene' to a relatively lengthy part of a play marked by its own dramatic unity, and incorporating any number of exits and entrances. Today, moreover, a scene is reckoned as happening throughout in one place which is represented by an artificial background – the 'scenery' of the scene. If the next scene is supposed to be happening in a different place, a change of scenery (a 'scene-change') is involved.

But the interludes were played without scenery. *Magnificence* has neither scenery nor division into scenes. But the thirty folios (or sixty pages) of the text can be divided for convenient discussion here into six equal sections, each of ten pages (with the second and third bracketed together to make a double section). Whether this equality of parts occurs by chance or by Skelton's intention is not to be decided here, but it does help to make a description of the action easier to outline.

As one reads, it becomes clear how very important the entrances are, each in its turn, as the plot unfolds. Every time a character comes in he arrives with a significant purpose and creates a significant (often deliberately contrived) effect in the development of the action and the maintenance of the interest. He does, in fact, initiate a new 'scene'. In the first ten-page section of *Magnificence* there are six entrances; the whole passage may be thought of as an episode in six entrances, or – had the convention been established so early – as an act in six scenes.

To describe the opening section in detail (referring to the reproduction in the Tudor Facsimile Texts series, of 1910, from a Rastell print undated but about 1533): the script begins without any preliminary direction save the name of the speaker of the opening lines – Felicity. Since there is no indication otherwise, he is to be pictured walking into a torchlit hall among the sitting and standing guests, and arresting their attention simply by declaiming his twenty-three opening lines.

In them he speaks of the problems of wealth – its value but also its uncertainty, how it is essential to nobleness but may, uncontrolled, bring its possessor to ruin. And he announces that he stands for money-with-happiness – 'For welthfull felicite truly is my name'.

Another man now walks into the hall (but still with no entrance direction) and greets Wealthful Felicity with acclamation, thus stirring the interest with his hail-fellow exuberance:

> Mary[!] welthe and I was apoynted to mete
> And eyther I am dysseyued or ye be the same
> FEL. Syr as ye say: I haue harde of your fame
> Your name is lyberte as I understande
> LYB. Trewe you say syr gyue me your hande

This situation has brought to attention another characteristic feature of the setting of early interludes: that of a meeting and converse between men, not in some fictional place elsewhere, but in the here and now, where those for whom they are playing are normally assembled in everyday life. Polonius's 'The actors are come hither my Lord' (*Hamlet*, II.ii) admirably expresses it; the audience does not go to the theatre, the players come to the people and they act in a room of the people – costumed and declaiming, preaching or up to any sort of ribaldry, but otherwise themselves among people, come to entertain them just where they are. Hence there cannot be any conception of scenery; it would be 'from the purpose' of that sort of playing. Let us see what follows.

Felicity remains throughout the play the kind of reasonable fellow he sets out to be here, but Liberty is to prove a more intractable character and in the end he takes a bitter part in the plot. All this is hinted to the audience in the ensuing dialogue in a way specifically calculated to hold the attention.

The two shake hands. Where have you been? asks Felicity. I'd better not say, laughs Liberty. Felicity turns to the audience with: Listen to this gentleman joking! But Liberty says if he told he might get locked up.

Felicity objects: But liberty locked up is not liberty. Then he checks and admits that

> ... lyberte may somtyme be to large
> But yf reason be regent and ruler of your barge

Thus Felicity reasons, and then Liberty is piqued; argument threatens, albeit courteously as yet. Then the third entrance occurs with dramatic effect and marked now by a Latin direction in the text, '*Hic intrat Measure*'.

Measure, the reasonable exponent of moderation, exclaims: Christ assist you in your altercation. And the others check before Measure's reproof that their language is like the pen of him that writeth too fast.

There follows a brief exposition on what is the main theme of the play – that measure should govern in all things, even in using wealth or in allowing liberties. Liberty demands: Would they make him subject to Measure? But he reluctantly affects to agree with them. Measure is reassured, Felicity says they will gladden their master, and Liberty sums up with

> There is no prynce but he hath nede of us thre
> Welthe with measure and plesaunt lyberte.

Then Measure intervenes and ushers them aside so as to clear the way for the fourth entrance 'here at hande'. And then we have '*Hic intrat magnyfycence*'. The entrance is thus dramatically built up; the others stand back leaving the floor to the new figure. He begins by assuring the audience of his 'noble porte and fame' and tells them his name. Then he calls his friend Measure out of the shadows and, looking past him as he comes, asks who the others are. Measure introduces them. Magnificence invites them to join his household but makes it very clear to them that they are to be under Measure's authority. Measure accepts the charge. Liberty is clearly very reluctant, but Magnificence sends him off under Measure's guidance. They leave the place together. Then Magnificence has a few words with Felicity about Liberty's wilfulness. They agree that Measure must be in control if they are all to live together.

All this is pretty serious dialogue but it is made dramatically effective by a clear implication as it continues that the speakers do not – or soon will not – agree between themselves on the matters discussed. But something still more calculated to quicken the interest follows immediately in the particularly significant fifth entrance – a small, active, aggressive young figure runs in, greatly daring, and in his first three lines says they are all talking nonsense and will they listen to him! '*Hic intrat Fansy*'.

Immediately there is a new atmosphere; for two pages Fancy argues and criticizes them until Magnificence is so outraged at his impertinence that he orders him out. But Fancy at once apologizes and reveals that he really came to bring a sealed letter to Magnificence. It purports to be from someone he calls Sad Circumspection living abroad in Pontoise. Magnificence is instantly intrigued and mollified. He first sends Felicity away so that he can open and read the letter in private, but at the same time he tells Fancy to stand by and wait. Then he begins in silence to open the letter. Obviously this is just ideal theatre – a very pregnant silence after squabbling, and then what next?

Following upon this calculated build-up comes the most unusual sixth entrance. It is unusual both in its kind and in its description. The description is in one of the most specific acting directions in all Tudor drama, and it surely could not have been conceived without great under-standing of the capabilities of suggestive acting and of audience effect. It is again in Latin, but translated it reads (or appears to read, for neither the Latin nor the printing is free from error):

> Here let him [Magnificence] act as if he were reading the letter to himself. In the meantime let Counterfeit Countenance run in, trolling and tripping. When he sees Magnificence let him check [and] stealthily draw back for a moment [then] after a brief space let Counterfeit Countenance again approach, looking upon them and speaking from a distance, and let Fancy motion silence with his hand.[1]

Who is this Counterfeit Countenance? He is in fact the first of the four arch-conspirators who are to plot the downfall of Magnificence. But it is worth a note in passing that he and his companions are liable to cause some confusion in the mind of a reader of the script because their odd names are all so alike, especially when abbreviated in the speech ascriptions: 'Cou*n*terfet cou*n*'; 'Crafty conuay'; 'Clokyd colusyo*n*'; 'Courtly abusyo*n*'. (Moreover each assumes an alias during the course of the presentation.) Skelton might be held to be at fault in this, but only by a reader of the script, not by a spectator at a performance, because then each of these very distinctively characterized villains would be quite clearly

---

[1] 'Hic faciat tanqu*am* legeret litteras tacite: Interim superueniat cantando cou*n*terfet cou*n*tenaunce suspenso gradū q*ui*[?] viso magnyfycence sensū [? sensim] retrocedat ad te*m*pus post pusillu*m* rursum accedat counterfet cou*n*tenaunce prospectando et vocitando a longe et fansy animat [? annuat] silentium cum manu' (f. v).

singled out from the others by his features, his manner and his costume, about all of which matters there are suggestive hints in the lines. For the present, the first of them, Counterfeit Countenance, can be taken alone; he is to be seen as a swaggering cheat, gay and plausible, anxious to gain a position in Magnificence's household.

He enters, then, singing and dancing, checks at the sight of Magnificence reading, and of Fancy waiting on the side, draws back, pauses, approaches again, and then tries to attract Fancy's attention from a distance by hissing his name in an undertone. Surely a gift of an entrance for any actor, coming in a dramatic pause and deflecting the attention from the prinicipals to himself! In addition, the situation is heightened because Magnificence, in his absorption, scarcely notices him and so, after all this, the newcomer goes off again with nothing said. Next Magnificence recollects himself and murmurs: Did someone call you, Fancy? Fancy says it was nothing, and goes on to angle for a substantial tip from Magnificence for having brought the letter through many dangers on the way from the Continent. Meanwhile, the anxious intruder hovers in the shadows among the crowd of amused spectators – clearly awaiting a more favourable moment.

Fancy and Magnificence talk on, Fancy suggesting he himself would make a much more appropriate courtier than Measure (as apparently the mysterious letter has hinted), and at length Magnificence agrees to accept him and take him away to his palace. After this, Magnificence is out of the action for the next twenty-one pages. But just as the two go out we have a further attempt at interruption from Counterfeit Countenance, who hisses to Fancy, 'What I say herke a worde.' To which Fancy retorts in contempt, 'Do away I say the devylles torde.' And leaves him.

This brings to an end the first section of six entrances. Sufficient has been said to give an idea in some detail of the character of a fairly distinguished interlude. Not all early interludes are as well wrought as this but all of them are in this key and make similar technical exploitation of the means at their disposal. The remainder of this play must be described more briefly.

The second (double) section is now to begin. It will run for some twenty pages and it is concerned with the extensions of the plotting against Magnificence. It is mostly in comic, even farcical, terms, with quarrels, satire and backchat, and must have been played with much the atmosphere of a music-hall programme. It is rather on the lines of a theme with seven variations; generally each variation consists of a dialogue about the means to ruin Magnificence, with a new character brought in each time to add his own particular corruption, and in most cases the newcomer draws apart at the end and concludes with a soliloquy describing his own particular corruption and style – rather in the manner of a soloist's cadenza.

Counterfeit Countenance, left alone in the place after Fancy's rebuff, turns unabashed to the audience and gloats over the prevalence of 'false faces' in this life. Next he is joined for the second entrance by another rogue, Crafty Conveyance, who is indeed the craftiest villain of them all – the personification of deceitful contrivance.

The next entrance is of yet another rogue, named Cloaked Collusion, a proud, hooded courtier and master surveyor. He is later to play the chief part in setting Magnificence against his own good servant, Measure. In the fourth entrance, a rash, gay spark enters singing and spouting French; his name is Courtly Abusion. All of them conspire to their one end, then all leave save the latest comer. He, alone in the place, addresses to the spectators possibly the most informative of aᴜ the soliloquies – a detailed description of his costume, fashion and manners. He stays for the fifth entrance in which Fancy comes back to join him, now carrying a 'hawk' (really an owl). He hints of a quarrel beginning to rise between Liberty, Measure and Cloaked Collusion. Courtly Abusion leaves. The sixth entrance is made by a new figure leading a dog. He is dressed as a jester and his name is Folly. He jokes with Fancy about their boyhood exploits and then proposes to barter his dog for Fancy's 'hawk' – and much other backchat. To them, finally, Crafty Conveyance returns for the seventh entrance but, after suffering some of Folly's practical jokes, he retires into the shadows while Fancy and Folly go off together, presumably to see what is happening to the conspirators at court. Crafty Conveyance then emerges and treats the audience to a soliloquy on his personal world of underhand practices.

Now a new turn comes in the play, beginning a fresh section – the third – in which the plot against Magnificence matures and climaxes. The section can be divided into three main entrances. The first is the magnificent return into the hall of Magnificence himself, but he comes at a loss as to how to hold a balance between Felicity and Liberty. He is biased towards Liberty and so he snubs Felicity. Crafty Conveyance takes this moment to sidle out of the shadows and gives his unqualified approval of whatever Magnificence may say. Still dispute goes on, Magnificence swaying to one side and then to the other, incapable of a final decision. At length the others go and leave him alone. He declaims a grand soliloquy affirming his superiority to Alexander, Julius Caesar, Hercules and fourteen other heroes. Interrupting him comes the second entrance in this section; it brings in Courtly Abusion again, elegant and the very embodiment of pleasure. He comes 'doynge reuerence and courtesy' and he introduces to Magnificence (with the greatest respect) the subject of 'carnall delectacyon', and advises him on the means to achieve it.

Fast on the end of this discussion, the third entrance takes place at the far end of the hall – the entrance of the hooded snake, Cloaked Collusion, leading poor maligned Measure behind him. He whispers:

> Stande styll here and ye shall se
> That for your sake I wyll fall on my kne

So he makes use of the convention of differentiation of acting areas; he leaves Measure as it were in an anteroom and goes on his way to address Magnificence at (as seems most likely) the upper end of the hall. But his pleading on Measure's behalf is subtly couched so as to annoy Magnificence rather than effect a reconciliation, and despite Measure's subsequent approach and self-defence Magnificence flies into a rage against him and exclaims in disgust:

> Haue hym hens I say out of my syght
> That day I se hym I shall be worse all nyght

And, as Measure retires down the hall in ignominy, a cry comes from Courtly Abusion: 'Hens thou haynyarde out of the dores fast'; and so at the climax of the play we have a reminder of the major item in the setting of interludes – the screens with their two doors.

After this climax some dramatic touch is needed to drive it home and prepare for the anticlimax. Skelton handles it in this way: Magnificence is shocked into a revulsion of sickness by Measure's banishment, so much does it affect him (a good psychological point!). But now Cloaked Collusion steps to his aid and takes the opportunity to persuade Magnificence to give him Measure's place and authority; as soon as he is satisfied, he leaves Magnificence alone. Immediately Folly enters and (as it were in an anticipation of the Fool's scene with Lear) begins to talk wilder and wilder nonsense until Magnificence does not know whether to laugh or cry. But Folly suddenly breaks off at the entrance of Fancy announcing bad news and he runs away. Fancy, acting a tragic messenger in sixteen lines, says that the four rogues have robbed the coffers and decamped! Then Magnificence interrupts, as he catches sight of a new figure about to come in, 'Alas why [? who] is yonder that grymly lokys?' Fancy glances over his shoulder and is off like a shot crying: 'Adewe for I wyll not come in his clokys.' Magnificence stays transfixed in horror at the sight and murmurs: 'Lorde so my flesshe trymblyth nowe for drede'; for he is gazing into the very eyes of Adversity himself, who advances upon him with terrible effect and an eighty-line speech of reproach. During it, as a direction reads, 'Magnyfycence is beten downe and spoylyd from all his goodys and rayment'; he is stripped, humbled, down and out.

We are now in the fourth section. It consists of six entrances (one of which is of more than usual interest from the production point of view). After Adversity comes Poverty; then Liberty returns to mock the broken Magnificence. Next Cloaked Collusion and Crafty Conveyance come back to laugh at him together. Despair then enters; and finally Mischief comes in and offers Magnificence a grim choice between a halter and a knife.

The interesting technicality comes during Poverty's scene. There is a curious acting direction in Latin which means (presumably) something like 'Here let him approach to lift up Magnificence and he shall lay him on a spread place'.[1] This seems at first a puzzle, but an examination of some of the lines in the following dialogues offers at least a possible solution.

First, before he left, Adversity had said to the audience: 'Take hede of this caytyfe that lyeth here on grounde.' So Magnificence was at that point already stretched on the floor. Next, Poverty has a line in his opening speech, 'Nowe must I this carcasse lyft vp', and it is here that he is directed to take Magnificence to the *locum stratum*. A little later, Magnificence bewails his lot, using the words 'In mysery and wretchydnesse thus to be lapped', and subsequently Poverty takes up this figure of speech with 'Nowe lap you in a couerlet full fayne that you may ... Nowe must ye lerne to lye on the strawe.' Later again, Poverty proposes to go out to beg for food for Magnificence, and says as he leaves that he will 'happe you the whyles with these homly raggys'. And in the scene that follows, Liberty comes in without at first seeing Magnificence. Then he suddenly exclaims:

What a very vengeaunce I say / who is that
What brothell I say is yonder bounde in a mat

All the above put together seem to show that the explanation of the '*locum stratum*' is that Poverty when he entered dragged a sort of poor straw pallet with him and a rag of a blanket, and dropped them as he went by, until the moment came to help Magnificence to the place where

[1] 'Hic accedat ad leuandum magnyfycence et locabit eum super locum stratum.'

they had been spread – in other words, this is an early piece of 'scene-setting' with a bare palliasse to signify a dwelling (or at least a state) of poverty and degradation.

There remains now simply the fifth and last section, this time of four entrances, all of them concerned with reconciliation and rehabilitation.

First, Goodhope checks Magnificence's knife-hand. Second, Redress brings a fresh garment for Magnificence (significant use of costume again). Third, Sad Circumspection enters and, upon hearing about the letter Fancy had brought in the beginning, denies all knowledge of it – it was a forgery. Finally, Perseverance comes, chats pleasantly with his brother Virtues, and all gently chide Magnificence.

Perseverance turns to the audience and expresses his mind in a couple of beautifully typical Skeltonian stanzas:

> This treatyse deuysyd to make you dysporte
> Shewyth nowe a dayes howe the worlde comberyd is
> To the pythe of the mater who lyst to resorte
> To day it is well / to morowe it is all amysse
> To day in delyte / to morowe bare of blysse
> To day a lorde / to morowe ly in the duste
> Thus in this worlde there is no erthly truste
>
> To day fayre wether / to morowe a stormy rage
> To day hote / to morowe outragyous colde
> To day a yoman / to morowe made of [?a] page
> To day in surety / to morowe bought and solde
> To day maysterfest / to morowe he hath no holde
> To day a man / to morowe he lyeth in the duste
> Thus in this worlde there is no erthly truste

Magnificence adds, to the audience:

> This mater we haue mouyd you myrthys to make
> Precely purposyd vnder pretence of play . . .

They lead Magnificence off, back to his palace, to reinstate him and, as they walk quietly out, Redress adds a final couplet for the benefit of the spectators:

> And ye that haue harde this dysporte and game

Jhesus preserue you frome endlesse wo and shame
  (Amen)

One particularly notable fact about *Magnificence* is that though it comes so early in the period it seems already to bear witness to a direct appreciation and use, by the author, of the resources of alert acting, and of the dramatic effects that even at this date could be conveyed by the skill of the player himself, performing by-play in an interval of silence during the lines. This clearly belies the assumption often made that acting at this date would not be considered by intelligent people as capable of any subtleties of expression at all. And yet the fact now clearly seems to be that not only were some at least of the theatre men of the time quite capable of very considerable force in dramatic writing, with great ingenuity and music in the verse, but that in addition there was also a very keen observation of the finer nuances of an actor's expression as it could be employed in the presentation of a plot.

(ix) Further features of the first period 1500–1530

The next play of this first period which offers a suggestion of development in technical methods is the anonymous *Calisto and Melebea* (*c.* 1527). The development is a specialization in the use of the doors on occasions when the situation in the play might be made clearer thereby. The interluders now begin to take advantage of the existence of a pair of doors to suggest that one leads to one place and the other to a different place (here is the birth of a distinctive Elizabethan convention). The custom up to this time seems to have been to think of the doors as leading off to nowhere in particular – simply to 'outside'. But in *Calisto* there is no doubt that, in one passage at least, one door is considered as leading to a different place from the other. The convention is very lightly used as yet, it may or may not have been strictly maintained throughout the play, and in any case it is not so much a convention as simply an exploiting of reality – because one door is supposed to lead to the orchard in Calisto's house and the other to the neighbourhood outside his house; which, speaking generally, is just the kind of thing that the two doors of any normal screens in fact did do.

The distinction is made quite clearly in the play. Calisto woos but totally fails to move a certain Melebea. So he asks his servant to go to the nearby house of Celestina, the local procuress, and ask her to come to see him and discuss his problem. The servant goes out (let us say by the door on the audience's right). What now does Calisto do? His lines are quite clear. He says: 'To pas the tyme now wyll I walk / Up and down within myne orchard.... Thus farewell my lordys for a whyle I wyll go.' This last line is to the audience. The implication in his 'for a whyle' is that his absence is to be temporary and simply to fill in the time his servant is away on his errand. If the servant has left by the right-hand door to go abroad to another house, then it would obviously be appropriate for Calisto to leave by the opposite, or left-hand, door to go not to another house but into his own orchard, there to stroll and wait. Thus one door would be, for the time, accepted as leading to the outside world and the other as leading to the inner courtyard.

Such a distinction is not made in earlier plays, and even now it is, as I have said, not so much a newly created convention as an acceptance of ever-present reality. But it is to lead in a few decades to that 'licence' about which Sir Philip Sidney protested (see above, p. 77).

What follows now is particularly interesting. How is the scene of the servant's arrival at Celestina's house, and his explanation to her of Calisto's business, to be managed?

In fact, very simply. The hall floor is for a moment empty after Calisto's exit. Then a woman enters, almost certainly from the right-hand door. She addresses the audience, in the usual fashion of a newcomer in an interlude, and tells them her name; it is Celestina. She then describes the ups and downs of her profession at some length. After this she makes a remarkable statement: namely, that Calisto's servant is looking for her and that she has been told she might find him here! Obviously this is a contrivance on the part of the author and it has almost the effect of a scene-change. Where is she supposed to be speaking? At her home? At Calisto's house? In the street between? She goes on in her soliloquy for over sixty lines and then, and only then, is she interrupted by the entrance of the servant who has been bidden to go and find her.

He gives her his master's message, then after a brief talk with her he suddenly breaks in on what she is saying with 'Peas for me thynketh Calisto is nye'. And Calisto walks in, re-establishing that we are back in his house and that his perambulation of the orchard is over. There has been no definite indication whatever about where all this has taken place; the nearest to a suggestion of any locality, or journey between localities, is simply the distinction in use between the two doors – one to the orchard and the other to the outside world.

Of the six plays by or attributed to John Heywood, two are especially interesting technically. In one, *The Play of the Weather* (*c.* 1528), Jupiter sits in judgement at a court of complaints about the weather from a number of individuals who each want a different improvement. The Vice, called Merry Report, undertakes to organize the stream of appellants: some he allows to speak directly to Jupiter; some he checks, questions and turns away, promising to pass on the pleading himself to Jupiter, who all this time is apparently sitting in his seat of judgement. The problem is, how could it be convincingly represented that some of the suitors could see and speak to Jupiter directly, while some on the other hand could not see, or have any contact with, Jupiter at all? Yet Jupiter has not at any point a direction to exit. He does, however, make a proposal to the audience that he will 'withdrawe' and thereupon occurs the strange direction: 'At thende of this staf the god hath a song played in his trone or Mery report come in.' We are given no more in explanation.

It may be that (1) the throne was at the lower, or screens, end of the hall and had an actual small curtain in front that could be closed or opened like the traverse curtain of some medieval scaffolds. Or (2) it might have been achieved by what one could call an imaginary curtain instead of a real one, so that Jupiter *noticed* certain suitors but simply omitted to notice others. Or (3) it may be that Jupiter's throne was stationed at the opposite end of the hall (that is, near the high table), that Merry Report allowed certain suitors to advance up the hall directly to Jupiter and intercepted others as they entered through the screens, confining them to the lower end throughout their action. If it were the last method, then it would present another example of 'differentiation'. In any event there is a technical convention created by interlude conditions and here made use of by the players.

The other play of Heywood's is *Johan Johan* (*c.* 1520); here is an especially striking instance of realism amounting to reality in the setting. The play contains one of the most modern and complete plots so far, being in a sense a music-hall sketch of the eternal triangle. The household properties it calls for in its presentation of the kitchen setting are precisely those available in any hall – namely, a trestle table, stools, plates, mugs, a loaf, a pie, candlesticks and, particularly, a practical fire burning in a fireplace.

Yet, for all its realism, it is still possible for Johan the husband to invoke the 'differentiation of acting areas' convention and (in effect) to leave the house where he lives and go out to another house, knock at the door there, and invite the priest who lives there (with whom he has a doorstep chat) to come across and share the pie with him and his wife. All this business could be quite clearly put over to the audience by Johan's leaving that particular area of the hall where the trestle table had been set up, walking, in the torchlight, to one of the screens' doors, and rapping on the doorpost. When Johan, with his wife and the priest, are at length all seated at the table, the satirical passage of the play is all ready to begin.

To sum up this first period. There is by the end of the 1520s a common use of the 'place', by which is intended the whole available floor space of the hall up to the high table, as acting area. There is, too, a common use of the screens' doors as the cause of, or excuse for, a fairly elaborate conventional 'language' in the actors' vocabulary so far as meaning of plot and dramatic effect are concerned.

(x) Some features of the middle period 1530–1550

Much the same kind of differentiation happens – but with a variation – in a contemporary play, *Godly Queen Hester*. This variation introduces an innovation so considerable as to justify our noting a new period of advance, the second of the three in this chapter.

Godly Queen Hester (anon., *c.* 1527) is a far less intense and more narrative play than *Magnificence* but it has its dramatic moments. In it King Assuerus, speaking presumably in his palace, tells his chancellor, by name Aman, that he proposes to marry, and he instructs Aman to go through the land 'to seke faire maidens . . . to the intent among them we may chose a quene'.

The dialogue that follows now, immediately on the King's words, is entirely different. It is between Hester (one of the maidens) and her uncle, and in it the uncle tells her of the King's decree and advises her how she should behave supposing she were chosen queen. Obviously neither the King nor Aman should be present at this private talk. But what has happened to them? Fortunately the script supplies the answer: just before Hester and her uncle come in (say, by Door B) to begin their talk there is a direction in the margin reading – 'Here the kynge entryth the trauers & aman goeth out'. Leaving aside for the moment the first part of this direction, the second part is clear – 'aman goeth out'. It is pretty certain he must go out by Door A because immediately afterwards Hester and her uncle have to come in, and Aman must not meet her yet. This is satisfactorily disposed of by Aman's using the opposite door. But what about the King? He cannot follow Aman because he has to wait for his return; he is not due to meet Hester yet, and cannot remain on view through what follows.

The first part of the direction supplies the (possibly unexpected) answer to the question – namely, that the King 'entryth the trauers'.

Difficulty certainly exists in proving with finality just what a traverse then meant, but the very strong likelihood is that it was a pair of simple draw-curtains on a rod put up for the occasion, most probably before the centre element of the screens and a couple of feet away. Such a device would be a very important step forward and would solve many problems in later interludes. But whatever the 'trauers' was, it was certainly used in *Hester* in 1527. Unfortunately I have not been able to find it actually named in any play again until Jonson's *Volpone* (V.iii), but that of course does not mean that it was not in use during the intervening seventy-eight years. In fact, the traverse (and the scaffold or stage, and indeed any technicality) may have been used earlier or more widely than suggested here, but I have confined myself to actual text mentions in surviving plays which can be studied.

Taken in conjunction with the problem in *Calisto* described in Section (ix) above, it seems clear that the interluders found a need to supply themselves on occasion with a 'retiring place' for a character who had to withdraw temporarily from the action but *not* make a definite exit. The solution in *Calisto* – namely, to go off into one's 'orchard' – would clearly not be suitable in all cases, even if the playwright were to add the phrase 'or some other place' as in fact he did in a precisely parallel situation in *Godly Queen Hester* (see l. 634, 'For a season we wyll to our solace / Into our orcharde or some other place'). The curious and awkward phrase suggests how the need had been felt before but had not been met. Now, however, the traverse would supply that need for a place to 'retire' – and conversely, of course, for a place from which to 'advance' again. Thus it would become the ancestor of the 'discovery space' occasionally required in the Elizabethan playhouse later. And, since it was a temporary device and therefore to be set up only when the play required it, it would explain satisfactorily the absence of any permanent 'inner-stage' opening, or 'discovery space', in De Witt's drawing of the Swan stage.

(xi) Features of the third period 1550–1576

There is only one more great innovation in presentation technique before the building of The Theatre in 1576, and it opens the third and last period of this present chapter. The first indication about it comes on the title-page to *Gammer Gurton's Needle* (*c.* 1553) where we read that this comedy was 'Played on Stage, not longe ago in Christes Colledge in Cambridge'. The innovation, of course, is in the mention of its being played *on stage*. This is the first direct reference to a stage in all interlude scripts, so far as extant plays are concerned.

There is very little in *Gammer Gurton* beyond this bare remark to explain what shape or size of stage it might be or how it was used. Summing up the very scanty evidence to be found in this period, the stage was – at first, anyway – not a large one. It was probably more like what we would call a dais, or what was then called a 'footpace' or step up, some 6 inches or a foot high, and probably correspondingly small in area, say some 6–8 feet. It would stand against the centre part of the screens in such a way as to leave the two doors free, and it would not interfere with any action played out, as formerly, on the hall floor.

What it in fact amounts to is a special development of the 'differentiation' idea, stressing the fact that action taking place upon it, and action taking place upon the hall floor, should be understood to be in some way separate. This the following references will show.

There is a situation in John Phillip's *Patient and Meek Grissil* (*c.* 1559) which appears to offer some confirmation of the details mentioned above concerning the nature of a stage. In it a Messenger leaves the Marquis's palace and goes to the house where Grissil lives, to deliver to her a summons to come to the palace. He is just about to reach her house when he hears her singing and pauses to listen before going on to make himself known and deliver the message.

From the principles set out earlier in this chapter, it would seem very likely that there will be examples here of differentiation of acting areas and of distinction between doors. Suppose Door A represents the palace (or the way from the palace), and suppose Door B represents Grissil's house (or more specifically the entrance door to that house); how may the place where Grissil comes to sit and sing be represented? For this is what the script unmistakably directs that she must do. The place may be thought of as a room indoors, or it might be supposed that she comes out onto a porch outside. But the problem is the same in any case, for the Messenger must hear her, yet must not interrupt her before his cue – which is two stanzas away. The most promising suggestion would seem to be that a still closer application of the differentiation idea was invoked; that the area between the doors and directly against the centre screen was temporarily allocated to Grissil's little singing act, and that she came to that area from her house door, carrying her distaff and a stool, sat down and immediately began (unconscious of the Messenger). Whether in fact the space was supposed indoors or outdoors would have mattered not at all to a Tudor spectator; the 'place' he would have in his mind would be simply the hall he sat in, and all the happening would signify for him would be the presence of entertainers come to amuse him. But this theorizing does not settle what is the immediate practical point of the presentation of the scene: where in fact *was* the Messenger while he listened to her, and what was he doing during those two stanzas of her very devotional and hymn-like song?

The answer is given us in the accompanying acting direction where he is told to 'Go once or twise about the Staige', and the same direction adds, 'Let Grissill Singe some songe, and sit Spinninge'; the stage is then definitely brought into the picture and Grissil must have mounted it when she came from her door to sing. The words of the song now follow, and it is during that song therefore that the Messenger must go once or twice *about the stage*. Once the song is over he can approach Grissil and ask: Who lives here? And she tells him: My father and I. As soon as that happens all distinctions of place are dissolved, and the dialogue returns to normal, until the next occasion for differentiation occurs. It is worth noting that the stage supposed here would come just on the area supposed for the stage in *Gammer Gurton's Needle* on independent evidence. It is also worth noting that the phrase 'to go about the stage' does *not* mean 'to walk to and fro *upon* the stage', but 'to go this way and that on the floor *beside* the stage'.

The word 'about' is obviously an equivocal adverb to use for a stage action, but it would be hard to be more precise. To say to go 'around' would be equally equivocal. In *Susanna* there is yet another equivocal adverb, 'to go *afore*', relating to actors leaving the stage to go (apparently) in front of it (see below, p. 97).

Apius and Virginia (*c.* 1564) is much more melodramatic both in its plot and in its verse. Concerning its mention of a stage (or 'scaffold' as it is here called), the situation leading up to it is this: Judge Apius lusts after

Virginius's daughter, Virginia. In order to get her in his power he summons Virginius and has him accused of stealing the girl when she was a child. Virginius, greatly perturbed, indignantly denies this.

Now Apius has an acting-direction to 'go forth'. Surprisingly, however, this direction is immediately followed by a further speech by him telling Virginius, on pain of death, to deliver his daughter to Apius for a private interview. After this speech Apius again has a direction but this time to 'exit' (not 'go forth'). And only then does he finally go out.

The oddness here may be explained if Apius had at the beginning mounted a low rostrum, of the sort described above, to hear the accusation made against Virginius. Then having heard it he would step off the stage in order to 'go forth' according to the direction but, on his way out, pause to address his devastating command to Virginius as he passes him on the floor.

However that may be, Virginius is now duly upset, and the significant direction follows: 'Here let Virginius go about the scaffold'. He briefly but vehemently bewails the case and then announces that he must go home. But just then he is made to pause by the entrance of a strange figure. The kind of action suggested in the above direction would seem to be a parallel to the action when the Messenger came to Grissil; if so, the 'going about' would not be *upon* the stage but on the floor *around* it. There is a similar sort of reason here too – namely, the need to leave the stage itself clear for an intervening piece of business. In this case it is the entrance of the personified figure of Rumour, who comes to reveal to all the world the extent of Apius's villainy in a twenty-eight-line speech. It would clearly be helpful to have Rumour – a non-human, omniscient figure – kept separate in some respect from the very human Virginius. For one reason it would distinguish the human being from the abstraction; more important, perhaps, Virginius has to hear Rumour but, in the nature of things, not to reply to or question her, and Rumour herself has no call to address any person directly. But if Rumour speaks from the rostrum she can convincingly overlook Virginius; while if Virginius keeps to the floor he can the more effectively pause on the way out and stay to hear the details of his daughter's fate. When Rumour has finished she goes out. Virginius speaks seven lines in a diatribe of bitter cursing, at the climax of which his daughter enters and asks what it is all about. The rest of the play rather falls to pieces.

In John Pickering's *Horestes* of 1567 there is an interesting direction concerning the use of a stage. The situation is as follows: just before it, King Idumeus has entered together with his 'Councell', and it would seem inevitable that they would take the stage. The King explains that they are about to see the muster of Horestes' army but asks, 'Where is Horestes why stease [stays] he'? 'Councell' replies, 'Oh soferayne lord me thinkes I here, him for to be at hand / yft please your grace, he is in sight, euen now withal his band' – so now the soldiers are approaching through one of the doors into the hall. As they come Idumeus calls, 'Com on Horestes we haue stayd, your mouster for to se.' It is at this point that we have in the margin the following direction: 'Let ye dru*m* play & enter Horestis w^t his band marche a bout the stage.' Surely it would seem most unlikely that Horestes and his army (however few soldiers represented it) would enter and then *mount the stage* where the King and 'Councell' were waiting to review them, and march about *on* that very stage, to what would appear to be everybody's confusion! Not only would it be less confusing and more suitable to march up and down on the floor beside and before the stage, but the very presence of the rostrum for King and court to stand on would help the atmosphere of a review and of the final address to the troops that Idumeus makes after it.

The general evidence seems clear that the interluders' stage of this period did not take up a great deal of room; did not interfere with the doors; left a considerable amount of acting area still free on the hall floor; and was low and quite easy to mount without steps. All this can be affirmed only as general usage because, naturally, the details of a performance would depend on the place where it was played, and some places such as the royal court could have offered greater facilities.

The last reference within this period is to an even more elaborate use of the stage. It comes in Thomas Garter's *The Most Virtuous and Godly Susanna* of *c.* 1569. In the relevant passage the two salacious Elders (speaking on the kind of small stage already described) discuss Susanna's daily habit of washing in her orchard, and propose to go and hide there to watch her. Then one of them says, 'O Lord that she were there', and then adds, 'Away apace, go on afore, me thinke she commeth here' – obviously 'heralding' an entrance for Susanna. But before she enters there appears this direction concerning the Elders: 'Here they go afore into the Orchard, and Susanna and her two maydes come vpon the stage.' The Elders must therefore step down and go *afore* into the orchard (which we shall find has a practical fence and gate). And so it must be that we have here not only one 'differentiated' area on the stage but a further one on the hall floor in front of the first and isolated from the remainder of the floor by some sort of gate.

Susanna and her two maids now step up and take their places 'vpon the stage' where the Elders had previously been, while the Elders themselves enter the orchard before (and presumably a little below) that stage. And there they hide. After a short talk the three women step down and also 'goe into the Orcharde'. There Susanna finds she has forgotten her 'sope and oyle' and tells the maids to fetch them, adding: 'make fast the Orchard dore'. This they do and one of them even enjoins the other to 'Proue with your foote, if that the Dore, as we were bad be lockt'. So Susanna is locked in with the two old men.

It seems there can be little doubt that in all the above there is a growing scope of presentation ranging from nothing beyond the two doors, and the floor itself, at the beginning of the century; on through distinct meanings for the two doors; then to the addition of a traverse; and then to the provision of a small 'stage', footpace, dais, rostrum, whatever is the most informative name for it. And it may well be that the very smallness of this dais (forced upon it by the need to leave the greater part of the hall floor free for other action and for the general circulation of the servants and others attending the event) was one, at least, of the pressures which decided Burbage to have done with temporary resorts to occasional great halls, and to build instead a theatre where he could have a proper stage nearly as big as the footpace and the acting area of the hall floor put together, and where he might be free from the interference of spectators crowding his players. In the first respect he was to be successful; in the second he was unfortunately less so.

It ought perhaps to be repeated in closing that not all Tudor perform-ances were in private halls; other sites were certainly used on occasion – guildhalls, colleges, inns, village greens, even churchyards, and of course the court itself. How much these occasions contributed to the eventual form of the theatre building in and after 1576 is matter for discussion elsewhere. The playhouse shape itself and the arrangement of the auditorium most probably derived from inn-yards or animal-baiting rings. But equally prob-able does it seem that the experience gained from seventy-five, and more, years of performing before hall screens must have influenced the arrange-ment of the stage and of the tiring-house façade which backed it.

As a footnote to this chapter, and as some confirmation of the theory about the stage offered here, it seems relevant to quote the opening direction to an elaborate play by the professional comedian, Robert Wilson (reputed as rare a one as Tarleton), written probably for presentation at court, *The Cobbler's Prophecy* – dated about 1589 and thus thirteen years beyond the period of this chapter. The play is (among other things) a skit on the morals of the Roman gods, and the opening direction reads (I italicize the words especially relevant to what has been said above): 'Enter Iupiter and Iuno, Mars and Venus, Apollo, after him, Bacchus, Vulcan limping, and after all Diana wringing her hands: they *passe by*, while *on the stage* Mercurie from one end Ceres from another meete.'

III The companies
and the repertory

T. W. Craik

1 Varieties of performers

The history of acting from 1500 to 1576 may be briefly and broadly described as the history of a transition: from occasional, private and itinerant performances to regular public performances in a permanent theatre. It was in 1576 that James Burbage built The Theatre in Shoreditch as a London headquarters for the Earl of Leicester's Men;[1] later in the same year Richard Farrant leased a building in the Blackfriars as a playhouse for the Children of the Chapel Royal.[2] From then onwards the drama in England virtually means the plays acted by the London companies in their London theatres, though plague and prohibition might send the companies travelling as far afield as Exeter and York, and though royal command might call them to perform at court to enliven the Christmas holidays or to grace a noble wedding.

However, the history of acting in this period is not only that of the

[1] E. K. Chambers, *The Elizabethan Stage* (Oxford, 1923), Vol. II, pp. 384–8.
[2] Chambers, op. cit. Vol. II, p. 36. Sebastian Westcott, the master of St Paul's choir school, is known to have superintended public performances by the Paul's Boys (on unidentified premises belonging to the cathedral) before December 1575. See T. Lennam, *Sebastian Westcott, The Children of Paul's, and 'The Marriage of Wit and Science'* (Toronto and Buffalo, 1975), pp. 43–50.

professional companies (if we define professionalism for the present as giving performances for gain, irrespective of whether the actors' whole income was made in this way). In several grammar schools the performance of plays was regarded as a profitable academic exercise; and schoolboys, university students and members of the Inns of Court acted before invited audiences, including royal spectators, on special occasions. Besides this academic amateurism, there persisted the civic amateurism of the miracle cycles until their gradual discouragement and discontinuance under Elizabeth's government. This chapter will not be concerned with performers of miracle cycles, since their history belongs to medieval drama. For the same reason nothing will here be said of actors of folk plays.

Alongside the development of English drama from medieval times runs the course of various sub-dramatic entertainments: performances which, while not plays in any strict sense of the word, nevertheless involved an element of impersonation. Such were the Christmas processions of Boy Bishops and of Lords of Misrule, the civic street pageants of welcome provided for royal visits, and the courtly disguisings or masques which were to culminate in Jacobean splendour. The relationship between the disguising and the drama of the early Tudor court is particularly intimate, as will be seen in discussing the actors of the Chapel Royal. These sub-dramatic spectacles employed a miscellaneous range of performers. The Boy Bishop and his retinue were choristers. The Lord of Misrule was a member of a king's or nobleman's household, appointed for the occasion of the Christmas holidays to preside over the revels: he might himself be a gentleman (as, for example, George Ferrers in 1552–3 at court), and, when he processionally entered upon his duties, amateurs and professionals might rub shoulders in his retinue (John Smith, who took part as a 'disard' or jester in George Ferrers's revels, was very probably the Court Interluder of that name).[1] When street pageants employed live performers (for often model figures were used), they were recruited from schoolboys, choirboys and the general public in the same manner as in the miracle cycles; women and girls might occasionally appear in these shows,[2] though they did not act in true plays until the seventeenth century. (I take it that the 'worshipful wives' of Chester, who provided the miracle play of the Assumption of Our

---

[1] Chambers, op. cit. Vol. II, p. 82.
[2] G. Wickham, *Early English Stages 1300–1600*, Vol. I (London, 1959), pp. 271–2, cites payments of 8d. apiece to named girls for appearing in pageants at the London Lord Mayor's Shows of 1523 and 1534.

Lady, financed, but did not themselves act, their play.)[1] The court disguisings were performed by lords and ladies nobly dressed, who entered the
hall usually with a mobile pageant such as a ship or a castle, an arbour or a
mountain, took part in some short symbolic encounter like the attempted
storming of the castle, and then danced with each other and with the spectators: on at least some of these occasions the Children of the Chapel
Royal came in as singers upon the pageant, and sometimes the same
evening's entertainment included a regular play by regular actors.

Returning to the true drama of the early sixteenth century, we may divide
it, with Glynne Wickham, into two types: 'that of worship, appealing to a
universal audience; and that of social recreation, appealing to a small
sectional audience'.[2] This is not to say that all private acting was wholly
secular: the singers of the Earl of Northumberland's chapel in the 1520s
were expected to perform a nativity play before him annually at Christmas
and a resurrection play at Easter.[3] However, the large distinction is useful
as a reminder that the body of English secular drama originates in the
performances of professional entertainers to noble households. The connection between the unattached travelling entertainer and the entertainer
who was officially retained is obscure, but it is likely that a travelling
troupe who casually arrived, performed and pleased might be invited to
stay, or offered a welcome at their next visit, and might so become attached
to the household in question. Alternatively, persons originally employed
in other duties may have emerged (during Christmas festivities, for
instance) as talented entertainers, and been thereafter formally recognized,
and regularly paid, as players. It is not known how early the travelling
minstrel added acting to his accomplishments: we hear of 'layking of enter-
ludez' (interlude playing) at Christmas in *Sir Gawain and the Green Knight*
in the fourteenth century, though apart from the dialogue *De Clerico et
Puella* (early fourteenth century) no such early texts survive. Nevertheless,
the tradition of travelling performers, itinerant minstrels, was an important
influence on the English professional theatre.

In discussing the groups of actors who performed plays during the
period, no very rigid and systematic procedure can be adopted. The division
– so clearly marked today – between the professional and amateur company
was in the sixteenth century much less distinct. Even the local actors in the

---

[1] G. Wickham, op. cit. Vol. I, pp. 271–2, 346, on the contrary, thinks that they were
themselves the performers.
[2] Ibid. Vol. I, p. xliii.
[3] E. K. Chambers, *The Mediaeval Stage* (Oxford, 1903), Vol. II, p. 193.

miracle cycles were paid for their labours, and it is also possible that some of the principal roles were taken by regular actors, that is, actors who made a living out of their art. Moreover, a group of town actors might take their miracle play to various houses, noble and religious, and there perform it for reward.[1] Thus, although there is a sense in which the acting of miracle cycles is amateur, there is another sense in which it is not. Again, the two chief companies of boy actors, the Children of the Chapel Royal and the Boys of St Paul's choir school, did not support themselves by their performances: acting was originally an occasional and incidental function of theirs. But by the end of the century both were established as famous acting groups giving frequent public exhibitions and charging for admission just like the adult companies in the public theatres. As for the men who have been called in this paragraph regular actors, it was not unusual for them to have a trade besides acting. George Maylor or Mayler, one of the Court Interluders of Henry VIII, provides an instance. In a lawsuit of *c.* 1530 about playing garments he is described as a merchant tailor, being then aged forty, and in another lawsuit of 1529 he is described as a glazier; his professional status as an actor is, however, quite clear from the subject of the latter lawsuit, which is his agreement to take a tailor called Thomas Arthur as apprentice for one year, undertaking not only to teach him to play but also to secure his employment as one of the Court Interluders.[2]

The division between companies of men and companies of boys, like the division between professionals and amateurs, is convenient but not absolute. It is true that we hear of school performances given wholly by boys, and it is probable that when the master of a grammar school or choir school brought his boys to court during Elizabeth's reign he was not himself an actor in their play. On the other hand it is a fact that in 1515, when the Children of the Chapel Royal gave *Troilus and Pandar* before the court, their master William Cornish played Calchas.[3] As for the adult companies, their traditional early constitution was from four to six men, sometimes supplemented in the middle of the sixteenth century by one or two boys, though the boys are, of course, to be considered in the light of apprentices who will graduate to men's roles with years.

However, though these divisions must not be oversimplified, they provide some method of classification, and so we may distinguish between

---

[1] E. K. Chambers, *The Mediaeval Stage*, Vol. II, pp. 184–5.
[2] Ibid. Vol. II, p. 187 (note 3); Chambers, *The Elizabethan Stage*, Vol. II, p. 81. Another Court Interluder, John Young, was a mercer: ibid. Vol. II, p. 80 (note 5).
[3] See below, pp. 118–19.

two types of company: first, those whose acting was their speciality, who were retained by a patron as actors, and who, being the heirs of the itinerant minstrels, would travel when their patron did not need their services; and, second, those whose acting was (at least originally) their secondary function, their primary one being singing (in the case of choristers) or study (in the case of grammar school boys or students at the universities and Inns of Court).[1] Practical distinctions, then, can be drawn between regulars and occasionals, professionals and amateurs, men and boys, always bearing in mind the fact that the actual history is much more complex.

In the following pages there will be given accounts, first, of the chief companies of players and their known repertory, beginning with the adult groups and proceeding to the children; second, of amateur acting at the universities, Inns of Court and elsewhere; third and finally, of some extant plays of the period which cannot be positively ascribed to particular companies.

[1] That the second group might occasionally borrow the itinerant habits of the first is shown by a payment at Norwich (1580–1) to 'the Earle of Oxenfordes lads' and by that group's appearance at Bristol (September 1581) in the form of nine boys and a man. (Chambers, *The Elizabethen Stage*, Vol. II, pp. 100–1. He comments: 'These were probably boys of the Earl's domestic chapel, travelling either with the Duttons [chief members of the then Earl of Oxford's Men] or as a separate company.')

2 Men's companies

The Court Interluders came into existence in Henry VII's reign, their first recorded payment being in 1493. There were four of them in 1494, and five in 1503. Nothing is known of their activities before they became royal actors, except that the name of one of them, John English, occurs in 1485 as the recipient of certain 'stuffures' paid for by a royal warrant. If this John English ('apparently a royal tailor or valet', according to Chambers[1]) later became the actor, as is probable, he provides an instance of recruitment of players from the household servants. The process certainly took place in reverse, for one of English's fellow actors in 1494, Richard Gibson, became Porter and Yeoman Tailor of the Great Wardrobe early in Henry VIII's reign, in which capacity he supervised the costumes and properties used in court shows, and apparently ceased acting in them.[2] English himself, who seems to have led the company from the first, took them to Scotland in 1503 in the train of Princess Margaret when she married James IV in Edinburgh; there they played 'a Moralite' and other unrecorded pieces. Henry VIII increased the company to eight or ten players who received varying annual fees according to seniority, from £6. 13s. 4d.

[1] *The Elizabethan Stage*, Vol. II, p. 78 (note 1).
[2] Ibid. Vol. I, p. 72; Vol. II, p. 80.

to £2. 4s. 5d., exclusive of 'rewards' for performances, Christmas presents, and what might be picked up on tour: for from 1526–7, usually under the name of the Queen's Men, they are recorded as performing as far north as Durham and as far west as Bristol.[1] At Norwich in November 1546 the title of their play is known: *The Market of Mischief*. During Edward VI's reign they are reported only at Maldon (1549–50), but acted fairly frequently at court, requiring an oven and weapons of wood at Shrovetide 1548 and a seven-headed dragon at Shrovetide 1549 (probably for an anti-papal play), besides other unspecified properties and costumes for Christmas plays in 1551–2. During the following Christmas they were rehearsing, and presumably presented, 'a play of Esop's Crow, wherin the moste part of the actors were birds', and some time between 1551 and the end of Edward's reign they were paid on a Shrove Monday for playing 'the play of Self-love'.[2]

Apart from a reward for a performance before Elizabeth, perhaps in January 1559,[3] there are no further records of their giving plays at court. Chambers thinks, however, that they 'no doubt took their share in court revels during the earlier part of Mary's reign'[4]: certainly there are no records of provincial performances by them between October 1547 and the year 1555–6. Thereafter they reappear frequently on tour, in every year of Mary's reign and of Elizabeth's until 1573. Then there is one solitary appearance at Ipswich between 29 September and 6 October 1581.[5] A new company called Queen Elizabeth's Men came into existence in the spring of 1583,[6] and it is doubtless to this company that all later provincial records refer.

During this period of their decline at court, the Court Interluders continue to be numbered as eight in the fee-lists, but their actual numbers seem to have been seven after 1552 and four after 1556, and after the beginning of Elizabeth's reign vacancies that occurred were left unfilled. The last of the actors, John Smith, died in 1580, having been in service for some thirty-three years. Whether he was still touring the provinces up to 1573 is unknown. Two of his colleagues had died in 1563 and the third in 1568,[7] so it is evident that the company calling itself the Queen's

[1] *The Elizabethan Stage*, Vol. II, p. 81.
[2] Ibid. Vol. II, p. 83; Chambers, *The Mediaeval Stage*, Vol. II, p. 201.
[3] Chambers, *The Elizabethan Stage*, Vol. II, pp. 83–4.
[4] Ibid. Vol. II, p. 83.
[5] J. T. Murray, *English Dramatic Companies 1558–1642* (London, 1910), Vol. I, p. 19.
[6] Chambers, *The Elizabethan Stage*, Vol. II, p. 104.
[7] Ibid. Vol. II, p. 84.

Men was partly unofficially constituted during the ten years before 1573, while at Ipswich in 1581 it must have been wholly so.

It is regrettable that so little of the Court Interluders' repertory is known: a morality at the Scottish court in 1503; *The Market of Mischief* at Norwich in 1546, which sounds like a moral interlude employing allegorical characters; the two Shrovetide plays, with their properties listed, of 1548 and 1549 at court; *Aesop's Crow*, presumably a dramatized beast-fable, at court during Christmas 1552–3; and *Self-Love*, also given at court by 1553, which may have been a moral allegory, but may equally have been a discussion in John Heywood's manner between differentiated typical persons. To these may be conjecturally added *Wealth and Health*, a political moral interlude which, I have elsewhere argued, belongs to Mary's court at the beginning of her reign,[1] at which time the company is not recorded as travelling the provinces. The title-page claims falsely that the seven characters can be distributed among four actors, whereas, even with doubling, five actors are required (six if there are to be no awkward pauses). The seven Court Interluders of 1554, however, would not have needed to double the parts at all.

Collier's account of this company's playing before Henry VIII in 1513 a moral interlude written by Medwall and called *The Finding of Truth*, which displeased the king by its length, is now universally discredited.[2] This fictitious anecdote no doubt influenced Chambers's belief that the Court Interluders were 'unwisely wedded to the old methods' and cultivated allegory when it had 'had its day'.[3] Allegory, however, continued not only to exist but also to be fashionable (particularly in the hands of the boy actors) well into the middle of Elizabeth's reign; and, as for the repertory of the Court Interluders in her father's time, we must not conclude that because they played moral plays they would or could play nothing else.

The royal company of players was not the first to enjoy noble patronage, though doubtless its existence encouraged other groups of players to seek patronage and other great households to provide it. In 1482 there already was a company belonging to Henry Bourchier, Earl of Essex, and another belonging to Richard, Duke of Gloucester.[4] Whether the latter company

[1] T. W. Craik, 'The Political Interpretation of Two Tudor Interludes', *Review of English Studies*, N.S., IV (April 1953), pp. 98–108.

[2] J. P. Collier, *The History of English Dramatic Poetry to the Time of Shakespeare; and Annals of the Stage to the Restoration*, 2nd ed. (London, 1879), Vol. I, p. 69. The story was repeated by Chambers, *The Mediaeval Stage*, Vol. II, pp. 188 (note 1), 201, 443, but later rejected by him in *The Elizabethan Stage*, Vol. II, pp. 79–80.

[3] Chambers, *The Mediaeval Stage*, Vol. II, p. 201.

[4] Ibid. Vol. II, pp. 186–7.

continued to perform as the king's players when their patron became Richard III is not known. The existence of these and other early companies of players claiming noble patronage is known not through wages from the patron but through rewards from noble households, religious houses and towns which they visited with their plays. The patronage, in short, did not necessarily give them a sufficient salary and a continual playing place: it gave them the *entrée* to many places where they could play and be paid.[1]

From these records of payments we can deduce that in the early sixteenth century there were many such companies on the road. The Northumberland Household Book estimates that 33*s*. 4*d*. was spent in rewards to visiting players during the Christmas holidays of 1511–12, and states that 20*d*. was the fee for each play.[2] This means that twenty plays were given that Christmas at the Earl of Northumberland's house. The volume of performances in the environs of London during this period can also be guessed, from a statement in the lawsuit of *c*. 1530 already mentioned:[3] the costumes in question had been hired out, since about 1525, at least twenty times every summer and twenty times every winter.[4] Not a trace of all these performances is left, and it may be noted here that, apart from *The Market of Mischief* (at Norwich in 1546 by the Court Interluders), *Barbarous Terryne* (at Ipswich in 1563 by an unknown company),[5] *Samson* (at the Red Lion Inn, Stepney, in 1567 by an unknown company),[6] *The Cradle of Security* (at Gloucester some time between 1565 and 1575 by an unknown company),[7] and *The Red Knight* (at Bristol in 1576 by the Earl of Sussex's

---

[1] It gave them, furthermore, a legal status when they were on their travels: not being masterless men, they were not liable to the late medieval laws against vagabonds, which were severely reinforced by statutes of 1531 and 1547. The 'service' which they officially rendered their patrons was often very nominal, and, to guard against their abuse of this loophole in the law, new legislation was introduced in 1572. Players had now to be bona fide household servants of their patron, and no patron below a baron was recognized as conferring legal protection on travelling players. Mayors and country justices were, however, empowered to grant local travelling licences to players who lacked this baronial protection. The matter is fully discussed by Chambers in *The Elizabethan Stage*, Vol. I, pp. 269–82.

[2] Chambers, *The Mediaeval Stage*, Vol. II, p. 187. By 1522–3 the fee was 10*s*. for every Lord's player, and 20*s*. for the players of the Earl's special friends and kinsmen.

[3] See above, p. 106.

[4] Ibid. Vol. II, p. 183 (note 2).

[5] Murray, op. cit. Vol. II, p. 288.

[6] Chambers, *The Elizabethan Stage*, Vol. II, p. 380.

[7] D. M. Bevington, *From 'Mankind' to Marlowe* (Cambridge, Mass, 1962), pp. 13–14. Chambers wrongly titles the play *The Castle of Security* (*The Mediaeval Stage*, Vol. II, p. 189; *The Elizabethan Stage*, Vol. I, p. 333).

Men),[1] even the titles of all these touring plays up to 1576 are lost. It is only the Revels Accounts at court which preserve with any frequency the titles of plays given by the companies of adult actors under noble patronage.

The first such titles occur when Lord Rich's Men (active 1564–70) appeared at court at Christmas 1567–8.[2] The plays prepared by the Revels between Christmas and Shrovetide were *The King of Scots* (described as a tragedy), *As Plain as Can Be*, *The Painful Pilgrimage*, *Jack and Jill*, *Six Fools*, *Wit and Will*, *Prodigality* and *Horestes*; but, as four companies of boys were also acting at court during that period, it is not known which of these plays belonged to Lord Rich's Men.[3] Sir Robert Lane's Men (active 1570–2) played *Lady Barbara* on 27 December 1571, and *Cloridon and Radiamanta* on 17 February 1572.[4] The Earl of Leicester's Men (active (1559–88) played *Predor and Lucia* and *Mamillia* on 26 and 28 December 1573, *Philemon and Philecia* on 21 February 1574, *Panecia* during the Christmas of 1574–5, and *The Collier* (not identifiable with Fulwell's *Like Will to Like, quoth the Devil to the Collier*) on 30 December 1576.[5] The Earl of Lincoln's (Lord Clinton's) Men (active 1566–77) played *Herpetulus the Blue Knight and Perobia* on 3 January 1574, and *Pretestus* during the Christmas of 1574–5.[6] The Earl of Sussex's Men (active 1569–94) rehearsed *Phredrastus* and *Phigon and Lucia* for Christmas performances in 1574–5 which did not take place.[7] The Earl of Warwick's Men (active 1559–65, 1575–80) played *The Painter's Daughter* on 26 December 1576.[8] Lord Howard's Men (active 1576–1604, latterly as the Lord Admiral's Men, and

---

[1] Chambers, *The Elizabethan Stage*, Vol. II, p. 93.
[2] Ibid. Vol. II, p. 92. At Christmas 1560 Lord Robert Dudley's (later the Earl of Leicester's) Men played, as also did Paul's Boys. No title is given in the Revels Accounts, but a contemporary letter-writer says 'at the corte new plays, which lasted almost all night – the name of the play was huff-suff[*sic*]-and-ruff, with other masks both of ladies and gents' (ibid. Vol. IV, p. 79 (note 6)). Chambers assumes that this was Preston's *Cambises*, as does Bevington (op. cit. p. 60), who ascribes the performance to Dudley's Men. But as Huff, Snuff and Ruff appear only in one brief episode of Preston's play, it is very unlikely that a spectator should state that it was named after them, and more likely that *Cambises* drew upon this earlier lost play for three of its minor characters.
[3] *Wit and Will* is probably *The Marriage of Wit and Science*, *Prodigality* The Contention *between Liberality and Prodigality*, and *Horestes* the *New Interlude of Vice containing the History of Horestes* by John Pickering. All the other court plays mentioned in this paragraph are lost.
[4] Chambers, *The Elizabethan Stage*, Vol. II, p. 96.
[5] Ibid. Vol. II, pp. 85–91.
[6] Ibid. Vol. II, pp. 96–7.
[7] Ibid. Vol. II, pp. 92–6.
[8] Ibid. Vol. II, pp. 97–8.

afterwards under various patrons to 1641) played *Toolv* on 27 December 1576.[1]

It must be repeated that these are their court performances of named plays, not their only appearances at court; nor is this a complete list of the adult companies who appeared there. Companies of players had visited the court since at least 1427, when both the 'jeweis [i.e. *joueurs*, players] de Abyndon' and 'Jakke Travail et ses compaignons' were rewarded for 'entreludes' during the Christmas revels.[2] The surviving accounts of payments in the early years are incomplete, but it is clear from those for the period 1492–1516 that every two or three years would bring one or another visiting company to court.[3] Not all of these claimed noble patrons: 'four Pleyers of Essex' (on 1 January 1494) and '3 Pleyers of Wycombe' (on 31 December 1494) were presumably local groups, and Chambers suggests that such groups may have been non-professional actors travelling with their miracle play.[4] The household accounts of noblemen and religious houses, and the financial records of towns, show the same variety among the visiting companies of players.

The distinction between professional and non-professional actors, in these early days, was (as already remarked) an indistinct distinction, when the local actors as well as the troupe under a patron's name could take to the road. Such details as are known of John Bale's dramatic career may throw more light, though of a dim kind, upon the formation and the activities of companies of players.[5] Bale, who became one of the most prolific and violent attackers of the Roman Catholic Church, was a priest of Thorndon in Suffolk before and after his conversion to Protestantism. This occurred before 1534, in which year he was examined once by the Archbishop of York and again by the Bishop of London as to his views on honouring and praying to saints. On both these occasions Bale was got out of trouble by Thomas Cromwell, who he sympathized with plays of his: 'ob editas comoedias me semper liberavit'. Bale had written English comedies and tragedies for John Vere, Earl of Oxford, who like Cromwell supported the Protestant party at court. The Earls of Oxford had players in

[1] Chambers, *The Elizabethan Stage*, Vol. II, p. 134.
[2] Chambers, *The Mediaeval Stage*, Vol. II, pp. 186, 256–7.
[3] Ibid. Vol. II, pp. 257–8.
[4] Ibid. Vol. II, pp. 184–5. Chambers points out that the fifteenth-century Croxton *Play of the Sacrament* 'appears to be intended for the use of a travelling troupe', since it concludes with a statement that nine actors may play it.
[5] For Bale's biography, see J. W. Harris, *John Bale* (Urbana, Ill., 1940).

1492 and again in 1547,[1] and it is reasonable to infer that Bale wrote his plays for the Earl's company to act: perhaps it was through performance that Cromwell knew of them. After Bale was deprived of his living of Thorndon in 1537 or 1538 he turned his chief energies to writing plays, and composed or revised the five that are extant: *God's Promises*, *John the Baptist's Preaching in the Wilderness*, *The Temptation of Our Lord*, *Three Laws of Nature, Moses and Christ* and *King John*. To act these plays he recruited a company, and (it seems) himself performed the role of the expositor in the first four, whose speeches are headed 'Baleus Prolocutor'.[2] Thomas Cromwell, Lord Privy Seal since 1536, now re-enters the history. His account books show payments of 40s. on 8 September 1538 and 30s. on 31 January 1539 to 'Bale [1539: 1538 Balle] and his ffelowes', 'for playing before my lorde'. The former performance, and probably the latter also, took place 'at saynt Stephens besydes Caunturbury'. At the same time a company, variously described as Lord Cromwell's Players and the Lord Privy Seal's Players, gave performances at Thetford Priory, Norfolk (between 1536 and 1540), Cambridge (1537–8, 1539–40) and Barnstaple (1538–9).[3] It has been convincingly conjectured[4] that this company consisted of 'Bale and his ffelowes' (who might be so described by Cromwell's treasurer, even if they had already gained his employer's patronage), and that Cromwell's payment to Bale's company on 31 January 1539 was for a performance of 'an enterlude co[n]cernyng king Iohn / aboute viij or ix of the clocke at nyght on thursdaye the seconde Daye of Ianuarye' at Cranmer's house.[5]

After Cromwell's fall from power and execution in 1540, his players cease to be heard of. Bale, who had fled to Germany in 1540 and returned in 1547 to become Rector of Bishopstoke in Hampshire, makes his next theatrical appearance there, rehearsing *Three Laws* in 1552. He recounts that a local priest protested against the play by making his servant, who had a part in it, learn instead a speech in which Bale was called heretic and knave.[6] This

[1] Chambers, *The Elizabethan Stage*, Vol. II, p. 99; *The Mediaeval Stage*, Vol. II, pp. 222, 257.

[2] At the end of the anonymous children's play *Jacob and Esau* (1554?) the epilogue is delivered by 'the Poete', who also was possibly the author.

[3] Murray, op. cit. Vol. II, p. 36.

[4] J. H. P. Pafford and W. W. Greg (eds), *King Johan*, Malone Society Reprint (London, 1931), p. xvii.

[5] Ibid. p. xviii. The play is identifiable as Bale's *King John* from a contemporary account: Harris, op. cit. pp. 102–3.

[6] Bale, *An Expostulation (etc.)*, quoted by Harris, op. cit. p. 103.

was evidently a scratch company assembled from local actors. Bale used local actors again when in 1553 (being then Bishop of Ossory in Ireland) he celebrated Mary's coronation in a highly characteristic way, by having his Protestant trilogy *God's Promises*, *John the Baptist's Preaching in the Wilderness* and *The Temptation of Our Lord* performed at the market cross of Kilkenny, 'to the small contentacion of the Prestes and other Papistes there'. The actors were 'the yonge men', who provided 'organe playinges and songes very aptely'.[1] The organ would be a portative organ, and, with the singing, suggests that the young men may have included, or indeed consisted of, choirmen and choirboys. There is some evidence pointing to a revival of *King John* at Ipswich for Elizabeth's visit in 1561, but no hint by whom it was played, if at all.[2]

Cromwell's players have been here discussed in some detail because of their probable connection with a known author of extant plays. But in the general circumstances of their brief career – their acknowledging a patron and their travelling when he did not require their services – they were representative of many such small troupes which will not be discussed at all because nothing is known of them except their patrons' names and parts of their itinerary. I cannot here do better than quote David Bevington's admirably concise account of the life of such travelling players in the late fifteenth and the sixteenth century.

> Like the minstrels, the players traveled at first in groups of four or less, on foot, with packs or packhorses, and perhaps a wagon for the more prosperous. Later, the leading troupes could afford mounts. Whereas common or unlicensed players were accounted vagabonds and so handled, those who wore noble livery enjoyed the prestige of such endorsement without lengthy commitments to their master's service. By the late fifteenth century the best of these players were sufficiently well-to-do to provoke comment upon the splendor of their dress. Besides the occasional performance for their lord, they visited other patrician banqueting-halls, and performed in towns within the municipal buildings and on village greens. Often they presented the first show in a town before the mayor or bailiff and members of the council. Visits to London during the winter season became increasingly common in the sixteenth century, for participation in the court revels and performances in the inn-yards of the city. Even the provincial churches and church-

[1] Chambers, *The Mediaeval Stage*, Vol. II, p. 374; Bevington, op. cit. p. 56.
[2] Pafford and Greg, op. cit. p. xix.

yards were not excluded as impromptu theaters for the ubiquitous players, with the proceeds from the selling of ale going to church benefit. At first the actors usually performed on a stage of trestles and barrels with a hanging backdrop for exits and entrances. Their scene was fluid and open, without stage properties to indicate setting. Their playing area was a single *locus*, and they operated almost entirely without stage machinery. Such rigorous economy was necessary not only for mobility, but for keeping operating costs at a minimum. Payment came in the form of wages or local collections, out of which the players had to meet their own staging costs – unlike the purveyors of disguisings or pageants at court, who were fully subsidized for their elaborate decorations.[1]

The three most important Elizabethan companies, the Earl of Leicester's Men, the Lord Chamberlain's Men and the Lord Admiral's Men, became important only in the period after 1576, during which they had established a permanent foothold in London and were acting regularly before their actual patrons, the London public, while their nominal patrons might procure their annual invitation to entertain the queen at court. It is true that by 1576 (when its two chief competitors appeared) the Earl of Leicester's Men was a company of some continuance, having begun in 1559. However, there was no necessary continuity of membership in the typical Elizabethan company: a patron's name might in turn shelter various groups of players; and conversely a group of players might circulate from patron to patron, as did the group led by Laurence and John Dutton, who from 1571 to 1583 successively served Sir Robert Lane, the Earl of Lincoln, the Earl of Warwick and the Earl of Oxford.[2]

[1] Bevington, op. cit. pp. 12–13.
[2] Chambers, *The Elizabethan Stage*, Vol. II, pp. 3, 98–9.

3 Boys' companies:
the Chapel Children

In the period beginning in 1576 the adult professional companies shared (or, more properly, disputed) the public's favour with the two principal companies of boys, the Children of the Chapel Royal and the Boys of St Paul's choir school. To the early history of these companies, usually abbreviated to the 'Chapel Children' and the 'Paul's Boys', we now turn.

The Chapel Royal itself had existed from the beginning of the twelfth century, but its connection with drama dates from the Tudor period. By this time its membership consisted of a dean, from twenty to thirty-two gentlemen, from eight to twelve children, and a master of grammar. The instruction and the keep of these children devolved upon this latter official, and the successive masters became responsible also for the boys' dramatic performances.[1]

The boys were originally, of course, recruited for their singing voices, and the masters had authority to impress boys from other choirs into the royal service. It is as singers that they first appear in court entertainments, in the pageants provided for the wedding festivities of Henry VII's elder son Prince Arthur to Katherine of Aragon in 1501.[2] One of these was a castle

[1] Chambers, *The Elizabethan Stage*, Vol. II, pp. 24–7.
[2] H. N. Hillebrand, *The Child Actors* (Urbana, Ill., 1926), p. 45.

containing eight ladies; on each of its four turrets was 'a little child, apparelled like a maiden', and these four children sang sweetly as the pageant was drawn into the hall by four beasts of gold and silver (in each beast being two men, presumably court servants). The singing boys doubt-less came from the Chapel Royal, as the ones in another of these pageants are stated to have done. This other pageant, representing 'a goodly Chapell', introduced artificial mermaids, 'one of them a man mermaide the other a woman', the man being in armour from the waist upwards, 'and in every of the said mermaides a Childe of the Chapell singing right sweetly'.[1]

The first plays of the Chapel Royal were given not by the children but by the gentlemen. From 1506 to 1512 payments were made in reward to the Gentlemen of the Chapel for acting once or twice a year, during the Christmas holidays, before the king.[2] The usual reward was £6. 13s. 4d. (ten marks, which continued customary for court plays till 1572)[3]; each gentleman also received annual wages of £13. 6s. 8d. (20 marks). The children received no wages apart from their board, but they had a secure position and good prospects of a future career, either at court as Chapel Gentlemen or in other offices, or elsewhere; many were sent to the university.[4]

Nothing, apart from the payments, is recorded of these plays by the gentlemen, except that in some instances the number of actors is stated: four players appeared on two occasions, five on another, 'divers' on another; at Christmas in 1508, 'Mr Kite, Cornish, and other of the Chapel' played before Henry VII at Richmond.[5] John Kite, who later became Archbishop of Armagh (1513), was at this time subdean of the Chapel. William Cornish, whose name first appears in 1493, became master of the children in 1509 (succeeding William Newark, who had held the office since 1493). It was during his mastership (1509–23) that the children began performing plays.

The first such performance known took place at Christmas 1515, when Cornish and the children played an interlude of *Troilus and Pandar*. A short but important description of the show, with an inventory of costumes, is provided by Richard Gibson (formerly a Court Interluder and at this time Yeoman Tailor of the Great Wardrobe) in his account book.[6] From this

---

[1] Hillebrand, op. cit. p. 46.
[2] Chambers, *The Elizabethan Stage*, Vol. II, p. 28.
[3] Ibid. Vol. I, p. 217: thereafter, it varied between £6. 13s. 4d., £10 and £13. 6s. 8d. until 1575, when £10 became the normal payment.
[4] Ibid. Vol. II, p. 29; Hillebrand, op. cit. pp. 42–3.
[5] Chambers, *The Elizabethan Stage*, Vol. II, p. 29 (note 6).
[6] Printed as Appendix III by Hillebrand, op. cit. pp. 324–5.

description it is clear that the play was, in the fashion of the time, combined with a pageant. Gibson specifies the setting as 'a castel of tymbyr fyx and fast in y^c kyngs hall'. He thus emphasizes the fact that it was permanent and not a mobile pageant on wheels such as was usual. It was evidently used for all three parts of the performance: Cornish's play; a fight at barriers of three against three with spears and with swords; and a disguising in which appeared a queen and six ladies, seven minstrels, six lords and gentlemen, and six other ladies. The six last-mentioned ladies would be ladies of the court, to dance with the six gentlemen. The queen and her six ladies, on the other hand, who issued from the castle 'w^t spechys aft[er] y^c devyes [device] of m^t kornyche', must be taken as child actors.[1] Gibson's inventory mentions a costume (not described) for 'y^c lady y^t playd faythe'. The phrasing is ambiguous, but the sense is presumably that a boy played a lady personifying Faith. Whether Faith was one of the queen's ladies in the disguising or a morality character in the interlude is uncertain: in favour of the latter view (to which I incline) it may be noticed that no other lady's costume except Cressida's is itemized, and that Faith would appropriately appear in a play of which Cressida's faithlessness was a principal theme. Other costumes are for Troilus, Pandar, Ulysses (the unnamed actors of whom are stated to be children), Diomed 'and hys felow[es]', Calchas (played by Cornish), a herald who introduced the fighting at barriers (Cornish again), and 'm^t harry of y^c chappell y^t playd in thys dysgysyng'. This last-mentioned person was Harry Kite, a Gentleman of the Chapel (distinct from John Kite, the subdean mentioned above): his part is not stated, and it is not quite clear whether he played in the disguising proper (in which it is hard to find a part for him unless as leader and spokesman of the minstrels) or in the play (if Gibson's 'disguising' loosely refers, as it may well do, to the whole entertainment). In a final list of the number of costumes to be provided, Gibson states that fifteen personages appeared in the play, though it is unlikely that all of these were speaking parts. A point to be noted is that to perform the parts (fourteen without Cornish) two of the Chapel Children would have to appear twice, unless they were supplemented by two of the gentlemen. A number of them would also appear again (like Cornish as the herald) in the subsequent disguising.

[1] As in the pageant of 4 March 1522 (at Wolsey's house), where eight ladies – Beauty, Honour, Perseverance, Kindness, Constance, Bounty, Mercy and Pity – defended a *château vert* against eight lords led by Henry VIII. Rosewater, comfits and fruits were the missiles. See Hillebrand, op. cit. pp. 57–8.

From this time onwards the children performed regularly at court. Their next play of which any description survives[1] was also part of a composite entertainment including a masque, presented on 3 September 1519.[2] Seven children took part, as Gibson's list of their costumes shows, and they played Summer, Winter, Sun, Moon, Wind, Rain and Lust (i.e. Pleasure). Gibson also states that the author was Cornish.

On 6 May 1527, at the king's new banqueting house at Greenwich, under Cornish's successor William Crane (master, 1523–45), the gentlemen and children combined again in a dialogue with songs, leading to a triple combat at a barrier in the manner of the Christmas revels of 1515. The account in Hall's *Chronicle* (that invaluable record of Tudor pageantry) is less detailed than that of a Venetian eye-witness, summarized by H. N. Hillebrand:

> After the spectators were seated, there entered eight singers, forming two wings, singing certain English songs; among them was a handsome youth alone, clad in blue taffeta, sown with eyes. The singers having made obeisance and withdrawn, the youth declared himself to be Mercury, sent to the king by Jupiter, and proceeded to deliver a Latin oration to the glory of his majesty; after which he announced that Jupiter, having frequently listened to disputes between Love and Riches, and being unable to decide their superiority, had appointed the king judge, to pass final sentence in the controversy. Thereupon Mercury went off, and on came eight young choristers (the children) of the chapel, four on each side; those to the right were led by Love ('Amor') and the other wing by Riches ('la Richezza'). In the center walked a man alone, in the guise of Justice, and sang. Justice commenced narrating the substance of the dispute in English; thereupon Love and Riches began their debate, each being supported by the choristers on his side, who recited verses.[3]

Hall does not mention Justice, though perhaps he is to be identified with the old man with a white beard who appeared after the combat and concluded that love and riches are both necessary to princes. Such a figure might be a disguised boy actor, but the Venetian account shows that on this occasion it

---

[1] Ignoring Collier's fictitious *Triumph of Love and Beauty*, which he attributed to Cornish, alleging that it received royal favour when Medwall's *Finding of Truth* was disliked. See p. 110, n. 2.

[2] Hillebrand, op. cit. p. 57.

[3] Ibid. pp. 62–3.

was in fact a man. (There is no instance yet of boys playing old men, and it is significant that the one old man in the Troilus story, Calchas, was played by Cornish; for Pandar, though he is Cressida's uncle, would be quite young, as in Chaucer's poem.) The author of this entertainment is unknown.[1]

Though there is occasional mention of garments (for four children in a play at New Year 1541;[2] a prophet's costume for a boy, probably used in Edward VI's coronation revels, 1547;[3] white sarcenet for a Chapel Children's play some time between 1555 and 1560[4]), there are no records of named plays by the Chapel Children from 1527 to 1565. The gentlemen performed a morality of *Genus Humanum* at Christmas 1553 (originally intended as a coronation play for Mary), and perhaps also the coronation play of 'the story of *Orpheus*' for Edward VI on 22 February 1547, since the royal warrant for *Genus Humanum* mentions 'the gentlemen of the chappell of our progenitoures' as the customary actors of coronation plays.[5] It is important to remember that, though their early performances employed only four or five actors, the gentlemen could at need assemble a much larger cast, and augment themselves from the children, as perhaps they did for *Genus Humanum*, which had costumes for twenty-two characters, including five virgins.[6] They always outnumbered the children, and in 1553 there were some twenty gentlemen to some eight children.[7] To distinguish the men's performances from the boys' is not easy, as both belonged to the same organization, and in one document referring to the

[1] Collier, op. cit. Vol. I, p. 98, identifies *Love and Riches* with a pageant designed by John Rastell, *The Father of Heaven*, of which the expenses of performance (between 6 February and 7 May 1527) survive; these included payments to an unnamed person for poetical dialogue in English and Latin. So too does A. W. Reed, *Early Tudor Drama* (London, 1926), pp. 17–19. On the other hand, the Father of Heaven does not appear in the two accounts of *Love and Riches* (whereas he is prominent in Rastell's street pageant of 1522, of which Wickham, op. cit. Vol. I, p. 84, quotes a contemporary description). C. W. Wallace, *The Evolution of the English Drama up to Shakespeare* (Berlin, 1912), rejects the identification, but attributes *Love and Riches* to John Heywood on merely conjectural grounds. Hillebrand judiciously observes that William Crane, the master of the children, cannot be ruled out as the author (op. cit. p. 63).

[2] Hillebrand, op. cit. p. 63.

[3] Ibid. p. 65 (note 91).

[4] Chambers, *The Elizabethan Stage*, Vol. II, p. 32.

[5] Ibid. Vol. II, p. 29.

[6] E. Feuillerat (ed.), *Documents Relating to the Revels at Court in the Time of King Edward VI and Queen Mary*, in W. Bang, *Materialien zur Kunde des alteren englischen Dramas*, Vol. XLIV (Louvain, 1914), p. 289.

[7] H. N. Hillebrand, 'The Early History of the Chapel Royal', *Modern Philology*, XVIII (1920), pp. 239–40.

gentlemen's *Genus Humanum* the players are called the 'Children of the Chapel' (just as in 1574 Leicester's Men are called 'my Lord of Lesters boyes').[1] A 'playe of yeowthe at Crystmas' was acted either in Edward's reign or in Mary's. Probably it was the same as a dialogue between Riches and Youth (each claiming superiority) which is stated to have been played on 6 January 1552, thought there is no record of its actors. The resemblance between this dialogue's title and the debate between Love and Riches suggests that the Chapel Royal played it also.[2]

Richard Bower (master, 1545–61), who succeeded Crane, is not known to have written plays, though he quite possibly did so, and has sometimes been credited with *Apius and Virginia* ('by R.B.'), a play intended for boy actors but about the production of which nothing is known. The next master (1561–7) was Richard Edwards, known author of *Damon and Pithias* and of a two-part play of *Palamon and Arcite* which is lost. *Damon and Pithias* is stated on its title-page to have been acted before the queen by the Chapel Children, and can be safely identified with 'Edwardes tragedy' of the Revels Accounts (Christmas 1564), though it is actually a tragicomedy. Edwards had already presented at least one 'interlude' for which costume material was supplied at Christmas 1561[3]: probably he had presented many, as he enjoyed a high contemporary reputation as a playwright and was clearly an energetic producer. He is the first master who is known to have taken his boys to play to audiences outside the court. On 2 February 1565 and 2 February 1566 they acted at the Candlemas feasts of Lincoln's Inn (of which Edwards had become a member on 25 November 1564),[4] but what they played is unknown. *Palamon and Arcite* was not written for the Chapel but for a two-part performance at Christ Church, Oxford, by the scholars: it will be discussed later, along with other university plays.

William Hunnis (master, 1566–97) was a playwright whose interludes and lyric poems were praised by a contemporary,[5] and so it is reasonable to infer that he produced the Chapel Children in his own plays. Among the court plays between Christmas and Shrovetide 1567–8 already mentioned,[6] *The King of Scots* is probably his: at least, it is described as a tragedy, and the Chapel presented a tragedy between 29 February and

[1] Chambers, *The Elizabethan Stage*, Vol. II, pp. 29, 88.
[2] Hillebrand, *The Child Actors*, p. 66.
[3] Ibid. p. 82.
[4] Ibid. p. 83.
[5] C. C. Stopes, *William Hunnis and the Revels of the Chapel Royal*, in Bang, op. cit. Vol. XXIX (Louvain, 1910), p. 203.
[6] See above, p. 112.

2 March 1568.[1] A play of *Narcissus* was given by the boys on 6 January 1572, and a play calling for a country setting ('Holly, Ivye, firr poles & Mosse for the Rock'), and the equipment of three hunters and their dogs, on 13 February 1575.[2] To the great entertainment of the queen at Kenilworth in 1575 Hunnis contributed a 'device of the Delivery of the Lady of the Lake' (18 July), in which his boys may have taken part.[3] After 1575 his active connection with their plays seems to have lapsed till 1580. During this period (in which no Chapel performances occur until after 1576) the Chapel Children's plays were in the hands of Richard Farrant, a founder Gentleman of the Chapel, whose previous theatrical productions had been with the Children of Windsor. His first court play with the Chapel Children was a joint production with his Windsor Children of *Mutius Scaevola* on 6 January 1577.

[1] Stopes, op. cit. pp. 223–4; Hillebrand, *The Child Actors*, p. 85. Thomas Warton's *History of English Poetry* (1774–81) has quotations purporting to come from a lost pamphlet of 1569 called *The Children of the Chapel Stript and Whipt*; in these, the boys are stated to give Sunday performances, in the queen's chapel, of 'bawdie fables gathered from the idolatrous heathen poets' (Chambers, *The Elizabethan Stage*, Vol. II, pp. 34–5). These quotations, and the pamphlet, are almost certainly Warton's inventions: see M. C. Bradbrook, *The Rise of the Common Player* (London, 1962), ch. 3, p. 294, n. 2 and reference. They are therefore unreliable evidence as to the Chapel Children's repertory or conditions of performance.

[2] Chambers, *The Elizabethan Stage*, Vol. II, p. 35.

[3] Ibid. Vol. IV, p. 62; Vol. II, p. 35.

4 Boys' companies: Paul's Boys and others

'Paul's Boys', as already stated, means the choir school of St Paul's Cathedral. (The known dramatic performances of St Paul's grammar school in Tudor times were not in English.)[1] This choir school had an establishment of ten boys under the supervision of an almoner, who during the sixteenth century combined this function with that of choir master.[2] The two masters who have a place in theatrical history are John Redford (almoner, *c.* 1534–47) and Sebastian Westcott (almoner, 1553–82: he was apparently Redford's immediate successor, and acting almoner, during the six years before his formal appointment).[3]

Redford's name is not connected with any recorded performance, but he is named as the author of one almost complete interlude, *Wit and Science*, and brief fragments of two others, which are extant in manuscript. It can be

---

[1] Their most ambitious was a play in Latin and French, on 10 November 1527, before Henry VIII and the French ambassadors, in which 'the heretic Luther' was attacked and Wolsey praised. An enormous cast of at least forty-eight boys took part. Chambers, *The Elizabethan Stage*, Vol. II, p. 11; *The Mediaeval Stage*, Vol. II, pp. 196, 219; Hillebrand, *The Child Actors*, pp. 16–17.

[2] Chambers, *The Elizabethan Stage*, Vol. II, pp. 9–11.

[3] A. Brown, 'Three Notes on Sebastian Westcott', *Modern Language Review*, XLIV (1949), pp. 229–32.

assumed that these were written for his boys. *Wit and Science*, it is true, calls for four players upon viols, but such instrumentalists could be provided from among the boys, because at Mary's coronation progress through London in 1553 there was 'a pageant made against the Dean of Paul's gate, where the choristers of Paul's played on vialls and sung'.[1]

The first dramatic performance which Paul's Boys are unequivocally stated to have given took place at Nonsuch on 7 August 1559, when Queen Elizabeth saw 'a play of the Chylderyn of Powlles and ther Master Se[bastian], Master Phelypes, and Master Haywod'.[2] However, the boy actors whom Westcott had brought to Hatfield to entertain her during her brother's reign, on 13 February 1552, must also have been Paul's Boys. On the same occasion 'Mr Heywoode' and the king's drummer and fifer were paid, presumably for their part in the same entertainment. The association of Heywood (John Heywood, the dramatist) with the Paul's Boys, while not an official one, was evidently a close one – not close enough, however, to warrant the assumption that he wrote all or any of his plays for them to act, nor even that he wrote always for children, though in his *Play of the Weather* he certainly did so.[3] His apparently freelance writing and un-attached career draws attention to the interrelationship of those connected with court entertainment. It has been mentioned already that Richard Farrant went from the Chapel Royal to the other royal chapel at Windsor, from which he returned to direct the Chapel Children. Sebastian Westcott, whose dramatic career is linked throughout with Paul's Boys, is first heard of at court as a yeoman of the king's chamber (1545).[4] The court is obviously the centre of the theatrical world during the early Tudor period.

Paul's Boys played regularly at court, sometimes two or three times a year, between 1560 and 1582 when Westcott died. Their only plays which are definitely known up to 1576 are two: *Iphigenia*, a 'tragedy' (28 December 1571 or 1 January 1572), and *Alcmaeon* (27 December 1573), neither extant.[5] A number of the plays which are extant have been conjecturally

---

[1] Stow's *Annals*, quoted by Reed, op. cit. p. 4.

[2] Chambers, *The Elizabethan Stage*, Vol. II, p. 13.

[3] T. W. Craik, *The Tudor Interlude* (Leicester, 1958), p. 31. This is also his only play to demand a specially constructed setting, a curtained throne for Jupiter; Bevington, op. cit. p. 40. On Heywood's career, see Chambers, *The Elizabethan Stage*, Vol. II, pp. 12–13, 32; Hillebrand, *The Child Actors*, pp. 67–8; Reed, op. cit. pp. 38–62.

[4] Chambers, *The Elizabethan Stage*, Vol. II, p. 12. Westcott had previously been in holy orders: dispossessed at the dissolution of the monasteries, he was receiving a pension in 1541 and was employed by the churchwardens of his native Chulmleigh, Devon (T. Lennam, op. cit. p. 10).

[5] Chambers, *The Elizabethan Stage*, Vol. II, p. 14.

attributed to them, but a strong case can be made out for only two: *The Contention between Liberality and Prodigality* and *The Marriage of Wit and Science*. These have already been connected with two court plays of 1567–8, *Prodigality* and *Wit and Will*.[1] The case for *Prodigality* implies that the play given on 2 February 1575, for which the Revels Accounts specify a feathered costume for 'vanytie in sabastians playe' and other costume items and properties evidently belonging to *The Contention between Liberality and Prodigality*, was a revival of the *Prodigality* given in 1567–8[2]; but it is reinforced by the fact that the 'Pallace of prosperitie', listed among the 'houses' required for the plays of 1567–8, corresponds with Fortune's palace, into which Prodigality tries to break, in the printed play.[3] *Wit and Will* seems to be so called after the chief characters in *The Marriage of Wit and Science*, Wit and his page Will.[4] This play is a reworking, in accordance with Elizabethan taste in style and staging, of Redford's *Wit and Science*,[5] and the fact that Redford's play is not known ever to have been printed is a further argument that the reworked play came from St Paul's choir school. It is always to be borne in mind, even if we accept the probability that these two plays belonged to the St Paul's repertory, that their producer Sebastian Westcott need not have been the author of either of them.[6] However, the fact that Paul's Boys are known to have performed twice during this particular season gives them a very strong claim on the two plays.

The theatrical career of the Children of Windsor (Boys of the Chapel Royal at Windsor) belongs to the mastership of Richard Farrant. Their independent performances at court, before the joint *Mutius Scaevola* with the Chapel Children on 6 January 1577, took place once or twice a year between 1567 and 1576. Three titles of their plays are known: *Ajax and Ulysses* (1 January 1572), *Quintus Fabius* (6 January 1574) and *King Xerxes* (6 January 1575).[7]

These three companies of choirboys, all of whom acted chiefly at court during the period 1500–76, are the only ones who make any significant contribution to secular drama. (The court performances of the choir of

---

[1] See above, p. 112, n. 3.
[2] Hillebrand, *The Child Actors*, pp. 29–30.
[3] Craik, *The Tudor Interlude*, p. 16.
[4] Chambers, *The Elizabethan Stage*, Vol. IV, pp. 29–30.
[5] Craik, *The Tudor Interlude*, p. 13 (note 23), 15–16; Bevington, op. cit. pp. 22–3; Lennam, op. cit. pp. 90–2.
[6] A. Brown, 'A Note on Sebastian Westcott and the Plays Presented by the Children of Paul's', *Modern Language Quarterly*, XII (1951), pp. 134–6.
[7] Chambers, *The Elizabethan Stage*, Vol. II, pp. 61–3.

Westminster School will be discussed later with other grammar school productions.) There are notices of religious plays given by the choristers of Magdalen College, Oxford, and by the choristers of the Earl of Northumberland's Chapel, in the early years of the century.[1] Another instance of a chorister group comes perhaps from Suffolk in 1537, when Thomas Wylley, Vicar of Yoxford, writes thus to Thomas Cromwell:

> The Lorde make you the instrument of my helpe, Lorde Cromwell, that I may have fre lyberty to preche the trewthe.
>
> I dedycat and offer to your Lordeshype A Reverent Receyving of the Sacrament, as a Lenton matter, declaryd by vj chyldren, representyng Chryst, the worde of God, Paule, Austyn, a Chylde, a Nonne callyd Ignorancy; as a secret thyng that shall have hys ende ons rehersyd afore your eye by the sayd chyldren.
>
> The most part of the prystes of Suff. wyll not reseyve me ynto ther chyrchys to preche, but have dysdaynyd me ever synns I made a play agaynst the popys Conselerrs, Error, Colle Clogger of Conscyens, and Incredulyte. That, and the Act of Parlyament had not folowyd after, I had be countyd a gret lyar.
>
> I have made a playe caulyd A Rude Comynawlte. I am a makyng of a nother caulyd The Woman on the Rokke, yn the fyer of faythe a fynyng, and a purgyng in the trewe purgatory; never to be seen but of your Lordshyps eye.
>
> Ayde me for Chrystys sake that I may preche chryst.
>
> Thomas Wylley
of Yoxforthe Vykar
fatherlesse and forsaken.[2]

Cromwell's interest in propagandist drama against Rome has already been mentioned in relation to Bale's plays; it seems that Wylley also is looking to him as a patron. Wylley proposes to give a private performance of *A Reverent Receiving of the Sacrament* (a play against the doctrine of transubstantiation?). I do not think that he binds himself to give no more, but rather that he seeks Cromwell's opinion of the play before doing so. Likewise, *The Woman on the Rock* is not a closet-drama for reading only[3] but a script for scrutiny before performance. The play against the Pope's

---

[1] Hillebrand, *The Child Actors*, p. 12.
[2] Chambers, *The Mediaeval Stage*, Vol. II, p. 221 (note 1).
[3] As Chambers suggests: ibid. Vol. II, p. 186 (note 1).

counsellors, which incensed Wylley's fellow priests, seems, however, already to have been shown.

Wylley's plays are an instance of Tudor Protestantism. Acting in grammar schools in the sixteenth century is an aspect of Tudor humanism. Many of the plays given by grammar school boys were Latin ones, either classical or neoclassical, and accordingly do not directly concern the history of drama in English. In other cases there is an element of doubt. Bale reports that Ralph Radcliffe converted the dissolved Carmelite priory at Hitchin into a grammar school in 1538.[1] He constructed a 'theatrum' (which implies at least a permanent stage) in the lower part of the building (perhaps the refectory), and there presented plays to the public ('plebi'). It has been presumed that these plays were in Latin,[2] but in view of the public performances I do not think that the vernacular can be ruled out. It is true that Bale gives their titles in Latin, but then the whole text of his *Scriptorum Catalogus* is in Latin, and when he quotes the opening lines of his own English plays he does so in Latin translation. The subjects of Radcliffe's plays were: *The Patience of Griselda*; Chaucer's *Melibeus*; *Titus and Gisippus*; *The Burning of Sodom*; *The Condemnation of John Hus*; *The Disobedience of Jonah*; *Lazarus and Dives* ; *The Courage of Judith*; *The Afflictions of Job*; and *The Deliverance of Susanna*. The play about Hus suggests a controversial spirit, and, if so, there is some piquancy in playing it in a dissolved priory; but, though some of the others may have included anti-Catholic thrusts, Radcliffe does not seem to have been, like Bale and Wylley, a dedicated controversialist.

Thomas Ashton, headmaster of Shrewsbury School (founded 1552), gave a series of Whitsuntide plays in the 1560s, of which it is supposed (though nowhere definitely reported) that his scholars were the actors. A local quarry, a natural amphitheatre in which a Whitsun miracle play had been annually performed for some time, was the setting; and the town continued to finance Ashton's productions, which attracted large audiences, including noblemen. The plays, which must have been in English, included *Julian the Apostate* (1565 or 1566) and *The Passion of Christ* (1561, revived 1569).[3]

The records of five or six corporations contain payments to local school-boys for playing before the mayor and council: at Plymouth, 1564–74 (boys of Totnes); Beverley, 1566–72; Ludlow, 1562, 1575–6; Norwich, 1547;

---

[1] Chambers, *The Mediaeval Stage*, Vol. II, p. 197; Hillebrand, *The Child Actors*, pp. 18–19.
[2] Ibid. p. 19.
[3] Ibid. pp. 20–1. Chambers, *The Elizabethan Stage*, Vol. III, pp. 210–11.

Louth, 1556–68.[1] The schoolmaster is named on several of these occasions as presenting the play, which at Louth in 1568 was 'an enterlude', [2] and evidently in English, as all these civic performances may be assumed to have been. In London, the boys of the Merchant Taylors' School (founded 1561) played in 1572–3 and 1573–4 before the Merchant Taylors Company. Its headmaster, Richard Mulcaster, also brought his boys to court at various times between 1573 and 1583: they played *Timoclea at the Siege of Thebes by Alexander* on 2 February 1574 and *Perseus and Andromeda* on 23 February 1574.[3] Other school companies to appear at court were from Eton (on 6 January 1573)[4] and Westminster (between 1567 and 1574). The queen had already seen the grammar school boys of Westminster in Latin plays in 1564–5 and 1565–6; for the English plays at court, however, payment was made to the masters of the choirboys of Westminster School, who therefore must have given *Paris and Vienne* (19 February 1572) and *Truth, Faithfulness and Mercy* (1 January 1574).[5]

[1] Hillebrand, *The Child Actors*, p. 15.
[2] Murray, op. cit. Vol. II, p. 324.
[3] Chambers, *The Elizabethan Stage*, Vol. II, pp. 75–6.
[4] Ibid. Vol. II, p. 74.
[5] Ibid. Vol. II, pp. 72–3.

5 University and Inns of Court performers

At the universities, as in the grammar schools, much of the acting was of old or new Latin plays. Besides the stimulus of humanism, college drama was fostered by the increasing number of gentleman commoners, the sons of wealthy gentlemen, in the sixteenth century,[1] who would be familiar with the interlude playing that accompanied festive occasions at great houses and at court. Of such courtly splendour Edwards's two-part play *Palamon and Arcite* at Christ Church, Oxford, was a conspicuous example. Edwards not only provided the text but spent two months at Oxford preparing the production: the queen could spare him from court because she was to be guest of honour at the performance, which took place on 2 and 4 September 1566.[2] Two years before, on 8 August 1564, she had been entertained at Cambridge with a King's College production of 'an English play called *Ezekias* made by Mr Udal' (Nicholas Udall, the author of *Ralph Roister Doister*).[3] No other performances of named English plays appear in the college records. *Gammer Gurton's Needle* is stated on the title-page of its first known edition (1575) to have been 'Played on Stage,

---

[1] F. S. Boas, *University Drama in the Tudor Age* (Oxford, 1914), pp. 13–14.
[2] Hillebrand, *The Child Actors*, p. 76; Bevington, op. cit. pp. 34–5.
[3] Chambers, *The Mediaeval Stage*, Vol. II, p. 452.

not longe ago in Christes Colledge in Cambridge' and 'Made by Mr. S. Mr. of Art'. This comedy is generally agreed to belong to the years 1550–3, during which time several plays were organized by William Stevenson (who may have been the author, though the college records are concerned with him only as a producer).[1] *Thersites* will be mentioned later as a play attributable to Oxford on internal evidence.

The lawyers' society of Lincoln's Inn has been mentioned already as engaging Edwards's Chapel Children to act at the Candlemas (2 February) feasts of 1565 and 1566. Sometimes adult actors were engaged for this occasion (Lord Rich's Men on 2 February 1570).[2] Besides entertaining visiting companies, the Inns of Court furnished amateur actors in plays of their own. Like the sixteenth-century universities – perhaps more so – they drew upon the gentry for their members. Their Elizabethan productions were elaborate and expensive, like their Jacobean masques later. An earlier-recorded play was that given at Gray's Inn at Christmas 1526–7. It was a political interlude written by John Roo, serjeant-at-law, and its theme was the corruption of Lord Governance by Dissipation and Negligence, his consequent separation from Lady Public Weal, and their final reconciliation and the banishment of the evildoers. Wolsey interpreted this play as a satire on his administration (which it evidently was), imprisoned the author, and rebuked and threatened 'the yong gentlemen, that plaied in the plaie'.[3] In the middle of the sixteenth century, William Baldwin, who had superintended and perhaps written an otherwise unknown 'Irisshe playe of the state of Ierland' for a court performance at Easter 1553,[4] was in 1556 preparing a play called *The Way to Life* for a joint performance at court (which did not take place) by all the Inns. The synopsis of it shows that it was an elaborate morality involving sixty-two characters.[5] Thomas Sackville and Thomas Norton collaborated in *Gorboduc*, which was an Inner Temple play, part of the Christmas celebrations of 1561–2, and was shortly afterwards shown at court (on 18 January 1562) in conjunction with a great masque. With its dumbshows and choruses, and with musicians (who would be professionals) playing between the acts, it required at least twenty-one actors, and probably

[1] Boas, op. cit. p. 82.
[2] Chambers, *The Elizabethan Stage*, Vol. II, p. 92.
[3] Hall's *Chronicle*, quoted by Wickham, op. cit. Vol. I, p. 237. See above, p. 15.
[4] Wallace, op. cit. p. 74. The costumes include 'develles apparell'. Who acted the play is unknown. Wallace conjectures the Court Interluders.
[5] Feuillerat, op. cit. p. 215.

employed more.[1] Later productions were George Gascoigne's two translations from the Italian, the comedy *The Supposes* and the tragedy *Jocasta*, both played at Gray's Inn in 1566, the latter with another very large cast, most of them supernumeraries;[2] and *Gismond of Salerne*, by Robert Wilmot and others, played in 1566 or 1568 at the Inner Temple.

[1] Bevington, op. cit. pp. 36–7.
[2] Ibid. p. 37.

6 The unattached plays

We have now surveyed the types of organized acting companies, professional and non-professional, from 1500 to 1576. It remains briefly to consider the very considerable number of extant plays of the period which are not known to belong to the repertory of any particular company. A few – *Tom Tyler and His Wife*, *Jack Juggler*, *Respublica*, *The Bugbears*, *The Contention between Liberality and Prodigality* – contain statements in the text that children played them, but usually these plays of unknown origin can be assigned even to a type of company only by the use of conjecture upon internal evidence. The limitation of this kind of conjecture is obvious. The temptation to pair off extant plays too readily with titles in the Revels Accounts and elsewhere must be withstood (*Youth* was not the Edwardian court 'playe of yeowthe'), as must the temptation to identify extant plays with plays of which even the title is lost and to which only some vague reference survives: for instance, it is idle to ask which play Richard Edwards means when he writes, in his prologue to *Damon and Pithias*, of his earlier comedy which gave offence, since there are high odds that it no longer exists.[1] Topical allusion is another unsafe criterion, for

---

[1] F. G. Fleay identified it first (1890) with *Misogonus* and later (1898) with *Like Will to Like*: Hillebrand, *The Child Actors*, p. 78.

we have to be sure that the allusion is not of our own making. With local allusion we are upon safer ground. *Thersites* contains references to places in Oxford, as well as to the proctor and his men, which make it (in my opinion) unmistakably a college play. It has also a final prayer for the queen and the young prince, which fixes the date between the birth of the future Edward VI and the death of Jane Seymour, 12–24 October 1537. However, other references in the same play point to a Christmas production (notably the line 'I wyll geue the somewhat for the gifte of a new yeare'), and suggest that the prayer may have been added for a revival.[1]

Addresses to the audience, either in the final lines or elsewhere, also help to identify the occasion, or at least the type of audience addressed, and hence help in identifying the company or type of company which acted the play. The evidence can, of course, be variously interpreted. David Bevington thinks that a queen is personally addressed at the end of *The Disobedient Child* and is'not so addressed at the end of *Wealth and Health*,[2] whereas I think that the contrary is true. It is reasonable to suppose that, when the spectators are addressed, individually or collectively, in ribald and insulting terms, we are not dealing with a court play. On the other hand, we cannot carry the argument from tone too far, bearing in mind what even courtly Tudor ears would tolerate and courtly Tudor lips could utter. But a preponderance of classical allusion and a general graciousness of tone point to court or academic performance.

Reference to a paying audience implies, naturally, a professional company. The actors of Lewis Wager's *Mary Magdalene*, who 'haue ridden and gone many sundry waies' and offer value for money 'whether you geue halfpence or pence', are a travelling troupe.[3] No other play that I recall in this period mentions an admission charge, but perhaps one is implied in the prologue of Rastell's *Four Elements*, where he states that the comic elements are included to gratify and attract spectators who will 'resort' to the play.[4] Rastell, who had himself built a stage on his own land in Finsbury Fields[5] and possessed costumes, may have engaged professional actors to act his plays.

The evidence most valuable in assigning plays to acting companies,

[1] Boas, op. cit. p. 20. He attributes it to Magdalen College, between 1530 and 1537.
[2] Bevington, op. cit. pp. 29–30, 53 (note 19).
[3] Craik, *The Tudor Interlude*, p. 30.
[4] Bevington, op. cit. p. 46.
[5] Reed, op. cit. pp. 230–3.

however, is the twofold evidence of the dramatis personae and the stage. The Tudor stage has been discussed earlier in this volume, and so it will suffice here to make the general point that any demand in the text for specially constructed scenery proclaims the play as not being written for a travelling troupe to take from town to town. Such players would require plays calling simply for a hall, preferably equipped with two doors, or for an improvised trestle stage with a back curtain.[1] The converse argument – that a play needing no scenery was therefore written for strolling players – does not follow.

The evidence of the dramatis personae has two aspects: the number of the characters and their distribution through the play; and their age and sex. Most professional troupes of the first half of the sixteenth century, and some throughout it, seem to have included no boys.[2] In consequence, their plays, while not always excluding women and children as characters – which would restrict their material too severely – did so whenever this was possible, and, where it was not, kept them to a minimum. The choristers' companies, on the contrary, were under no such necessity (their problem being, at least in their early days, rather the presentation of old men), so that a play which contains a high proportion of women and children, especially when songs are provided for them, bears strong marks of being written for boys. Indeed, to judge from the way in which some of the boys' plays call attention to the femininity or the boyishness of the characters, their authors seem to rejoice in the scope which writing for children has given them.

The boys' companies could call upon more performers than could the adult groups. The Chapel Children numbered twelve on average during the sixteenth century, Paul's Boys ten. Most adult troupes before 1576 consisted of half a dozen players or fewer, though thereafter their numbers might be a dozen or more.[3] The Earl of Leicester's Men were six in number when they applied to him in 1572 for a certificate of appointment as household servants in order to conform with the new statute[4] and when they received their letters patent in 1574 they were five.[5] They may have

[1] See also Section II, p. 72.
[2] Bevington, op. cit. p. 79.
[3] Murray, op. cit. Vol. II, pp. 396–7 (payments at Southampton in 1576–7).
[4] See above, p. 111, n. 1.
[5] Chambers, *The Elizabethan Stage*, Vol. II, pp. 86–7. They were James Burbage, John Perkin, John Laneham, William Johnson, Robert Wilson and Thomas Clarke (the last is omitted from the list of 1574).

had one or two boy apprentice players as well,[1] but there is no evidence
that they had. The Earl of Sussex's Men numbered six when they were
paid for playing at Ludlow in 1569–70.[2] The Court Interluders, as has
been stated, were increased from four to eight or ten by Henry VIII, but
this seems exceptional, and thereafter their numbers dwindled. Consequently the adult actors required either plays in which the same few
characters appeared throughout, or plays in which there were never more
characters on stage together than the company's resources could muster.
In the latter case, the roles were 'doubled' by the actors, as is still done
in the modern theatre, with the difference that now it is only the minor
parts which are so combined, whereas in plays of the 1560s, with their
growing number of roles, only one principal actor, and not always he, is
limited to one principal role. When the resources of a company were
particularly taxed, two different actors were forced to take the same part
in different scenes,[3] but this is so very rare as to make it a certainty that
many plays were most efficiently designed for doubling by their authors
(though there do exist instances of plays faultily doubled, presumably by
their printers).[4] The common size of a professional troupe may be deduced
from the title-page divisions of the roles. Of the plays of 1500–76 printed
with such divisions, seven are aimed at a company of four, three at a
company of five, five at a company of six, one at a company of seven,
three at a company of eight, and one at a company of ten.[5] This last,
Misogonus, bears signs of being a Cambridge college play;[6] and, of the
three plays for eight actors, only one, *Cambises*, bears probable marks of
popular repertory. Accordingly, a play carrying a practical scheme of
doubling on its title-page presents a case, but only a *prima facie* case, for

[1] Bevington (op. cit. p. 60) assumes so in ascribing to them *Cambises* (divided for six men
  and two boys).
[2] Chambers, *The Elizabethan Stage*, Vol. II, p. 92; Murray, op. cit. Vol. II, p. 324.
[3] Craik, *The Tudor Interlude*, p. 41.
[4] Ibid. pp. 29–30, 36.
[5] Bevington, op. cit. pp. 265–73, reprints the title-pages. The plays are as follows. For
  four: *Impatient Poverty*, *Mary Magdalene* (Lewis Wager), *The Longer Thou Livest the
  More Fool Thou Art* (William Wager), *Lusty Juventus* (R. Wever), *New Custom*, *The Tide
  Tarrieth No Man* (George Wapull), *Wealth and Health*. For five: *Like Will to Like* (Ulpian
  Fulwell), *Three Laws* (John Bale), *The Trial of Treasure* (William Wager?). For six: *Common
  Conditions*, *The Conflict of Conscience* (Nathaniel Woodes), *Horestes* (John Pickering), *King
  Darius*, *The Marriage of Wit and Wisdom* (Francis Merbury). For seven: *Enough is as
  Good as a Feast* (William Wager). For eight: *Cambises* (Thomas Preston), *Patient and
  Meek Grissil* (John Phillip), *Susanna* (Thomas Garter). For ten: *Misogonus* (Laurentius
  Barjona, i.e. Johnson?).
[6] Bevington, op. cit. p. 64.

an adult company as the original players. It must be remembered that one way for a company to equip itself with a repertory was to buy printed plays at fourpence or sixpence apiece, and that many plays must have been acted up and down the country by companies of actors of whom the original author had never heard. It must also be stressed that, because we know that professional men habitually doubled, we must not assume that boys and amateurs never did. If Paul's Boys played Redford's *Wit and Science*, I am sure that the four viol-players doubled the twelve instrumental roles.[1]

The use of supernumerary actors, or 'extras', also throws some light on the companies who originally played these unascribed pieces. From the setting-up of the public theatres may date the use of stagehands for this purpose (perhaps Barabas's carpenters in *The Jew of Malta* were the real stage-carpenters and the ancestors of Fielding's 'carpenters to walk on before King Pyrrhus');[2] but until 1576 a play which introduces the nine muses (*Damon and Pithias*) or twelve jurors (*Nice Wanton*) is most likely to be a children's play. If Paul's Boys played *The Contention between Liberality and Prodigality*, they probably augmented their numbers from St Paul's grammar school or their own probationers[3] to provide the kings drawing Fortune's chariot and the attendants singing in her train. Into *Ralph Roister Doister* are introduced 'two drummes with their Ensignes' (two drummers and two standard-bearers), and it has been suggested that Udall deliberately included these extra roles in order to allow as many boys as possible to enjoy a stage appearance.[4]

This may well be correct if Udall wrote his play for his grammar school pupils at either Eton (1534–41) or Westminster (1553–6).[5] It is unfortunate that so little is known of Udall's dramatic activities. They were clearly extensive. He wrote verses for London pageants at Anne Boleyn's coronation in 1532, was perhaps the author of a late miracle play called *Placidas alias Sir Eustace* in 1534 at Braintree, Essex (of which he was vicar, 1533–7; after 1534, however, his Eton duties must have kept him from his parish), brought his Eton boys to play before Cromwell in 1538 (nothing is known of the play, which may have been in Latin), and perhaps at this period composed the lost *Ezekias* which was later acted at the sister-

---

[1] Craik, *The Tudor Interlude*, pp. 47–8.
[2] *Tom Jones*, Book IV, ch. 1.
[3] As Chambers suggests they may have done on another occasion: *The Elizabethan Stage*, Vol. II, p. 13 (note 2).
[4] Bevington, op. cit. p. 33.
[5] Another suggestion is that it was for the Windsor Boys in 1552 or 1553: W. L. Edgerton, 'The Date of *Roister Doister*', *Philological Quarterly*, XLIV (1965), pp. 555–60.

foundation King's College, Cambridge. He had produced court 'dialogues and enterludes' before Mary 'at soondrie seasons' before 1554, when he was authorized to receive 'apparell' for his forthcoming 'devises' at Christmas.[1] He died in 1556. Substantial resemblances between his known extant play *Ralph Roister Doister* and *Respublica* suggest that the latter was one of his court interludes. Internal evidence shows that it was written to be acted before Mary by children in the first Christmas of her reign. It is not, however, known who these children were; they may have been the Chapel boys.[2] Like Heywood's, Udall's talents seem to have been at the disposal of actors with whom he had no official association.

Returning, after this digression, to the use of supernumerary actors, we may notice that the early Tudor combination of play and masque in the same entertainment has left its marks on some plays. Rastell's *Four Elements* contains on the title-page a statement that the complete play takes an hour and a half to act, but that by omitting much of the scientific instruction the playing time can be reduced to three-quarters of an hour, whereas 'if ye list, ye may bring in a disguising' to make a more substantial entertainment. In Medwall's *Fulgens and Lucrece*, a Spanish dance, and a shouted instruction in Flemish to the musicians who play for it, are complimentary recognitions of the Spanish and Flemish ambassadors' presence at a banquet in Cardinal Morton's house in 1497.[3] The dancers and musicians, who are casually introduced – one of Lucrece's two suitors asks her:

> Wyll ye see a bace daunce after the gyse
> Of spayne, whyle ye haue nothynge to do?

– are evidently not members of the small acting company which the play requires. There are seven parts, two of them combinable by the same actor,[4] thus calling for a professional company of six. But, as with the actors of Rastell's *Four Elements*, there is nothing to tell us who they were, for we do not know whether Cardinal Morton had his own professional company or engaged someone else's.

It is thus possible, on internal evidence, to go some distance towards assigning unattached plays of the period to types of company. Bevington

---

[1] Chambers, *The Mediaeval Stage*, Vol. II, pp. 451–2.
[2] Hillebrand, *The Child Actors*, p. 69.
[3] F. S. Boas and A. W. Reed (eds), *Fulgens and Lucres* (Oxford, 1926), Pt II, ll. 380–1. Medwall was Morton's chaplain.
[4] Craik, *The Tudor Interlude*, p. 31.

has attempted such a classification,[1] and his conclusions are generally acceptable, though it is important to remember that they are and must be tentative. In the absence of external evidence, this conjectural assignment of plays to players is as much as can at present be done; and it is unlikely that such external evidence will be produced, in any quantity, in the future.

[1] Bevington, op. cit. pp. 65–7.

IV The plays
and the playwrights

Lois Potter

1 Pre-Reformation dramatic traditions

(i) Introduction: the nature of allegorical conflict

The stage plan for *The Castle of Perseverance* (1405–25) seems a good starting point. It is circular, probably symbolizing the world.[1] In the centre is a castle; round the circumference are five scaffolds. One of these is God's, which, for most of the play, is occupied only by musicians dressed as angels. The other four are the homes of the Three Enemies of Man – the World, the Flesh and the Devil – and of one of the Seven Deadly Sins: Avarice, whose special role in the play is thus indicated. Following tradition, the diagram puts God in the east and the Devil in the north. The World's scaffold is located in the west. This means that, unlike the mystery cycles, this morality play is suspended between God and the world. Man, the hero of the story, is born into the centre of the circular world at the beginning, but his Good Angel at once offers him the opportunity of escaping from it by turning to God. Instead, Man chooses to follow his Evil Angel. In travelling to the west to receive food and clothing from

[1] See Catherine Belsey, 'The Stage Plan of *The Castle of Perserverance*', *Theatre Notebook*, XXVIII (1974). Unless otherwise indicated, the dating of plays follows that of A. Harbage (ed.), *Annals of English Drama*, rev. S. Schoenbaum (London, 1964).

the World, he is (like Donne in 'Good Friday, Riding Westward') forced to turn his back on God. He is also heading, literally and symbolically, towards death.

The events which follow correspond to a view of the archetypal human life which can also be found in virtually every other morality play. The harmless-looking minions of the World, Pleasure and Folly, introduce Man to the delights of wealth, which lead to his mounting the scaffold of Avarice. There, he is joined by the other Sins. Since the scaffold probably had to be reached by a ladder, each Sin had to make the ascent on his own, a fact which the author uses to stress the inevitability of the sequence:

> Thus euery synne tyllyth [attracts] in othyr,
> And makyth Mankynde to ben a foole. (ll. 1032–3)[1]

From Pride, the first Sin to mount the ladder, Man passes through both spiritual and fleshly evils, finally succumbing to Sloth, whose special province is not only laziness but apathy and the despair which keeps sinners from repenting. However, Man does awake from his sinful state, not for any psychologically explicable reason but because he has reached the age of forty and is no longer susceptible to the vices of youth. In order to persevere in his repentance, he enters the Castle of Perseverance, where the Seven Virtues, fighting on his behalf, beat off an attack by their opposing Sins. But with the coming of age he is lured out of the castle by Avarice, in whose service he dies. His final agonized call for mercy brings Mercy, one of the Four Daughters of God, and leads to a debate over the fate of his soul with Mercy and Peace on one side and their sisters Truth and Righteousness on the other. God at last appears to judge the case; Man is saved, the sisters reconciled, and God addresses the audience in the last words of the play:

> Evyr at the begynnynge
> Thynke on youre last endynge! (ll. 3647–8)

The circular shape of the acting area is itself an embodiment of this familiar message. So is God's speech: it can hardly be an accident that it so closely resembles the false self-glorification of the speech with which the World opened the play. Man's own life is also shown to be part of a constantly recurring cycle. As he lies dying, he discovers that all his worldly wealth is to be taken from him and given to a boy called 'I Wot

[1] For details of editions used, see Bibliography. Line numbers will be given only for the longer plays quoted.

Neuere Whoo'. On one level, the boy stands for a topical rather than a universal evil – the legal corruption which allows a man's estate to pass into the hands of total strangers. But on another, surely, he is what Man himself once was: a new arrival in the world who, being young, cannot understand the reality of death and believes that worldly gifts will last for ever. The message of the morality play is thus, in the strictest sense, life-denying.

Yet the morality, despite its allegorical nature, is firmly based in the very world which it urges Man to reject. The combat at the centre of *The Castle of Perseverance* is probably a serious parody of something which the church had long condemned: the tournament with an allegorical framework. At Treviso in 1214 there was a siege of the Castello d'Amore, whose defending ladies held out successfully against a bombardment of flowers and perfumes but finally succumbed to gold.[1] A similar siege, performed at a wedding celebration, is described in *Don Quixote* (Pt II, ch. xx). Glynne Wickham cites an account of a tournament at Ghent, which must have been roughly contemporary with *The Castle of Perseverance*; the challenger travelled from the Kingdom of Childhood through Youth to 'the great plain of Happiness, which is situated between the castle of Beauty and the noble mountain of Grace, called High Renown.'[2] It is quite possible that the same tournament lists erected for such spectacles, with their pavilions, forests and mountains, also served for the combat in which the Virtues defeated all symbols of worldly pleasure.[3]

Journeys and battles are the very essence both of romance and of the earliest moral plays. The fragmentary *Pride of Life* (late fourteenth century) breaks off as the king's messenger is travelling around the acting arena in search of a champion to answer his master's challenge to single combat with Death. The Digby *Mary Magdalene* (*c.* 1480–1520) borrows the allegorical siege from *The Castle of Perseverance* as well as sending its heroine and other characters on a number of non-allegorical voyages to and from the Holy Land. Even the much less ambitious Digby play about the conversion of St Paul requires him to make a journey on horseback, '*goodly besene in the best wyse lyke an aunterous knyth* [adventurous knight]'. In *Mundus et Infans* (*c.* 1500–22, also called *The World and the Child*)

---

[1] Sidney Anglo, 'The Evolution of the Early Tudor Disguising, Pageant and Mask', *Renaissance Drama*, N.S., I, ed. S. Schoenbaum (Evanston, Ill., 1968), p. 12.

[2] *Early English Stages*, 2 vols (London, 1959, 1963, 1972), Vol. I, p. 24.

[3] P. D. Arnott, 'The Origins of Medieval Theatre in the Round', *Theatre Notebook*, XV (1961), pp. 84–7.

the Deadly Sins are kings and the hero serves as their knight. A similar pattern of swaggering challenges followed by battle also occurs in mummers' plays and Robin Hood plays, to such an extent that it is often difficult to know whether the word 'play' is being used to mean combat or drama.

Because one kind of show borrowed so freely from the 'devices' (visual effects) of another, the relation of words to spectacle was largely explanatory. There were practical reasons why this should be so. No dialogue could be heard above the sound of a combat, and the fighters would in any case probably be too out-of-breath to speak. At the same time, the very openness of medieval and Tudor staging, the fact that the eye was not directed where to look, as we are accustomed to being directed by the proscenium arch or the camera, made it necessary to crystallize the meaning of the action either through words or through a tableau. Allegorical pageants and mummings were explained by a presenter. Sometimes a written explanation was appended to a triumphal arch to help spectators interpret the symbolism; sometimes a royal visitor was given a copy of explanatory verses. Guessing the meaning was part of the fun, no doubt, but it was easy to go wrong: the flowers which bowed down to Adam and Eve in the York mystery cycle also bowed down to the Tudor rose when Henry VII entered the city in 1486.[1] The *impresa*, the emblem, the dumb show, the pageant, were like so many riddles for which language alone could provide an answer.[2] There was an almost complete divorce between eye and ear.

The notion that seeing is believing pervades both mystery and morality plays. As one critic has noted, the constant verbal formula is '*you shall see, thus you see* and *thus you have seen*'.[3] The N-Town Banns constantly stress the importance of the visual experience in creating belief; the description of the pageants may have been illustrated by a picture or by actors in tableaux. No one seems to have been struck by the irony of the account of Christ's appearance to doubting Thomas –

And thomas euyn ther as ye shal se
Shal put his hand in his woundys dere.

[1] J. C. Meagher, 'The First Progress of Henry VII', *Renaissance Drama*, N.S., I (1968), pp. 52–3.
[2] See Dieter Mehl, *The Elizabethan Dumb Show* (Heidelberg, 1964; trans. London, 1965), esp. Pt 1.
[3] Bernard Spivack, *Shakespeare and the Allegory of Evil* (New York and London, 1958), p. 176.

– even though the biblical moral of the episode is 'Blessed are they that have not seen and yet have believed'.

If words made visual images intelligible, visual images made words memorable. This was the assumption behind the classical art of memory, as explained, for example, in Book II of Cicero's *De Oratore*. The master of this art controlled words and abstract concepts by visualizing them in some striking image; to remember them in the right order, he was to make a mental tour of a large building, revisiting, from room to room, the various figures which he had previously placed there in imagination. The procession of the stations of the cross in a church, the movement of pageant carts in a procession, the journey of the spectator from one allegorical tableau to another – all have affinities with the kind of memory journey suggested by Cicero.[1] It is possible that the elaborate stanza forms of the N-Town Cycle and *The Castle of Perseverance* may have been designed to make them easier to remember; the actor could have a mental picture of the shape of his lines, since a stanza was seldom divided between speakers. The sixteenth-century love of proverbs and *sententiae* is another example of the almost magical power attributed to any device which condensed experience into a memorable form. Virtuous precepts, Erasmus recommended, should be made available to a young prince 'now by a fable, now by example, now by maxims, now by a proverb. They should be engraved on rings, painted in pictures, appended to the wreaths of honour...'.[2]

Morality drama is most commonly said to be derived from the sermon pattern of text followed by exemplum.[3] As we have seen, there were other precedents for the separation of verbal meaning from visual illustration. A further one should be mentioned: the medieval belief that the comedies of Terence had originally been mimed by masked actors while the dialogue was read by the poet or by his friend Calliopus.[4] A similar technique was used in some medieval liturgical drama where a narrator spoke or chanted both dialogue and stage directions while the more lyrical part of the

---

[1] See Robert Edwards, 'Techniques of Transcendence in Medieval Drama', *Comparative Drama*, VIII (1974), pp. 157–71. Thomas Wilson's *Art of Rhetoric* (1553), paraphrasing Cicero, notes that the images in Catholic churches might be compared to the memory figures of the ancients.

[2] *The Education of a Christian Prince* (1516), trans. and ed. L. K. Born (New York, 1936; 1968), p. 145.

[3] See, esp., G. R. Owst, *Literature and Pulpit in Medieval England* (Oxford, 1933; 1961), p. x.

[4] Mary H. Marshall, '*Theatre* in the Middle Ages: Evidence from Dictionaries and Glosses', *Symposium*, IV (1950), pp. 1–39 and 366–89.

performance was carried out by singers, dancers or instrumentalists. A survival of the Terentian theory may be seen in the frequent descriptions of the prologue-speaker in sixteenth-century drama as a 'Poet', or even, in Bale's plays, as 'Baleus Prolocutor'. He is a fusion of the classical prologue, the preacher, and the presenter of the pageant. The morality play was only one of many forms in which, because there was always more than met the eye, there was always the need for extra-dramatic explanation.

Where it differed from those other forms was in the nature of the conflict portrayed. The world and death, rather than God and the Devil, are the agents with which its embattled hero has most to do. Biblical drama deals with a time when the forces of good and evil walked openly on the earth, but the morality is true to average human experience in allowing man little first-hand contact with spiritual forces. Indeed, God appears as a character in only a few plays. By keeping him out of sight until the end of *The Castle of Perseverance*, the dramatist is able to remind the audience that they, like Man, are in danger of forgetting the constant presence of the one spectator for whose benefit all human lives are enacted. As Death sardonically points out to the hero of *Everyman*,

> Thoughe thou have forgete hym here,
> He thynketh on the[e] in the hevenly sp[h]ere.

The Devil, also, rarely acts except through lesser agents; as Mercy warns in *Mankind*, he 'goth invisibull and will not be sen'. But the world is presented in all its most familiar and attractive forms, emphasizing the universality of evil among the spectators. Hence, in *The Castle of Perseverance*, Man's sense of safety in numbers:

> We haue etyn garlek everychone.
> Thou[gh] I schulde to helle go,
> I wot wel I schal not gon alone. (ll. 1369–71)

Vice is instantly recognizable in songs, feasting and satire on topical sins, whereas virtue has no existence except as an ideal. So the sharpest dramatic contrast in the morality play is not that between virtues and vices but between the pleasures of the world and the coming of death, which forces the protagonist to recognize the truth. Herod's feasting just before he is struck down by Death in the N-Town play; the feasts of all the earthly rulers in the Digby *Mary Magdalene*, followed by the sudden death of one of them, Mary's father: these have their counterpart in the tavern scenes which represent earthly pleasure for the Everyman type of hero.

What gives these plays their temporal framework is always the prospect of death and the fear that the hero, blinded by the world's deceptions, may not repent in time to be saved.

The Castle of Perseverance, the Digby plays and the mystery cycles all belong to a tradition of large-scale outdoor theatre which continued to be popular and important in many communities during most of the sixteenth century. However, there is only one surviving example of this type of play actually written in that century: Lindsay's *Satire of the Three Estates*. The greater part of the works we shall be looking at from now on were intended for indoor production at a time of year when plays were traditionally given: the period between Christmas and Lent. Hence, the contrast between the pleasures of the world and the underlying reality of death was given extra urgency by the sense that the play itself was part of a holiday that was coming to an end. Confession and penance were enjoined on everyone as part of the preparation for Easter, and dramatists, who for the most part were also churchmen, were eager to encourage spectators to undergo the ritual of repentance at Shrovetide rather than, as seems to have been all too common, postponing it until Holy Week.[1] Two late fifteenth-century plays – *Wisdom, Who is Christ* and *Mankind* – show two quite opposing ways of enforcing the moral that man must be in the world but not of it. What they have in common is their intensely black-and-white contrast between worldly and other-worldly values.

In *Wisdom*, a highly intellectual and formal play, the contrast is made visual in the costume of the heroine, Anima: a white robe covered by a black mantle to represent the cloud which the body casts over the soul. When Lucifer corrupts her by working on her three faculties, Mind, Will and Understanding, he does so by directing them away from contemplation of God and towards this world, arguing plausibly that Christ himself led an active life as well as a contemplative one. All three are soon wearing foppish dress; they also present a series of dances by costumed figures symbolizing the particular worldly forms in which their spiritual corruption may be found. What begins as a desire for pleasure ends with the three faculties fighting among themselves. When Anima next appears she is literally full of sin (seven little boys in devils' costumes crawl out from

---

[1] See M. Philippa Coogan, *An Interpretation of the Moral Play, Mankind* (Washington, DC, 1947). W. K. Smart, in 'Some Notes on *Mankind*', *MP*, XIV (1916–17), first suggested the Shrovetide associations of this play. J. J. Molloy argues that *Wisdom* needs to be seen in a similar context: *A Theological Interpretation of the Moral Play, Wisdom, Who is Christ* (Washington, DC, 1952).

beneath her skirt) and looks 'fowlere than a fende'. The very sight is enough
to convert the sinners and they go offstage to confession while Wisdom
delivers a sermon, but it is clear that repentance will be a long process.
The apparent impossibility of leading a virtuous life within the world,
as depicted here, has led to the suggestion that *Wisdom* must have been
intended for performance before members of a religious order.[1] But its
spirit is not very different from that of other moral plays. When Man
goes to the World for food and clothes, in *The Castle of Perseverance*, his
action is only a natural result of the fall of man and a symbol of original
sin, yet it is treated as an evil decision.

The hero of *Mankind* is undoubtedly an ordinary layman, whose spade
and rosary indicate his participation in both active and contemplative life.[2]
He at first resists the temptations of this world, represented by the clownish
New Guise, Naught and Nowadays, and gives in to them only when the
devil, Titivillus, has tempted him to give up work for sleep (sloth, or
despair) and then told him in a dream that his protector and adviser,
Mercy, is dead. The riotous living into which Mankind then plunges is
supervised by Mischief, the dramatic opposite of Mercy. The humour in
this part of the play is not merely coarse and mindless; there is sophisticated
irony, for example, in Mischief's description of the illiterate Naught as
'owr Tulli [Cicero]' (l. 692). But its verbal contrast with Mercy's language
is as sharp as the visual contrasts in *Wisdom*.[3] The four scoundrels are
very much of this world – at one point, they set out to rob the Cambridge-
shire gentry, giving full names and addresses of members of their audience
– and their influence nearly transforms Mankind from an honest labourer
to a thief and murderer. He actually attempts to hang himself when he
hears that Mercy is alive after all and 'sekyth euerywere' for him: what
ought to be a comforting truth has become a threat. Mercy, like Wisdom,
has a multiple function: he is an abstract quality, a priest whose duty is
to give good counsel to man, and an aspect of Christ himself (which lends
a particular irony to the false report that he has been hanged for theft).
In his moving confrontation with Mankind, it at first appears that pride
and despair will keep the hero from repentance:

[1] Molloy discusses and disagrees with this view (op. cit.). There seem not to have been
any plays specifically about the temptation to leave the religious life, with the exception
of *Brother William*, a Lowlands Morality described by Merle Fifield in 'The Community
Dialogues in Late Middle English and Their Language', *Revue des Langues Vivantes*,
[2] See Werner Habicht, *Studien zur Dramenform vor Shakespeare* (Heidelberg, 1968), p. 36.
[3] See Paula Neuss, 'Active and Idle Language: Dramatic Images in "Mankind"', in Neville
Denny (ed.), *Medieval Drama*, Stratford-upon-Avon Studies (London, 1973), pp. 41–68.

What, aske mercy yet onys agayn? Alas, yt were a wyle [vile]
   petycyun.
Ewyr to offend and euer to aske mercy, yt ys a puerilite. (ll. 819–20)

Salvation becomes possible only when he can bring himself to cry out,
'mercy, good Mercy! What ys a man wythowte mercy?' (l. 835) – a question
to which the despairing debauchery of the earlier scenes has already
provided a sobering answer.

   By creating dramatic suspense from Mankind's own awareness of how
little he deserves mercy, the author of this play solves one of the chief
problems of the morality. Medieval drama was indeed, as Robert Potter
has called it, 'repentance drama';[1] it urges man never to despair, however
sinful he has been and however late he may be in asking forgiveness. As
Christ says in the Wakefield Resurrection play,

> If thou thy lyfe in syn haue led,
> Mercy to ask be not adred;
> The leste drope I for the[e] bled
> Myght clens the[e] soyn [soon],
> All the syn the warld with in
> If thou had done.

The dramatic embodiment of this doctrine, however, tends to be a depiction
of man's life on earth as an unrelieved orgy, ending with so late a repentance
as to create real suspense about his future. It proves the greatness of divine
mercy by testing it to the utmost, as Mercy himself – ignored, insulted,
tripped up – is tested in *Mankind*. The effect is to transform Everyman,
the figure in whom the audience is supposed to see itself, into 'every man'
in the sense of Prince Hal's scornful remark to Poins: 'thou art a blessed
fellow to think as every man thinks' (*2 Henry IV*, II, ii). To prevent the
spectators from feeling too superior to the hero as he succumbs to one
vice after another, the dramatist often implicates them in the world of
villainy. In *Mankind* especially, Mischief and his three confederates keep
insisting that the audience wants the sort of fun they have to offer whereas
Mercy is an old bore whose departure everyone is eagerly awaiting. Vice
characters appear in groups of three, like New Guise, Nought and
Nowadays, in order to sing the three-men's-songs which Sloth, in *The
Castle of Perseverance*, describes as popular among his followers. All that

[1] *The English Morality Play: Origins, History and Influence of a Dramatic Tradition* (London
   and Boston, 1975), pp. 28–55.

Mercy and the other virtuous abstractions can offer in return is Latin, 'aureate' language and sermons. There are thus two possible traps for the morality writer. He can make Everyman a criminal type rather than a fallible human being, and he can use the more obvious attractiveness of worldly vice as an excuse for his failure to present virtue in a dramatically effective way.

One reason why *Everyman* (1495–1500) involves us, so much more than most other morality plays, with the fate of its hero is that he really does seem to be *every* man – guilty chiefly of too much love of this world and too little care for his own mortality – rather than a selfconscious compound of the Seven Deadly Sins. We do not, of course, see him with a wife and children – although, as Cawley points out in his edition of the play, affection for one's family is enumerated in the *Ars Moriendi* as one of the temptations of a dying man.[1] But his relations with Fellowship, Kindred and Cousin are almost totally free from the usual implication that all worldly friendships are really partnerships in crime. It is true that Fellowship, in a last attempt to prove that he would do anything for his friend except die with him, does say:

> But, and thou wyll murder, or ony man kyll,
> In that I wyll helpe the[e] with a good wyll.

But Everyman's reply, 'O, that is a symple [i.e. foolish] aduyse, in dede', restores an atmosphere of normality to the scene. The importance of repenting before it is too late is also integrated into the structure of the play, with its contrasting types of allegorical figures. At first, like Faustus, Everyman is mesmerized by the speed with which his life is ending:

> The tyme passeth. Lorde, helpe, that all wrought!
> For though I mourne it auayleth nought:
> The day passeth, and is almoost ago.
> I wote not well what for to do.

It is only when he has stopped seeking help from abstractions attached to this world – Fellowship, Goods, and so on – and turned inwards to Good Deeds and Knowledge that he can escape from the panic-stricken atmosphere of external time to the timelessness of the sacraments. Everyman's last moments stretch out in slow motion over the rest of the play, as if freezing the space 'between the stirrup and the ground'.

[1] A. C. Cawley (ed.), *Everyman* (Manchester, 1961), pp. xvi–xvii.

But there are a number of other 'sudden conversion' plays which set theological and dramatic requirements at odds. This is mainly because the hero is young and what makes him repent is not Death itself but only the *memento mori* language of some other character. Such plays fall vaguely into a 'prodigal son' pattern: elderly authority figures try in vain to persuade the hero of his mortality; refusing to believe them, he indulges in enthusiastic debauchery, insults his virtuous counsellors at great length, and then, for no apparent reason except that it is time to end the play, collapses into perfunctory repentance. The earliest dramatic example of this formula is found in a late fifteenth-century dialogue for Occupation, Idleness and Doctrine, where Idleness tries to pass himself off as Business, gives away his true name while drunk, and then abruptly repents and is renamed Cleanness.[1] It is a play calculated to bring out the Elder Brother in every member of the audience.

The underworld atmosphere of taverns, brothels and gaols must have been popular, for it is incorporated rather incongruously into *Mundus et Infans*, which, as we have seen, is primarily based on a metaphor from romance. The same colourful if unsavoury world is the background of *Youth* and *Hickscorner* (both written some time after 1513, though which came first is still debatable), which likewise deal with central characters whose exploits put them well below the spiritual level of every man. *Youth* is shorter and makes rather better sense allegorically, since its principal Virtue, Charity, actually does live out the quality he represents: he is long-suffering when put in the stocks by Youth and his companions, and he readily accepts the sinner's repentance, though it is so arbitrary as to take the Vices completely by surprise. *Hickscorner* is really not allegorical at all. It depicts a sick society, where 'Youth walketh by nyght with swerdes and knyves' and the delinquency of young people is as aimless as their reformation. The three scoundrels, Freewill, Imagination and their friend Hickscorner,[2] commit crimes as well as sins, and when Contemplation finds that they have set Pity in the stocks he forgets all about his other-worldly nature and advises his friend to get them arrested. In the circumstances, forgiveness seems beside the point, and the dramatist almost

---

[1] This play, still only in manuscript, is described in Norman Davis, 'Two Unprinted Dialogues in Late Middle English and Their Language', *Revue des Langues Vivantes*, XXXV (1969), pp. 461–72.

[2] Hickscorner means Dick Scorner, or scoffer, or indeed Vice in its later dramatic sense. There is an interesting use of the word in Udall's translation of the preface to Erasmus's *Apophthegmes* (1542): Socrates is said to have been called 'the hicke scorner of the citie of Athenes: because of his merie conceiptes and tauntyng'.

goes out of his way to show Imagination's self-interested motives for repenting:

> Nothynge drede I so sore as deth;
> Therfore to amende I thynke hyt be tyme.

Remembering the play's date and regarding it with hindsight, it would be easy to see it as a foreshadowing of the Reformation. We hear that

> prestes lack utteraunce to showe theyr cunnynge
> And al the whyle that clerkes do use so grete synne,
> Amonge the lay people loke never for no mendynge.

But such complaints had been commonplace for centuries. Both *Youth* and *Hickscorner* hover between the universal and the topical. Youth is portrayed as a typical young heir ready to squander his money; he is both a symbol of how the world deludes man and a social type. Though he is happy enough to consort with undisguised Riot and Lechery, there is also a suggestion of the Vice-disguised-as-Virtue theme in Lechery's pouting annoyance at having her real name known. In *Hickscorner*, the juxtaposing of real, allegorical and typical references is still more startling: a ship is bringing a cargo of vices into England, skippered by 'Ill Wyll, / Brother to Jacke Poller of Shoters Hyll'. The latter sounds real enough, but in fact is a type-name for a highway-robber.

With these later examples of medieval repentance drama we come to what is to be the dominant popular form: the short play written for a small company of actors who doubled as necessary to fill all the parts. This doubling and other aspects of presentation are discussed elsewhere in this book.[1] What we are concerned with here is their effect on the content of the moral play, and particularly on its depiction of conflict. In the more intimate atmosphere of the banquet hall, lacking the lavish spectacle of the arena plays and *Wisdom*, the symbolic actions of these small-scale moralities tended to become indistinguishable from real actions. Contrasts between Virtues and Vices could still be achieved by costume and verse form: in the first half of the period, this usually meant *rime royale* or couplets for the Virtues and short-lined couplets or tail-rhyme stanzas for the Vices. But the conflict between them inevitably became simpler. It was one thing for ladies symbolizing the Seven Virtues to defeat their enemies in a stylized tournament, with showers of roses or (for sins of

---

[1] See above, pp. 135–7, 71–99.

1 The hall screens, Hampton Court Palace, *c.* 1535

2 Conjectural reconstruction of a performance of Medwall's *Nature*

3 The hall screens, Penshurst Place

4 The hall screens, Trinity College, Cambridge

5 The hall screens, Lambeth Palace

6 A booth stage at a village fair; detail from Pieter Bruegel, 'The Village Fete'

7 Pieter Bruegel the Elder, 'Temperantia'; showing a booth stage

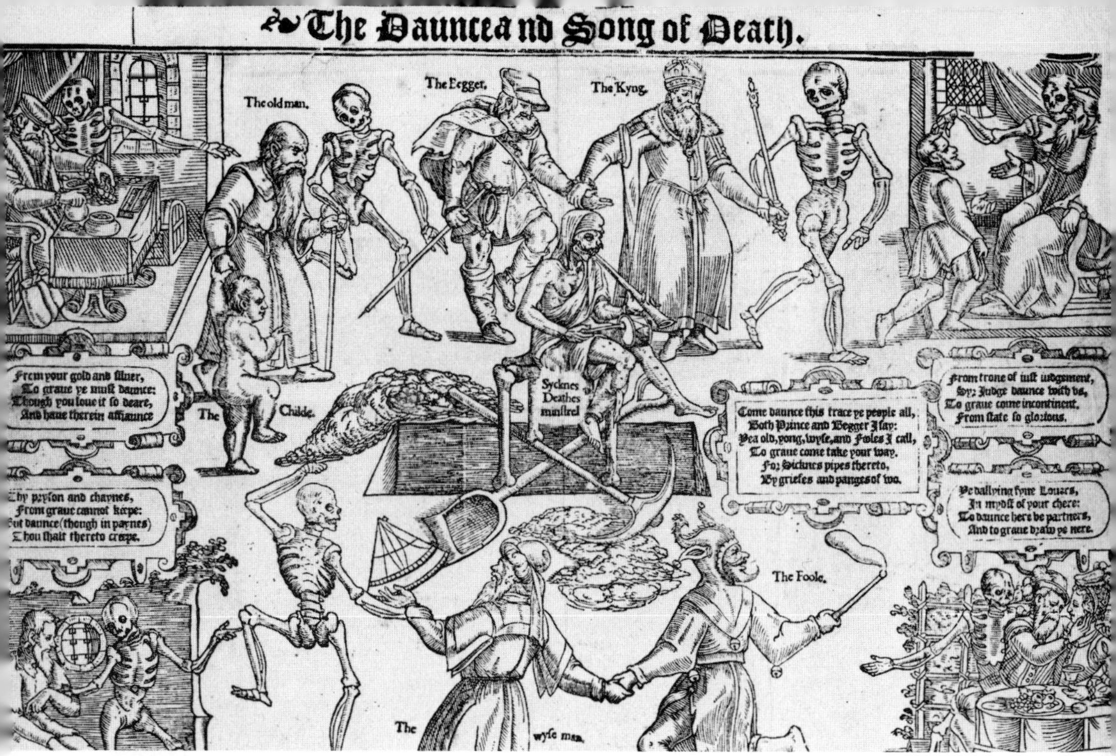

The old man.   The Begger.   The Kyng

From your gold and silver,
To graue ye must daunce:
Though you loue it so deare,
And haue therein affiance.

Thy prison and chaynes,
From graue cannot kepe:
Not daunce (though in paynes)
Thou shalt thereto crepe.

The
Childe

Syckness
Deathes
minstrel

Come daunce this trace ye people all,
Both Prince and Begger I say:
Yea old, yong, wyse, and Fooles I call,
To graue come take your way.
For, Syckness pipes thereto,
By griefes and pangtes of wo.

From trone of iust iudgement,
Say; Iudge daunce with vs,
To graue come incontinent,
From state so glorious.

Ye haltring fyne Louers,
In most of your chere:
To daunce here be partners,
And to graue draw ye nere.

The Foole.

The   wyse men

8 The Dance of Death; woodcut, *c.* 1569

9 The Dance of Death; woodcut by Hans
Holbein the Younger, 1573

10 John Heywood, 1556

11 The monk of Swinstead offering poison to King John, 1570

12 Time, Truth and Hypocrisy, 1535

13 Edward VI and the Pope, 1548–9

Thenterlude of youth.

¶ Charyte.
Esu that his armes dyd spred
And on a tre was done to dede
From all perylles ī, ℈ you defende
I do you spence tyll I haue made an ende
For I am come fro god a boue
To occupy his lawes to your behoue
And am named charyte
There may no man saued be

14 *The Interlude of Youth, c.* 1528

Theterlude of youth.

Charitie.   youth.

Iefu that his armes dyd fprede
And on a tree was done to dead
From all perils he you defende
I defyre audyence tyl I haue made an ende
For am come from God aboue
To occuppe his lawes to your behoue
And am named Charytye
There maye no man faued be
wythout the helpe of me
For he that Charytye doth refufe
Other vertues thought he do vfe

15 *The Interlude of Youth, c.* 1557

A very mery and

Pythie Commedie, called The longer
thou liuest, the more foole thou art.

A Myrrour very necessarie for youth, and
specially for such as are like to come to dig-
nitie and promotion: As it maye
well appeare in the Matter
folowynge.
Newly compiled by
VV. VVager.

℟ IMPRINTED AT
London, by Wyllyam Hovv
for Richarde Johnes: and
are to be solde at his shop
vnder the Lotterie
house.

16a *The Longer thou Livest, the More Fool thou Art*, title page, *c.* 1569

The Prologe.

Ristophones as Valerius doth tell,
Introduceth Pericles in a Commedie,
That he being reduced, againe out of Hell,
Unto Thathenienses did thus prophesie.
Bringe vp no Lyons in your Cities wantonly,
For as you bring them vp in actes pernicious,
So in the same you must be to them obsequious.
By this saith Valerius he doth admonish,
That rich mens sonnes be from euell manners refrained
Least that with profuse fondnes we do them norish,
Vertue of them euer after be disdained :
So that when authozitie, they haue obtained,
They them selues being giuen to inconuenience,
Oppresse their subiects vnder their obedience,
Oh how noble a thing is good education,
For all estates profitable: but for them chiefely
Which by birth are like to haue gubernation,
In publikque weales, that they may rule euer iustly :
For while the Romanes did forsee this matter wisely,
They had a wise Senate which preuailed alway,
And that being neglected, they fell soone to decay.
To be a good man it is also expedient,
Of good Parents to be begotten and borne,
In deede to all men it is most euident,
That a pleasaunt Rose springeth of a sharpe Thorne,
But commonly of good Seed procedeth good Corne,
Good Parents in good manners do instruct their childe,
Correcting him when he beginneth to grow wilde :
The bringing vp of a childe from his tender age,
In vertue, is a great helpe to be an honest man,
But when youth is suffred to haue his owne rage,
It falleth to much calamity now and than:
I would wish Parents and Masters to do what they can
Both to teach and correct their youth with reason,
That it may profit the publique weale an other season.

A ij   To

16b *The Longer thou Livest, the More Fool thou Art*, prologue

17 John Redford, *Wit and Science*, c. 1539

the flesh) bread and water; it was quite another for Charity or Pity to be accosted by a realistic thug who forced him either to join in a punch-up or be taken for a coward. In *Mankind*, although Mercy himself refuses to fight with the Vices, Mankind does take his spade to them. It has been argued that this episode makes him guilty of the sin of impatience, but it is Mercy himself who uses the biblical image of man's life as a war on earth and urges Mankind to fight against his enemies. The difficulty is that the allegorical significance of the fight is different from that of the literal scuffle. In *Mundus et Infans*, moreover, the fight between Manhood and Folly is treated as a game, a trial of skill; if it has an allegorical point, it is an ironic one, since Manhood wins the game. He then proceeds to give in to Folly after all – which, in fact, is what he has done by taking part in such a time-wasting activity as sword-and-buckler play. Apart from the wrestling match between Lust and Just in *The Trial of Treasure* (1567), there are no combats between Virtue and Vice in later moralities. Virtue sometimes suffers passively – Charity in *Youth*, Pity in *Hickscorner*, the ladies Chastity and Verity in *The Three Estates* – and sometimes makes a rather unheroic departure when confronted by Vice: Peace in *Impatient Poverty* (1547–58) is 'faced out of the place', and, in *The Longer Thou Livest the More Fool Thou Art* (1559–68), Piety is forced out by Wrath. But what happens far more often is that the representatives of evil fight among themselves. This naturally has the effect of further reducing the dramatic importance of virtuous characters: they become mere speakers of words, while the Vices have all the action.

The struggle for the soul of man, in these pre-Reformation interludes, takes place on the plane of language rather than through battle; in fact, it is largely a struggle *about* language. The forces of evil try to make man believe that there is no more to life than what he can see, that the gifts of the world are the only reality. Their virtuous opponents, on the other hand, have the more difficult task of making man believe in the reality of what he cannot see, and the illusory nature of the very things that seem most real to him. Whereas in *The Castle of Perseverance* all the characters shared the same figurative and allegorical language, as they also shared the same powerful visual symbolism, in the simpler, small-scale drama good characters are divided from bad by their ability to understand allegory. The Vices' favourite joke is to take literally the abstract language of a virtuous character: Mercy talks of separating the corn from the chaff and Mischief pretends that he is a corn-thresher; the hero of *Youth* can understand heaven only in a literal sense –

What, syrs, above the sky?
I had nede of a ladder to climbe so hie.

This particular joke is one of which the dramatists never tired: it recurs in *The Three Estates*, *Impatient Poverty* and, rather more wittily, in *Respublica*.

It is almost a sign of evil for a character to be aware of his own physical reality, as all the jokes about bodily functions indicate. The exchange between Charity and Youth is illuminating. Youth declares:

I florysh as the vine tre.
Who may be likened unto me
In my youthe and iolytye?
My heare [hair]¹ is royall and bushed thicke,
My body plyaunt as a hasel styck,
Mine armes be bothe bygge and strong,
My fingers be both faire and longe,
My chest bigge as a tunne,
My legges be full lighte for to runne
To hoppe and daunce and make mery.

Charity's response is:

You had nede to aske God mercye.
Why do you so prase your body?

And, turning Youth's own language against him, he points out that a tree in old age is cut down and thrown into the fire, a fate which is likely also to befall an unrepentant sinner. It is as natural for a virtuous abstraction to treat literal things allegorically as for his opponent to treat allegorical things literally.

The virtuous characters sometimes speak in a quasi-mystical style which probably derives, in more cases than have so far been identified, from specific examples of medieval devotional verse. Sometimes it is emotional and 'aureate'; an extreme example might be Mankind's outburst

O Mercy, my suavius solas and synguler recreatory,
My predilecte spesyall, ye are worthy to haue my loue. (ll. 871–2)

The Vices naturally comment on this extraordinary diction. Freewill's reaction in *Hickscorner* is typical: 'Nay, I have done and you lade out Latyn

¹ 'hearte' in the original text.

with scopes!'[1] A twentieth-century reader is likely to agree with him. But
at times the language of Virtue achieves an effective lyrical simplicity:

> When I go by my selfe ofte I do remembre
> The grete kyndnes that god showed unto man
> For to be borne in the moneth of decembre
> Whan the daye waxeth shorte and the nyght longe.
> Of his goodnesse that champyon stronge
> Descended downe fro the fader of ryghtwysnes
> And rested in mary the floure of mekenes. (*Hickscorner*)

The literal battles and journeys of the arena are absorbed into the language
of the characters. In what appears to be an incoherent attempt at a
repentance play, *John the Evangelist*,[2] there is a long, figurative description
of the journey to hell in terms of 'the elders of envye' and briars of back-
biting which grow along the path. Still more interesting is a speech from
the beginning of Part 2 of Medwall's *Nature*, performed some time between
1490 and his death in 1501. Like *The Castle of Perseverance*, it traces its
hero's progress from birth to old age, though not to death itself:

> I assemble [i.e. compare] the lyfe of a mortall creature
> To the assyege agayn[st] a strong town or castell
> In whyche there ys myche besy endevure
> Myche warly [worldly] polycy wyth dylygent travayll
> On every syde whyche parte shall prevayll
> By sleyght or ingyns or by strong power
> That other to subdue and bryng into daunger.

Language, here, is a substitute for action. A threatened battle between
good and evil forces comes to nothing, mainly because the Seven Deadly
Sins live up to their names so completely as to be useless as soldiers (Sloth
decides to stay at home; the Falstaffian Gluttony turns up armed only
with a cheese and a bottle). This episode has been described as a travesty
of the *Psychomachia*,[3] but it is also a clever solution to the problem of
staging a battle with the small cast that Medwall had at his disposal.

---

[1] Cf. 'What felowe Thersites, do ye speake latyn nowe – / Nay, then farewell' (*Thersites*,
1537), and Jaques's similar reaction in *As You Like It*: 'Nay then, God b'wi' you, an
you talk in blank verse!' (IV. i).

[2] Harbage and Schoenbaum date this play some time between 1520 and 1558, but the
language is pre-Reformation, as is the presence of two characters who apparently symbolize
the active and contemplative lives.

[3] E. N. S. Thompson, *The English Moral Play* (New Haven, Conn., 1910), p. 332.

A comparison of *Nature* with *The Castle of Perseverance* shows that the former is scaled down in the intensity as well as the size of its conflict. In its opening scene, Nature informs Man that she is God's minister on earth; she quotes Ovid, rather than Genesis, to explain man's position in the creation; and she gives him Reason and Sensuality, rather than Good and Evil Angels, as companions. This is not so novel as it appears. Medwall – about whom we know virtually nothing except that he was a chaplain – may have avoided biblical quotations out of reverence. And the conflict between Reason and Sensuality is traditional: a Latin closet morality by Thomas Chaundler (*c.* 1460) also begins with Man making a choice between Reason, who offers him a mirror, and Sensuality, who persuades him to accept the forbidden fruit. But in Medwall the conflict is a debate rather than a wholehearted struggle. Sensuality even suggests a compromise: if he can rule Man for the first forty years, Reason is welcome to have him after that. Neither of them is in disagreement with Nature's plan for the hero:

> thou art a passanger
> That hast to do a great and longe vyage
> And through the World most [must] be thy passage.

As in *The Castle*, Man then passes literally as well as symbolically to the World, who is seated at the other end of the hall. But there is no indication that he is making the wrong choice, or indeed that he has any choice. Unlike the boasting tyrants of *The Castle* and *Mundus et Infans*, the World is amiable, perhaps too much so. But he does remind Man that his new garments are a consequence of the Fall:

> Ye must consyder thys ys not paradyse
> Ne yet so temporate by a thowsand fold.

Man duly succumbs to Worldly Affection and the Seven Deadly Sins. With the approach of age, however, most of his Vices leave him and he returns to Reason almost *faute de mieux*. There is even a hint that he intends to entertain Avarice, the Vice of age, for a few years longer, without letting Reason know about it. Man's life, as he himself recognizes, has followed the law of nature and the way of the world.

But this is true of the play as well. Part 1, in fact, ends so abruptly as to suggest a last-minute change of plan on Medwall's part:

> And for thys seson

Here we make an end
Lest we shuld offend
Thys audyence....
Whan my lord shall so devyse
I shalbe at hys pleasure.

Unlike a preacher with a captive audience who expect to be made un-
comfortable by his sermon, Medwall was clearly aware that his function
was to provide amusement, and to provide it only when it was wanted.
'My lord' was Cardinal Morton, Henry VII's Chancellor, and his audience
may well have included the young Thomas More. As the World points out, a
man who intends to live under his rule must 'be of suche condycyon / As
all men be' and follow 'Worldly Policy'. Machiavelli's *Prince* was still a
generation away; 'policy' had not yet acquired its exclusively pejorative
meaning[1]; and Castiglione had not yet discussed the special problems
involved in combining the roles of Christian and courtier. But Chaplain
Medwall, carving his moral allegory into portions suitable for serving at a
banquet (itself, we have seen, the symbol of worldly pleasure), can hardly
have been unaware of the irony of his position.

(ii) Plays of compromise: Medwall, Rastell, Heywood

In *Mundus et Infans* there is a brief and unsuccessful attempt at reconciling the conflicting demands of God and the world. The hero, a knight
in the World's service, meets Conscience and decides to shift his allegiance.
His attitude to the World, however, is only slightly modified by his
conversion:

But yet wyll I hym not forsake,
For mankynde he doth mery make.
Thoughe the Worlde and Conscyence be at debate,
    Yet the Worlde wyll I not despyse;
For bothe in chyrche and in chepynge
And in other places beynge,
The Worlde fyndeth me all thynge
    And dothe me grete servyse.

---

[1] See N. W. Bawcutt, '"Policy", Machiavellianism, and the Earlier Tudor Drama', *English
Literary Renaissance*, I, 3 (1971), pp. 195–209.

In this kind of play, such an attitude is folly in the worst sense; Conscience has already explained that folly includes all the Seven Deadly Sins, and the Bible generally uses the word as synonymous with evil. Sure enough, the next character who enters is Folly himself. But the ambivalence of the Fool – irresponsible rascal, unconscious spokesman for truth, source of intentional amusement – is already present even in this play, where he deceives Manhood by giving his name as 'proper Folly', when in fact it is 'Folly-and-Shame'. Erasmus's *Praise of Folly*, the French *sotties*, and the sermon by Folly which concludes Lindsay's *Three Estates*, also embody a variety of techniques – from sheer nonsense to social satire – and a variety of attitudes to folly: on the one hand, a healthy sense of fun; on the other, a dangerous blindness to spiritual realities.

It was through a sophisticated use of folly that Thomas More (whose name in Latin, *Morus*, meant fool) attempted to reconcile the conflict between world and conscience. In *Utopia* (1516) he describes the kind of philosophy suitable for a prince's court. His examples are drawn from Latin drama, but they may also reflect on the mixture of comedy and moralizing in works, like Medwall's *Nature*, which he had seen in his youth:

> ... whyles a commodye of Plautus is playinge, and the vyle bondemen skoffynge and tryfelynge amonge them selfes, yf yowe shoulde sodenlye come upon the stage in a philosophers apparrell, and reherse owte of Octavia the place wherin Seneca dysputeth with Nero; had it not bene better for yowe to have played the domme persone [mute], then by rehersynge that, which served nother for the tyme nor place, to have made suche a tragycall comedye or gallymalfreye?[1]

More himself wrote comedies, but all that is known about them is that one dealt with the story of Solomon, which was not only a prime example of the application of philosophy to the affairs of this world but also, if More used the current legends of the wise king's wit combats with the fool Marcolphus, an exploration of the relation between wisdom and folly. In the history of Tudor drama, he is remembered as the invisible centre of a group of writers linked to him either through their presence in Morton's household (as with Medwall), through marriage (as with Rastell and Heywood), or through their posthumous reputation as pranksters, wits and jest-book heroes (as with Heywood, and also Skelton, who has little in common

---

[1] *Utopia*, trans. Ralph Robinson (1551), ed. J. H. Lupton (Oxford, 1895), Vol. I, pp. 98–9.

otherwise with this group).[1] All were men very much involved with the world. Those of them who survived to see the coming of the Reformation found, like More himself, that its effect was to put an end to the fragile compromise between world and conscience. Rastell became such a fanatical reformer as to embarrass even Cromwell and Cranmer, and probably died in prison as a result. Skelton ruthlessly satirized some young reformers, at a time when it was still safe to do so, but was remembered later as a reformer himself, probably because he had also satirized the unpopular Cardinal Wolsey. Heywood remained loyal to the old religion, took part in a conspiracy against Cranmer, and, though pardoned, finally exiled himself from his country some years after Elizabeth's accession. So the 'More circle', if it ever was that, existed only for a brief period before the pressure of history became too much for it. Its legacy is a small body of intellectual comic drama, based mainly on a formula dear to intellectuals: debate followed by compromise.

Some court entertainments combined intellectual debate with spectacle, as in *Love and Riches*, which Rastell produced at Greenwich in 1527. After a debate as to which of the two qualities was more important to a prince, there was a battle between warriors costumed to represent the two sides of the argument; an old man then appeared as adjudicator and announced, to no one's surprise surely, that both were equally necessary. Even without the spectacular element, however, debate was an entertainment in its own right. Queen Elizabeth was treated to many academic disputations when she paid her formal visits to the two universities. At a simpler level, there were other forms of verbal combat: the flyting, the riddle-contest, the lying competition, the mock-trial. Heywood's short plays make use of most of these devices, but the only 'trial play' of the period appears to be the *Processus Satanae* (*c.* 1570–5) in which Satan, acting as plaintiff, charges God with unfair tactics in sending his Son to earth in human disguise; the Four Daughters of God serve as the jury.[2]

What gave new life to this old form, in the sixteenth century, was the enthusiasm of More and Erasmus for the dialogues of the Greek satirist Lucian, of which they published a selection, translated into Latin, in 1506.

---

[1] This presumably explains why both Skelton and More were later to be favourably depicted in plays wholly or partly by the notoriously anti-Catholic Anthony Munday; like Chaucer, they occasionally ridiculed bad churchmen, and their religious beliefs were virtually cancelled out, in the popular mind, by their reputation as wits.

[2] At least, this is what can reasonably be inferred from the part of the actor who played God, which is all that remains of the debate.

Though Lucian was a sceptic about religion, his emphasis on the absurd contrast between man's pride and his mortality is not far removed from the *contemptus mundi* strain of medieval drama; a number of his dialogues deal with the fates of men after death. But his most interesting contribution to the early sixteenth-century drama lies in what he called his marriage of the techniques of comedy with those of the philosophical dialogue. His works were not written to be acted, and indeed call for utterly unstageable effects, like Charon and Hermes piling four mountains on top of one another. But action and setting are nevertheless clearly visualized, and implicit in the dialogue throughout, instead of merely providing a setting for abstract discussion as in most of Plato and Cicero. His technique, as well as his manner, is followed by Erasmus in his extremely popular *Colloquies* – at first (1518) designed only as conversation practice for students of Latin, but expanded over the next decade along the Lucianic pattern. These in turn influenced such works as William Bullein's *Dialogue Against the Fever Pestilence* (1564). More's own dialogues never become so dramatically visual as these, though the separation of the various chapters of *Utopia* and the *Dialogue Against Tyndale* by breaks for dinner gives them some resemblance to the court interlude. It is possible that the freedom with which Lucian moves his characters from place to place by means of dialogue alone may have suggested to sixteenth-century dramatists the possibility of achieving a similar temporary sense of place on an otherwise unlocalized acting area. It is in an adaptation of part of the Spanish dialogue novel, *La Celestina*, that, as Richard Southern has pointed out, we find the earliest English example of a character creating a setting simply by mentioning it.[1]

The earliest of the debate plays, Medwall's *Fulgens and Lucrece* (1497), is also the one which comes closest to being a play in the full sense of the word. But its starting point was a pair of Italian orations on the nature of true nobility, probably themselves based on Ovid's famous debate (in *Metamorphoses*, XIII) about whether brawn or brains had done more for the Greek cause. Caxton, who printed the orations in a translation by the Earl of Worcester in 1481, bound them with two works which he obviously considered similar, Cicero's philosophical dialogues *De Senectute* and *De Amicitia*. The rivalry of the two suitors, in the Italian work, is only an occasion for the debate; Lucrece's one contribution is to blush in a 'womanly' fashion and declare herself happy to leave the decision to her father and the Senate of Rome. Caxton himself, thinking of Chaucer's

---

[1] See above, pp. 89–90, and *The Staging of Plays Before Shakespeare* (London, 1973), pp. 223–4. Cf. 'Here is her father's house' in *Othello* (I. i).

Franklin's Tale, left the decision to the reader. When, in Part 1 of Medwall's play, B describes the plot to A, it sounds very much like that of the Italian original. What he leaves out are Medwall's own additions to the story: the considerable expansion of the romantic element, and the part played in it by A and B themselves.

Medwall's instinct for romantic comedy, indeed, almost works against the whole form of his play, since Lucrece has clearly made up her mind before either suitor opens his mouth. A surprising number of conventions familiar to readers of later plays can already be found here. The unsuccessful suitor, for example, is first seen approaching the girl's father instead of the girl herself (compare the County Paris and Romeo); he also gives presents, sends musicians to her, and uses a servant as go-between. The successful suitor, on the other hand, woos for himself, bluntly asking 'that I may have a plain yea or nay'. Lucrece, though slightly given to teasing, likes his frankness. Like the sympathetic pairs of lovers in later comedy, they are also linked by a sense of humour which enables them to fall in with the crude jokes of the servants A and B.

The more visual comedy with which A and B are involved, like the musical interlude in Part 2, may have been Medwall's attempt to accommodate his play to his audience. If, as is thought, *Fulgens and Lucrece* was given at a banquet whose guests of honour were the ambassadors of Spain and Flanders, marriage would have been a relevant topic, since the final outcome of the embassy was to be the betrothal of Prince Arthur to Katherine of Aragon. It seems unlikely that any further topical meaning lies behind Lucrece's choice of Flaminius in preference to Cornelius. But the presence of a large number of non-English-speaking guests might well have encouraged Medwall to surround his debate with as much action as possible. The wooing of Lucrece's maid by A and B, their grotesque duel on her account, and the surprise ending when she beats them both and then announces that she is already engaged elsewhere, may have been suggested by the wooing plays of English folk drama or by French farce, in which there are similar examples of a duel 'broche en cul'. Apart from their low-comedy function, however, A and B also move in and out of the dramatic scene with a freedom which is paralleled, in this period, only by the role of Diligence in Lindsay's *Three Estates*. They alternate between being naïve spectators who have no idea what is coming next, presenters who are completely in the author's confidence, and characters in the tradition of the medieval *garcio* – the incompetent and malicious servant. Medwall sometimes uses them, as Jonson uses his onstage 'spectators', to raise and answer awkward questions about the play's construction. Whereas the break in *Nature* was so arbitrarily foisted on the audience that they actually had to be told that there was more to come, in *Fulgens and Lucrece* the question 'Why might not this matter be ended now?' is not simply the recognition of a structural problem but also the expression of genuine suspense about the 'royal disputation' promised after the interval. At the end, a simple exchange between A and B neatly turns the play inside-out:

A. Why than is the play all do?
B. Ye[a] by my feyth and we were ons go
   It were do streght way.

The split between verbal debate and physical combat, which in Medwall is indicated in the division between main plot and subplot, can also be found, less skilfully discriminated, in the plays of Rastell and Heywood. The title of *Gentleness and Nobility* (1527–30), which has been attributed to both of them, describes it as 'A Dialogue ... Compiled in Maner of an Enterlude with Divers Toys and Gestis Addyd Therto To Make Mery Pastime and Disport'.[1] The one play definitely known to be by Rastell, *The Nature of the Four Elements* (*c.* 1517–18), also shows a division between words and spectacle, information and entertainment, such as one might perhaps expect from a man so experienced in the production of pageants both at court and in his native Coventry. His title-page, which gives a list of the useful things that can be learned from the play, notes that the dialogue can be cut by half if necessary and that 'also if ye list ye may brynge in a Dysgysynge'.

Rastell's varied and active career included the running of a press which printed Medwall's plays and at least some of Heywood's as well as (among other things) More's *Utopia* and the earliest English translations of Lucian. He learned a good deal from the writers whom he published; in fact, the word 'compiler', often used in this period as a synonym for author, would apply equally well to him in its modern sense. His *Nature* is evidently a companion piece to Medwall's, and he may have learned from *Fulgens and Lucrece* the flexibility that combined debate with disguising. Some of the ideas expressed in his dogmatic prologue can also be found in the unexpectedly dogmatic conclusions of two other plays from his press, *Gentleness and Nobility* and *Calisto and Melebea*. It has therefore been suggested that there were two hands in these works, the heavier of the two being Rastell's. But many of these ideas come from *Utopia* in the first

[1] See Elizabeth Merrill, *The Dialogue in English Literature* (New Haven, Conn., 1911), p. 33.

place and, like property in More's imaginary country, were held in common by a number of Tudor humanists. It seems unlikely that a printer who habitually tacked his own conclusions on to other men's works would have had so successful a career as Rastell apparently did.

Of the two *Nature* plays, Medwall's is the more accomplished but Rastell's, potentially at any rate, the more interesting. Medwall's title character is Natura Naturans, the (feminine) principle of life and being; Rastell's Nature, a man, is Natura Naturata, who embodies the workings of the universe. The figures corresponding to Medwall's Reason and Sensuality are called Studious Desire and Sensual Appetite, both of which are aspects of the hero Humanity. In the company of the former, Humanity listens happily to lectures on astronomy and geography from Experience, a great traveller, who illustrates his lessons with a map and perhaps – Rastell had made use of cosmic scenes in his pageants – with some illustrations as well. As a variety of source studies have shown, Rastell had a wide if superficial knowledge of basic books on his subjects, and Experience gives a digest of their contents. Experience has also heard about a recent voyage to the new-found lands, which ended in disaster when the sailors refused to make the journey and left their passengers stranded in Ireland. Rastell himself was one of those passengers and may well have written this play in Ireland, a fact which would explain his otherwise incongruous outburst against the treacherous mariners.[1] The play, then, is something of a catch-all for its author's personal interests. Luckily, these are so diverse that hardly anyone could fail to find something interesting in its contents. Though he had none of the poetic gift of his remote descendant, John Donne,[2] he had something of the same capacity for sensing a historic moment. Alongside Donne's lines about the effects of the 'new philosophy' one can put those of Experience as he points to the Atlantic Ocean on his map:

> This See is called the great Occyan
> So great it is that never man
> Coude tell it sith the worlde began
> Tyll nowe within this xx. yere

[1] See A. W. Reed, *Early Tudor Drama* (London, 1926), which is the source of most of our information about not only Rastell but the entire 'More circle'.

[2] Rastell married Thomas More's sister; Heywood married Rastell's daughter; Heywood's daughter married John Donne, the father of the poet.

Westwarde be founde new landes
That we never harde tell of before this
By wrytynge nor no other meanys
Yet many nowe have ben there.

Meanwhile, however, Humanity has gone off to the tavern with his other friend, Sensual Appetite. The comic side of the play is peopled with attractive figures like the Taverner ('Of all metes in the worlde that be, / By this light I love best drynke') and Ignorance, who dislikes all 'horeson losophers' and the 'great connyng extromers / That tell how far it is to the sterres'. Humanity's willingness to follow both sides of his nature –

I am indifferent to all company
Whether it be here or there

– would presumably have been corrected by Nature at last (some pages are missing at the end), but Rastell allows him to defend his conduct fairly convincingly. After all, it is only an extension of what Nature has said man ought to do with his God-given knowledge:

Knowe thy maker & cause of thyne owne beynge
And what the worlde is & wherof thou doest procede.

Allegorically, of course, it makes no sense that Humanity and his Sensual Appetite should go to meet a very un-Dickensian 'Little Nell' while his Studious Desire is conversing with Experience, but perhaps this blunder can be seen as Rastell's own peculiar way of effecting a compromise between God and the world.

In the long prologue to *The Four Elements* (it runs to six pages in the original edition) Rastell says that he wants to see more works written and translated on practical subjects, not on 'love or other matter not worth a myte'. *Calisto and Melebea* (1527–30) may or may not reflect this attitude to love stories. It would be hard to imagine anything more harshly moral than the way in which the original Spanish novel disposes of all its characters: young Calisto, the virtuous Melibea whom he seduces with the aid of the bawd Celestina, and the two servants who are corrupted to help in the love affair. The servants kill Celestina in a quarrel over money and are hanged for their crime; Calisto breaks his neck while climbing the garden wall to see Melibea; and she flings herself off the roof after having confessed the whole story to her father, who is left cursing the fatal power of love. Nevertheless, *La Celestina* was regarded as highly immoral. More's friend, the Spanish humanist Vives, said that if girls spent their time reading such books they would be better off not knowing how to read at all.[1]

The dramatic version is called 'A New Comedy in English in Maner of an Enterlude'. The Spanish novel, despite its tragic ending, was also called a comedy in its first edition (1499). But the word turns out to be more accurate when applied to the play. The adapter carries the story to the point where Melebea has received Celestina into her house and begun to take an interest in Calisto, at least to the extent of finding an excuse for the bawd to come again next day. Then, abruptly, the plot changes. Melebea's father tells her of an ominous dream he had the previous night. The stage direction specifies that she remains silent for a while after this, looking disturbed. She then confesses everything, presumably giving up all thought of Calisto for ever; her escape from sin is attributed to her habit of saying a prayer every morning; and the old man concludes the play with a speech about the dangers of idleness and bad upbringing.

Thus *Calisto and Melebea* certainly lives up to the promise of its title-page, offering both 'craft of rethoryk' (the extravagant speeches of Calisto, the persuasions of Celestina, and the racy brothel talk) and a display of the 'bewte and good propertes of women' as well as 'theyr vycys & evyll condicions with a moral conclusion & exhortacyon to vertew'. It seems quite probable that the moral conclusion was intended from the outset, not an afterthought, because the play's opening, with Melebea complaining of Calisto's repeated temptations, is likewise a departure from the novel, designed to make it into a morality play with Melebea as the Everywoman figure. At the same time, the truncated ending shows why the morality play was not really capable of dealing with Everywoman, except perhaps in the special case of Mary Magdalene. As the sixteenth century saw it, woman's virtue (i.e. chastity) differed from man's in that no amount of repentance could make up for its loss. Thus the heroine's sudden repentance and conversion had to occur, not after her sin, but in time to prevent it. The effect, not surprisingly, is undramatic.

John Heywood, who described himself in one of his epigrams as the maker of 'many plaies, fewe good woorkes in all my daies', did not write anything that we should call a play, with the possible exception of *Johan Johan*, a free translation from the French which has often been attributed

---

[1] *The Instruction of a Christian Woman* (first published in Latin, 1523; trans. Richard Hyrd, 1540), E-4 to F-2. See also H. Warner Allen's introduction to his edition of the interlude and the novel, in James Mabbe's translation of 1631 (Broadway Translations, n.d.).

to him. But of course, play, in the variety of meanings familiar to readers of Huizinga's *Homo Ludens*, is the essence of Heywood. His surviving writings for the stage, which date from 1519 to 1533, sometimes give off an amazingly capricious air, as when a character in *Love*, or *The Four PP*, suddenly begins hopping about the stage. Caprice likewise dictates both the beginning and the end of the debates. Not only are the characters in *Love* artificially polarized, but the hypotheses and analogies with which they explain their views are deliberately extreme in the manner of children's arguments; the words 'Put case that' generally lead to something like: Would you rather be up to your knees in water or fire? Would you rather be a horse or a tree? The long lists and sequences of alliterative or rhyming words are also a form of play; they have no purpose except to fill up time and perhaps display the actor's memory and speed of diction. This particular kind of writing is probably due to the influence of Skelton, but Heywood, a noted collector of proverbs, is also capable of telling phrases (e.g. in *Love*, 'I allow no love where sleep is not allowed') and of vivid arguments which get quickly to the point. He is fond of *double entendre*. 'Ye maye truste me at Syo [Chios, in the Aegean Sea] as well as here,' says the thoroughly untrustworthy Merry Report in *The Play of the Weather*, and the Pothecary in *The Four PP* assures his companions that

> Suche be these medycynes that I can
> Helpe a dogge as well as a man.

A love of punning carries over into the patterning of both plot and dialogue, as in this *tour de force*, where the buffoon No-Lover-Nor-Loved works out the permutations of his relationship with the other three characters in *Love*:

> Loving not loved, and loved not loving
> These partes can ioyne in maner rekening.
> Loving and loved, loved nor lover
> These partes in ioyning in like wise differ.
> But in that ye love ye twaine joined be
> And being not loved ye joyne with me
> And being no lover with me joyneth she
> And being beloved with her joyne ye.
> Had I a joiner with me joyned joyntly
> We joyners shulde joyne joynt to joynt quyckly.

The passage also illustrates the way in which characters in debate drama naturally fall into pairs, since a debate by its nature can have only two sides.

The speakers in *Love* never interact as a foursome, but only in pairs. Even in three-character plays a debate structure is preserved by having two speakers join forces against a third. The Knight and Merchant, who have been arguing at the beginning of *Gentleness and Nobility*, turn on the Plowman when he arrives with his own claims to dignity. In *Witty and Witless*, the two characters who are most radically opposed to each other never dispute at all. Instead, John, who has just conducted an unsuccessful argument with James about the relative merits of wit and folly, learns from Jerome what he really ought to have said. The play is a lesson in debating technique.[1]

In other plays the progression is linear: one character after another argues his claim to something – his right to have the weather of his choice, his superiority to the other characters – and the length of the discussion is limited only by the size of the cast. The most dramatic effect in these plays is likely to be the entrance of each new character to cap the remarks of the previous one, as happens in *The Four PP*; in *The Play of the Weather*, which is still more of a procession of characters, Heywood manages to vary their speeds and modes of arrival to a surprising extent. These are the most Lucianic of the dialogues. *The Four PP* may be based on the *Philopseudes*, one of the works translated by More, which makes fun of preposterous liars, especially on the subject of religion.[2] There is a still closer resemblance between *The Play of the Weather* and the *Icaromenippus*, in which Jupiter's difficulty in coping with a number of contradictory petitions from earth forms a small part of what Lucian's hero finds on his visit to Olympus. The Greek satirist consistently makes his Jupiter a pompous ass, and it is difficult to take Heywood's character seriously either. Far from showing the interdependence of all classes of society, the play shows their collective pig-headedness, and their stupidity in letting themselves be persuaded by Jupiter's 'solution' (which Merry Report accurately sums up: 'Syrs, now shall ye have the wether even as yt was').

The two plays with the most obvious French origins are also elaborately patterned; it is not certain whether Heywood wrote them but there is no other contender. *The Pardoner and the Friar* is essentially a shouting-match,

---

[1] Cf. More's *Dialogue Concerning Tyndale* (1528), where More tells the Messenger what he ought to have said in a dispute at the university. It has been suggested that this derives from St Augustine's combination of a specific argument with instruction in debating technique (Rainer Pineas, 'Thomas More's Use of the Dialogue Form as a Weapon of Religious Controversy', *Studies in the Renaissance*, VIII (1960), pp. 193–206).

[2] See also C. H. Herford, *Studies in the Literary Relations of England and Germany in the Sixteenth Century* (Cambridge, 1887), pp. 248–72, for lying competitions.

carefully orchestrated. The two speakers compete for attention, first alternately, then simultaneously, in a crescendo which ends, surprisingly, in a scuffle during which the two rascals join forces to defeat the two respectable citizens who have come to silence them. That is really all there is to the play, but the neatness of its pattern is extremely satisfying. *Johan Johan*, though more varied and interesting, is less skilfully constructed. The plot is the quintessential one of French farce about the henpecked husband whose wife is having an affair with the local priest. Obviously there are two possible sources of interest: the tricks played on the husband by the lovers, and the husband's reactions. The French author concentrates largely on the latter, but never quite decides how he would prefer to get his laughs: from the cuckold's rapid alternations between sullen passivity and outbursts of rebellion, or from the slow build-up of his fury to the point where the worm will turn at last. Each device is exploited to good effect, but the timing is not satisfactorily worked out. Jean Jenin puts up with so much, and also changes his mind so often, that his final outburst seems purely arbitrary. But the English translation makes a definite improvement on the original by having the husband return, after the explosion, to the vacillating mood of the opening. What are Tib and the priest doing, now that he has driven them offstage? He had better go and find out. And thus the fight goes on and the boundaries of the play are extended into the future and the offstage area.[1]

But the other plays in this category are neither amoral nor inconclusive. Their debates can easily be brought to an end, either through compromise or because the argument is one about which no correct conclusion can be reached in any case. Even when potentially explosive issues are raised – when the Laundress in *Weather* attacks the idleness of the Gentlewoman, or the Plowman in *Gentleness and Nobility* whips the Knight – they are defused by the context. Every argument has a counter-argument. The Plowman is given a good case for the virtues of the simple life (which may be partly based on Lucian's *Cynicus*: 'the gods have need of nothing, and those nearest to them have the fewest needs').[2] But he is wittily debunked by the Knight:

---

[1] See T. W. Craik, 'The True Source of John Heywood's *Johan Johan*', *MLR*, XLV (1950), pp. 289–95. It is difficult to prove parallels between commonplace lines, but the French play also contains a phrase – 'Ostez la torche de dessus', from a character who wants more light shed on him – which might have given Heywood the idea for Merry Report's entrance in *Weather*, with 'Brother, holde up your torche a little hyer!'

[2] *The Complete Works of St Thomas More*, ed. and trans. C. R. Thompson (New Haven, Conn. and London, 1974), Vol. III, Pt 1 (*Translations of Lucian*), p. 165.

In feyth, yf thou be a gentylman therfore,
Thou art a gentylman agaynst thy wyll full sore.

The Plowman himself recognizes that

all the grete arguments that we thre
Have made syth we resonyd here togedyr
Do not prevayle the weyght of a fether
For the helpyng of anythyng that is amys.
We can not help it; then, syth it so is,
I wyll let the world wagg and home wyll I goo
And dryf the plowgh as I was wont to do.

The Plowman accepts the social order, society in general accepts the weather, and the four PP accept the authority of the church, although the preceding discussion has clearly brought out the imperfections of all three.

So the final effect is conservative, as in the summing-up of *The Four PP*: 'No man hath loste nor no man hath woon.' The conclusion rises above the level of worldly debate by invoking a spirit of tolerance and calling on other-worldly values – as in the Pedlar's moving speech at the end of *The Four PP* or the reminder, at the end of *Love*, that the four attitudes to love represented by the debaters are all transcended by the divine love whose birth is celebrated in the Christmas season when the play was performed.

But one character usually stands outside this atmosphere of Christian reconciliation. In two of Heywood's plays – *Love* and *Weather* – he is called the Vice. The appearance of this name in non-religious drama, at least twenty years before it is again used to mean a particular type of dramatic character, has been a source of some embarrassment to scholars attempting to trace its history in the morality play. The proper translation of 'Vice', as Heywood uses it, would be 'jester'. Puttenham's *Art of English Poesy* (1589), in what is supposed to be an account of Greek and Roman theatre, describes the interlude and the Vice of the sixteenth century:

There was another kind of poeme, invented onely to make sport, and to refresh the company with a maner of buffonry or counterfaiting of merry speaches, converting all that which they had hard spoken before, to a certaine derision by a quite contrary sence, and this was done, when *Comedies* or *Tragedies* were a playing, and that betweene the actes when the players went to make ready for another, there was great silence, and the people waxt weary, then came in these maner of conterfaite vices, they were called *Pantomimi*, and all that had before bene sayd, or great part of it, they gave a crosse construction to it very ridiculously.[1]

The phrase 'conterfaite vices' suggests that F. H. Mares may be right in suggesting that 'Vice' comes from the vizard or mask of the clown, rather than from the agent of evil in the morality play,[2] though by mid-century the two meanings were probably confused in any case. Heywood's Vices, Merry Report and No-Lover-Nor-Loved – and also, though they are not called Vices, James in *Witty and Witless* and the atheistic Pothecary in *The Four PP* – are detached from the subject of controversy and turn the speeches of others to a 'contrary sense'. Even Medwall's A and B can be seen in this light. All these characters, like the more obviously evil ones of the moral interludes, steadfastly refuse to understand the language of abstractions and ideals. When the Gentleman in *Weather* tries to intimidate Merry Report by claiming to be his 'head', the Vice remarks naïvely that he is delighted to find that he has 'one hed more then I knew' and then makes a dirty joke about it. No-Lover-Nor-Loved uses the most grotesque and extreme argument – a hatful of exploding fireworks – to convince the idealistic Lover-Loved that a life of emotion makes one more susceptible to pain than pleasure.

Probably Heywood's greatest debt is to Chaucer, not only for his portrayal of the rascally Pardoner but for a view of life which, as in *The Parlement of Fowles* for example, can juxtapose idealistic and materialistic views of a subject and give full value to both. Heywood recognizes that some of the practices ridiculed by the Vice may deserve all that he says of them. The Pothecary's contempt for the Pardoner's absurd relics is obviously justified. But when this character goes on to attack the ideal in whose name the other three PP are, however stupidly, acting –

> For fere lest suche parels [perils] to me myght fall
> I thanke god I use no vertue at all.

– he is rebuked for his cynicism. It is characteristic, also, that the rebuke is accompanied by a witty paradox. The Pardoner's boast, says the Pedlar, proves that he does after all have one virtue: honesty. The separateness of the Vice from the other characters, in these plays, involves no serious moral condemnation. It is a joke, not a tragedy.

[1] Ed. Edward Arber (Westminster, 1895), Bk I, Ch. xi.
[2] 'The Origin of the Figure Called "The Vice" in Tudor Drama', *HLQ*, XXII (1958–9), p. 29.

(iii) *Magnificence*

Skelton's one surviving play is earlier than Heywood's works, on which, as we have seen, it probably had some influence. But it seems better to take it by itself because, like its author, it has little in common with the interests of the 'More circle'. It is true that it opens with a debate. Felicity and Liberty have arranged to meet for a disputation, and Measure, who has somehow heard of this, arrives in time to act as judge. Their conclusion is that both Felicity and Liberty are necessary qualities but that they must be ruled by Measure. This used to be thought of as a step towards the secularization of the morality play, because it implies that happiness can be achieved on this earth through the cultivation of the Aristotelian ideal of the golden mean. A useful corrective to this view has recently been provided by critics who point out that emphasis on the need for measure is neither particularly new nor specifically Aristotelian.[1] *Mankind* had already used the proverb 'Measure is treasure'. Nor is there any reason to believe that Skelton meant his play to have more than the most general application to contemporary events – the growing power of Cardinal Wolsey or the extravagance of the young Henry VIII.[2] Any man newly arrived in the world, as we have seen in *Nature* and *Youth*, may be compared to a rich heir or prince, susceptible to the influence of self-interested hangers-on.

The really novel feature of *Magnificence* is not its theme, the danger of living without measure, but the way in which Skelton uses this theme as an excuse for his own selfconsciousness as a writer. The devices which in Heywood are the reflection of a playful attitude towards language – alliteration, repetition, long lists of names, elaborate rhyme schemes – are here used to illustrate lack of measure. Still more than in other moral plays, even *Mankind*, the characters comment on one another's language, underlining the relation between verse form and moral implication. Thus, when Liberty starts arguing for the right to be himself, the verse changes, obviously on purpose, from *rime royale* to short-winded Skeltonics, and Measure comments,

> Your langage is lyke the penne
> Of hym that wryteth to[o] fast. (ll. 90–1)

[1] Cf. R. L. Ramsay's introduction to his edition of the play, EETS (London, 1908; repr. 1925) and W. O. Harris, *Skelton's 'Magnyfycence' and the Cardinal Virtue Tradition* (Chapel Hill, 1965).
[2] Cf. Ramsay, op. cit., and A. R. Heiserman, *Skelton and Satire* (Chicago, Ill., 1961).

Counterfeit Countenance offers to describe himself to the audience 'in bastarde ryme, after the dogrell gyse' (l. 408); of Courtly Abusion, Magnificence admiringly remarks, 'Mary, your speche is as pleasant as though it were pend' (l. 1538). Even Good Hope, who is presented in the 'aureate' style reserved for virtuous abstractions, draws a response in terms of language:

> Your wordes be more sweter than ony precyous narde ...
> There is no bawme ne gumme of Arabe
> More delectable than your langage to me. (ll. 2345–8)

Lack of measure is particularly evident in the treatment of the four court Vices. To some extent the length of their monologues can be explained by the extensive doubling which the play requires: each actor had to hold the stage long enough to allow the others to change costumes, and long enough, also, to establish his identity in one role before going off to reappear in another. If Ramsay's doubling chart is right, one man would have had to play both Counterfeit Countenance and Courtly Abusion. Skelton allows surprisingly little scope for his performers to fill out their roles themselves. Everything is done for them by description, their own and those of the other characters. Their clothes, their appurtenances and their behaviour all receive extensive comment. The actor playing Cloaked Collusion, for example, is told exactly what to do on his first entrance through the remarks of a fellow Vice:

> By Cockes harte, he loketh hye;
> He hawketh, me thynke, for a butterfly. (ll. 574–5)

His monologue is frankly presented both as a time-filler and as a virtuoso aria:

> To passe the tyme and order whyle a man may talke
>   Of one thynge and other to occupy the place,
> Then for the season that I here shall walke,
>   As good be occupyed as up and downe to trace
>   And do nothynge ... (ll. 689–93)

In his plot, as well, Skelton makes a virtue out of the arbitrariness of events by describing them in terms of his main theme:

> Somtyme without Measure he trusted in golde,
> And now without Measure he shal have hunger and colde. (ll. 1894–5)

It is a play of extremes:

> Sodenly Ryches, and sodenly Poverte;
> Sodenly Comfort, and sodenly Adversyte. (ll. 2521–2)

Skelton's play is thus skilfully devised to take account of the fact that he himself could neither write with measure nor construct a plausible sequence of events leading to the downfall of his hero. The emphasis on Fortune and 'this worlde full of Trechery' (l. 2020) is not necessarily incompatible with the vivid creation of an atmosphere of plotting and scheming by the court Vices who embody that treachery. But in fact the two are not clearly related. Heiserman rightly points out that the villains 'have no real plot up their sleeves'.[1] They rob Magnificence but there is no suggestion that they are to be caught and punished. Yet the virtuous abstractions promise that the prince will somehow be restored to Felicity.

The confusion arises because Skelton is writing two types of allegory simultaneously. His villains are of two different kinds. The four CC are external evils, recognizable caricatures of courtiers such as had already been portrayed in Barclay's *Ship of Fools* and Skelton's own *Bouge of Court*. Skelton insisted on four of them, despite the smallness of his cast and the fact that he did not, apparently, need them to sing. Presumably the reason was that, like the author of *Mankind* with his three NN, he wanted to give some sense of the numerical superiority, as well as the variety, of villainy.[2] But, above all, the bustling and whispering of the characters establishes an atmosphere, both sinister and comic, which can also be found in many later plays with court settings. The two FF, the brothers Folly and Fancy, belong to the tradition of psychological allegory; they are aspects of Magnificence himself. His victimization by the four CC is only possible because he has

[1] Heiserman, op. cit., p. 108.

[2] This taste for alliterative names is widespread in the sixteenth century. As F. P. Wilson notes (*The English Drama 1485–1585* (Oxford, 1969), p. 28), Heywood's *Witty and Witless* might as well have been called *The Three JJ* to match *The Four PP*. Much the most extreme example dates from the 1550s, though it exists only in the form of a description by its author, William Baldwin, the editor of the *Mirror for Magistrates*. It was called *The Way to Life* and consisted of sixty-two characters, each of whose names began with 'L'. (See his letter in A. Feuillerat, *Documents Relating to the Revels at Court in the Time of King Edward VI and Queen Mary* (Louvain, 1914), pp. 215–17.) There seems, moreover, to have been no objection to giving two characters similar or identical names: one thinks of the two Jaqueses and two Bardolphs in Shakespeare. So it is not surprising that the translator of the French *Farce du pâté*, whether Heywood or another, should have replaced the original name of the priest, Maître Guillaume (William), with the more typically English Sir John, without feeling any need to change the name of the husband, which was also John.

first been led astray by Fancy, who pretends to be sent by Sad Circumspection (Reason). In other words, Magnificence undergoes a kind of mental breakdown, in which what he takes to be rational activity is really delusion and self-deception. He is not only a prince, he is also a man playing (under the tutelage of Courtly Abusion) the part of a prince. The reality of his situation is not simply that better management would have kept him from going bankrupt but that 'the Welthe of this worlde can not indure'. As Magnificence lies in self-pity on the ground, Liberty enters singing, descants on his own ambivalent nature, and then runs out to answer the sound of an offstage horn: someone else is calling him. As with the appearance of the boy heir to Man's wealth in *The Castle of Perseverance*, the incident reminds us that the story is about to repeat itself yet again. Men learn nothing from examples, even though Adversity has just told the audience the meaning of Magnificence's fall:

> Take hede of this caytyfe that lyeth here on grounde;
> Beholde howe Fortune on hym hath frounde.
> For though we shewe you this in game and play,
> Yet it proveth eyrnest, ye may se, every day. (ll. 1946–9)

Adversity is surely not talking only about the falls of princes.

Still, it is Adversity and not Death that strikes Magnificence down. Felicity also seems to belong to this world and not the next, since his full name is 'Wealthful Felicity'. Yet Poverty's advice, when misfortune strikes, is that Magnificence should pray to God:

> Put your Wyll to His wyll, for surely it is He
> That may restore you agayne to Felycyte. (ll. 1997–8)

And when Redress and Sad Circumspection lead the prince back to his palace at the end, 'There to indever [endure] with all Felycyte', Magnificence does not behave like someone whose lost wealth has been restored to him; he simply says, 'I am content, my frendys, that it so be' (ll. 2564–5). What sort of happiness is being restored to him: worldly wealth, or peace of mind? Though its vivid depiction of the atmosphere of a prince's court may seem to bring a new, secular element into the morality drama, *Magnificence* is as much in the *contemptus mundi* tradition as its predecessors. For a real study of kingship and its special problems in this world, we have to wait until the Reformation encouraged dramatists to portray worldly power, not as an illusion, but as an important alternative to the spiritual power of the church.

2 The Reformation and the moral play

(i) John Bale

'The science of Printing being found,' wrote John Foxe in a memorable phrase, 'immediately followed the grace of God.'[1] It is hard to say whether the Reformation was more important in the preservation or the destruction of English dramatic tradition. What has survived from this period is only a small proportion of what once existed; for the most part, it survived because it got into print; and what got into print, at least after 1530, was largely conditioned by official encouragement on the one hand and censorship on the other. Hence a disproportionate amount of extant Tudor drama consists of short moral allegories intended to disseminate Protestant values to a popular audience.

It seems to have been possible to joke about doctrinal changes remarkably early, if one chose one's audience carefully. The farce *Thersites* (1537) has a reference to 'old purgatory' and its bragging hero threatens to get back at Robin Hood and Little John for their stealing of abbots' purses. But most of the plays which commented openly on events of this period have been lost or exist only as fragments. Some may also have been revised to take

[1] *Actes and Monuments*, 2 vols (1583), Vol. II, p. 840.

advantage of changed circumstances at the time when they were printed. This, at least, is the most charitable explanation of their incoherence.[1]

From the early 1530s, Cromwell and other leaders of the English Reformation were making use of the power of the press and the stage for propaganda. Though most of the results are lost, the titles give a fair idea of the work of men like Thomas Wylley (*Against the Pope's Councillors, A Reverent Receiving of the Sacrament, A Rude Commonalty*) and Ralph Radcliffe, schoolmaster at Hitchin, who turned out plays on subjects taken from Chaucer, legend, the Bible and history (John Hus is one of his heroes). Our information about these men and others comes from the extensive catalogues of British authors made by the one Reformation propaganda dramatist whose works have not totally disappeared: John Bale. It was largely thanks to this ex-Carmelite that many monastic records were preserved, reflecting his obsessive interest in the history and customs of the religion he hated.[2] He also seems to have been well acquainted with its drama.

One of the greatest obstacles to the popularizing of the new religion must have been the existence of the mystery cycles, which involved a whole community in the presentation of a version of the biblical narrative incorporating a great deal of romantic, legendary material. Performances of these cycles were eventually suppressed, though not until near the end of our period; in a few areas they even lasted into the seventeenth century. But, to begin with, it may have been hoped that it would be possible to save them by rewriting the more objectionable portions of the plays, suppressing only those which, like the episodes from the life of the Virgin, were too obviously contrary to reformed doctrine. It was presumably with this aim in view that Bale, some time in the 1530s, wrote a cycle of plays based on the life of Christ. He also wrote a Paternoster play, following another traditional dramatic form of which no examples remain. He then turned to more obviously polemical subjects: Catholic treachery, the knavery of Thomas à Becket, and the two marriages of the king. Such of his plays as have survived probably date from 1538, with some revisions from a later period. They include examples of all three types: the biblical

[1] See, e.g., T. W. Craik, 'The Political Interpretation of Two Tudor Interludes', *RES* (1953), and Rainer Pineas, 'The Revision of *Wealth and Health*', *PQ* (1965). R. B. McKerrow argues, in his introduction to *Impatient Poverty* (Louvain, 1911), that this play is an adaptation of a northern, Marian play to southern, Elizabethan circumstances.

[2] Both Foxe and Hall were indebted to Bale's work. See Jesse W. Harris, *John Bale: A Study in the Minor Literature of the Reformation* (Urbana, Ill., 1940).

cycle, the anti-Catholic morality, and the anti-Catholic history play.

These plays show Bale gradually coming to terms with the chief problem of any dramatist who wanted to use the theatre as a weapon against Roman Catholicism – the fact that the church was currently under attack precisely because it was so theatrical. The spectacular displays of relics by characters like Chaucer's Pardoner and Boccaccio's Friar Cipolla, the dove that was made artificially to descend when Cardinal Wolsey celebrated mass at the Field of the Cloth of Gold,[1] the pageantry of the mass itself, all represented ways in which, so Protestants claimed, religion was sacrificed to display:

> They ought not of the Church to make a Stage or Theatere,
> Nor for to pricke or prancke themselves, in such disguised geare.
> But all the popish state almost consists in this degree.[2]

In particular, there was the question of what constituted idolatry, the breach of the second commandment. Images in churches had been a subject of controversy long before the Reformation, but Tyndale's attack on them in the 1520s stirred up the discussion again and helped to make the contrast between Catholic and Protestant a contrast between visual and verbal means of worship. The emphasis on pictures instead of words is treated, in Protestant drama, as a sign of stupidity: the hero of *The Longer Thou Livest the More Fool Thou Art* (1559–68), when handed a Bible, immediately looks for the pictures in it. In *The Conflict of Conscience* (1570–81) it is Satan who quotes St Gregory's famous phrase about an idol being a layman's book, and an illiterate priest explains (in rustic dialect) how the pictures in his book help him keep up with the church calendar:

> As far Example, on the day of Chraistes Natyvitie,
> Ay [I] see a Bab in a Manger, and two Beastes standing by.

By contrast, the reformers insisted on the need for the *word*; the bad preacher was the one who did not preach. The more extreme advocates of this view lived up to it by inserting long sermons into their plays; even Lindsay, the last man to risk boring an audience, included one in *The Three Estates*. In plays based on Scripture, any slight concession to dramatic interest had to be carefully explained. Thus 'Appendix', the commentator in *The Resurrection of Our Lord* (a fragment which might date from any time between 1530 and 1560), gives long footnotes to each scene, apologizing for

---

[1] See John Stevens, *Music and Poetry in the Early Tudor Court* (London, 1961), p. 237.

[2] Naogeorgus (Thomas Kirchmayer), *The Popish Kingdom*, trans. Barnaby Googe (1570), sig. 10-v.

any details that are not strictly biblical. At the end of *King Darius* (1565) another commentator was used to make sure that nobody could possibly have missed the point:

> The sayenge, I suppose, you do understand;
> Yet to showe you agayne I will take in hand

– whereupon he proceeded to tell the entire story again.

This conscientiously deadly subordination of drama to sermon can also be found in Bale's scriptural cycle: *God's Promises, John the Baptist's Preaching in the Wilderness* and *The Temptation of Our Lord*. Each play begins and ends with a didactic speech by 'Baleus Prolocutor'; the one concession to spectacle is the descent of a dove at the moment of Christ's baptism, but there is organ music between scenes, as Bale did not subscribe to the more austere Protestantism which admitted only congregational psalm-singing. Despite the music, it would be hard to imagine a less attractive way of trying to win converts. Those who find Milton's God hard to take ought to read *God's Promises*. In this counterpart to the cyclic 'Procession of Prophets', God holds a series of duologues with biblical figures from Adam to John the Baptist, on the theme that man is getting worse and worse. This is how Bale dramatizes the decision to punish David for taking a census of the people of Israel:

> PATER COELESTIS. Thu shalt of these three chose whych plage thu wylt
>   have,
>   For that synnefull acte, that I thy sowle maye save.
>   A scarsenesse seven years, or els three monthes exyle,
>   Eyther for three dayes, the pestylence most vyle,
>   For one thu must have, there is no remedye.
> DAVID REX PIUS. Lorde at thy pleasure, for thu art full of mercye.

Nor is Bale's Christ any more sympathetic. Explaining that he has just spent forty days fasting in the wilderness, he clears up a doctrinal point for the audience:

> Thynke not me to fast, bycause I wolde yow to fast,
> For than ye thynke wronge, and have vayne iudgement.

The plays are liveliest when they are least scriptural and most allegorical – that is, when they turn from general doctrinal points to attacking the church of Rome, here embodied in Pharisees, Sadducees and Satan himself.

The latter shows his true allegiance by declaring, after Christ has resisted all his temptations, that 'Thy vicar at Rome, I thinke wyll be my frynde'. Most subsequent Protestant plays follow Bale's course, concentrating on abuse of the enemy rather than the exposition of theology (Lewis Wager's *Mary Magdalene* is an exception). None of them, however, fully exploited Bale's far more original idea: that of using the theatricality of the Catholics as a weapon against them.

In both his *Comedy Concerning the Three Laws* and *King John*, Bale makes use of a trick which is still found quite frequently in revue sketches. He introduces characters in formal, impressive costumes and then makes them break into incongruously vulgar dialogue, song or dance. The inventories of the Revels Office indicate that many costumes in its possession after 1530 were those of members of the church hierarchy, and they appear to have been used in many court entertainments. Bale obviously thought of them as capable of producing an effect in their own right, when worn by such revolting characters as the Vices in *The Three Laws*. But he also mocked the Catholic use of tropological and typological visual symbols by turning it on the 'tropes and types' of the bishop's costume worn by Ambition. When his mitre is bent downwards, Infidelity points out, it looks like the mouth of a wolf. In *King John* he found a different kind of joke. In the first scene between the Vice characters, 'Usurped Power' is wearing, not clerical dress, but some sort of light, indecent costume. Suddenly Sedition realizes who this unlikely-looking character really is: 'What? Usurpid Powr, cock's sowle, ye are owr pope!' and asks why the Holy Father is not equipped with his usual symbols, 'yowr thre crownys, yowr crosse keyes & yowr cope'. It turns out that the Pope happens to be travelling incognito, for private reasons. So a further point is made about the element of disguise in Catholicism.

The staginess of the Vices' behaviour is also frequently pointed out. King John calls churchmen 'dysgysed players', 'latyne mummers' and 'dysgysed shavelynges'. Sedition is an actor, whose doubling is built into his character:

> In every estate of the clargye I playe a part
> Sumtyme I can be a monke in a long syd cowle
> Sumtyme I can be a none [nun] & loke lyke an owle ... (ll. 194–6)

Dissimulation, as one might expect from his name, also 'plays his part' and 'plays the knave'. Thora Blatt has commented perceptively on Bale's parodies of religious ritual – the cursing of King John with bell, book and candle, the use (and abuse) of confession, the rite of absolution, and so on:

The irony works on two levels. First ritual, which is like juggling, is represented on the stage where, according to Bale, it belongs; next its pernicious influence is made clear by the fact that it is performed by the Vices, and contrasted with the language of the virtuous characters, who work mainly through godly words and a simple symbolism based on the Bible.[1]

A further point is that the parody has a desacramentalizing effect. It has been pointed out that, in both *Mankind* and *Everyman*, where the importance of confession is stressed, the dramatist refrains, probably out of reverence, from having the actual words of absolution spoken on the stage.[2] Bale deliberately removes this element of mystery from Catholicism. And yet he succumbs to the view that seeing is believing. The tableau in which Sedition is brought, literally and symbolically, into England is carefully prepared beforehand in case its meaning should be missed, but Bale also uses the visual effect as proof of the moral:

> Of me, Privat Welth, cam fyrst Usurpyd Powr;
> Ye may perseyve it in pagent here this howr. (ll. 785–6)

And the end of the play is full of such phrases: 'By thys example, ye maye see with your eyes', 'marke wele', 'Here was to be seane'.

Bale is the only representative in English drama of the apocalyptic tradition which related human to divine history. This seems to have been largely a German contribution; as early as the twelfth century, the Tegernsee *Antichrist* play had combined references to the current political situation with the legend of the false messiah who sends Hypocrisy and Heresy to corrupt the laity and clergy while the rulers of Europe fight vainly against him, until he is finally struck down by divine fire.[3] Antichrist was always available as a convenient symbol of one's most powerful enemy, and the Reformation determination to identify this character with the Pope led to a revival of Antichrist plays with the same universal sweep and topicality as this medieval prototype. 'Naogeorgus' (Thomas Kirchmayer) wrote the most famous of these plays, *Pammachius*, and dedicated it to Archbishop Cranmer in 1537, at a time when England's defiance of the papacy made her look like the best hope of Protestant Europe. When Henry

---

[1] Thora Blatt, *The Plays of John Bale* (Copenhagen, 1968), p. 133.
[2] M. Philippa Coogan, op. cit. pp. 15–16.
[3] The play is printed in Karl Young, *The Drama of the Medieval Church*, 2 vols (Oxford, 1933), Vol. II. See also the discussion of it in Richard Axton, *European Drama of the Later Middle Ages* (London, 1974), pp. 88–94.

VIII began to take a more reactionary course Kirchmayer reflected this in a sequel of 1541 by making the Antichrist-figure write a letter congratulating the English king on his recent moves against the reformers.[1] Bale made a translation of *Pammachius* (now lost), and his friend John Foxe wrote a Latin *Christus Triumphans* which was published in 1556, at a time when Antichrist must have seemed firmly established in England. Like the German plays, it treats historical and allegorical events as occurring simultaneously: thus, his opening scene introduces Eve and the Virgin Mary lamenting together, the Virgin over the death of her son, Eve over her children Psyche and Soma (the soul and body), who have been captured by Satan. This gives some indication of the historical sweep of the play. The heroine, Ecclesia, is persecuted first by the Roman emperors and then by Antichrist in the form of the Pope. At the end she is dressed as the bride of Christ, and the five wise virgins call to him to come quickly. 'Perhaps', the prologue says, 'it will not be long before stage representations will lie neglected; then indeed we will see all with our own eyes.'

Bale's *Three Laws* is a more original treatment of the *Pammachius* type of play, adapted for a small cast. God establishes his three laws: the Law of Nature, the Law of Moses and the Law of Christ. These correspond to the three persons of the Trinity and the three ages of human history; in other words, they exist both simultaneously and sequentially. Each of the three laws is corrupted by Infidelity the Vice and his two helpers, until God at last appears to punish sin and restore the laws to their original purity. In his note on costume, Bale gives the name of Vice both to Infidelity and to his subordinates. But the behaviour of Infidelity is different from that of the other Vices, whose names – Idolatry, Sodomy, Ambition, Avarice, False Doctrine and Hypocrisy – indicate the nature of Bale's targets as well as the unpleasant turn of his mind. They are all associated with Roman Catholicism, the evil genius which is shown attempting to destroy even the pre-Christian figures, the Law of Nature and the Law of Moses. But Infidelity is only using the church for his own ends, and consequently can act as its satirist even while working with its representatives. In this respect he shares the cynical detachment of Heywood's Vices.

Similarly, in *King John*, the chief Vice is a political figure, Sedition, who uses the disguise, and the help, of churchmen to accomplish his ends. This character was probably suggested to Bale by the recent uprising known as the Pilgrimage of Grace, which Protestants likewise saw as sedition disguised as religion. Here, the most astonishing merging of historical and

[1] Thora Blatt, op. cit. p. 31.

allegorical time occurs at the end, when, after the death of John, the three estates find themselves confronting a new character called Imperial Majesty, presumably Henry VIII. In subsequent revisions of the play Bale was able to take account of events since his first version of 1538. The Malone Society transcript of the manuscript makes fascinating reading. Whatever the precise dates of the revisions, it is clear that Bale's intention in them was not only, as one might expect, to heighten the anti-Catholic satire (he added to his already long list of religious orders and of 'holy' relics) but also to give a more heroic dimension to the character of John himself. The later version of the play thus makes him hold out longer against the humiliating demands of the church, and when he does give in it is insisted that he does so only for the sake of his kingdom:

> Shall my people shedde their bloude in suche habundaunce?
> Naye, I shall rather gyve upp my whole governaunce. (ll. 1738–9)

He is caught in a genuinely tragic dilemma, and his surrender to the church fills him with remorse from which he escapes only into a defeated and almost despairing death. Neither the parody deaths of Dissimulation and Sedition, who gloat over the prospect of becoming Catholic martyrs and working miracles, nor the eventual amends made to the king's reputation by Verity and Imperial Majesty, detract from the emphasis, in John's final scenes, on his suffering humanity. He is probably the first tragic hero in English drama. If, as seems likely, it was this play that was performed before Cranmer at Christmas 1538–9, it aroused one spectator to comment that 'king Iohn was as noble a prince as [ever] was in England'.[1]

Bale's ingenious reinterpretation of history to defend King John against the charge of tyranny shows to what extent reformers were prepared to tolerate royal absolutism as a bulwark against what they saw as the far greater danger of papal absolutism. His sympathetic portrayal of an earthly ruler is not unique in the period. The treatment of Pilate, in the fragmentary *Resurrection of Our Lord*, suggests how the mystery cycles might have been rewritten to accommodate the new relationship between church and state. Arnold Williams has shown that there was a medieval tradition which viewed Pilate sympathetically, but its main effect was to give the story of the Crucifixion an anti-Semitic emphasis; indeed, the unsympathetic Pilate of the Towneley Cycle actually forgets that he is a Roman and unites with

---

[1] Quoted in J. H. P. Pafford's introduction to his edition of *King John*, Malone Society Reprint (1931), xvii–xviii. See above, p. 16.

the Jews in trying to prevent Christ from overthrowing 'oure lawe'.[1] However, in the sixteenth-century *Resurrection* the Jews are not really Jews at all. They are shown to be primarily concerned with preserving their *old* traditions – and stress on antiquity is always a sign of Catholicism; Pilate is depicted as a good governor, sceptical of the power of the priesthood and concerned only with putting down sedition.[2] *Godly Queen Hester* (1525–9), though it does not attack the church as such (in fact it is a defence of the monasteries), can be seen as a foreshadowing of the new theme; its ending is clearly a hint that Henry VIII should take the reins of government into his own hands and get rid of his proud Chancellor, the most hated churchman of his time. King John, King Ahasuerus and the sixteenth-century Pilate form a startling contrast with the boasting tyrants who symbolized worldly power in medieval drama.

(ii) *The Three Estates* and *Respublica*

Popular and courtly drama adopt vastly different attitudes towards the Reformation. Despite the bitter tone of Bale's plays, at one level there was evidently a sophisticated society capable of enjoying the burlesque of the Roman Catholic funeral service in *Ralph Roister Doister* (which would have been equally daring whether produced in the reign of Edward or of Mary) or, like Mary of Guise, the Catholic regent of Scotland, the hilarious anti-clericalism of Lindsay's *Satire of the Three Estates*. It is also some indication of the complexity of religious attitudes that Nicholas Udall, the Protestant author of *Ralph Roister Doister* and possibly *Respublica*, collaborated with Mary Tudor in the project of translating Erasmus's *Paraphrases on the New Testament* (1548–9). Most humanists were able, without straining their consciences, to submit both to the government of Edward VI and to that of his Catholic sister.[3]

The issue is particularly confused by the popularity in drama of that ancient comic character, the clergyman who loves good living. Reformers were prepared to accept into their ranks almost any writer who satirized

---

[1] *The Characterization of Pilate in the Towneley Plays* (East Lansing, 1950), p. 21.
[2] His obvious resemblance to King John has led some scholars to attribute the play to Bale; Thora Blatt, however, thinks the apologetic discourses of 'Appendix' prove the contrary: Bale 'is never apologetic' (op. cit. p. 20).
[3] See J. K. McConica, *English Humanists and Reformation Politics* (Oxford, 1965).

such characters. Thus Foxe told of people who had been converted by the works of Chaucer, whom he described as 'a right wiclevian [follower of Wycliff] or els was never any'.[1] Heywood's plays also seem to have benefited from a confusion between anticlericalism and anti-Catholicism. Rastell (who by that time was a committed reformer) published four of them in 1533. While in some plays, such as those of Bale, William Wager and Thomas Lupton, bad priests are used to embody anti-Catholic satire, there are also a number of plays (such as *Gammer Gurton's Needle*) where the atmosphere seems pre-Reformation and there is no attempt to make capital out of the priest's inadequacies. By the Elizabethan period, the implication is that superstition and ignorance have been banished to remote rural areas (the ignorant Caconus in *The Conflict of Conscience* (1570–81) has a northern accent) or are confined to old women, like the one in *The Pedlar's Prophecy* (1561–3) who clings to the old religion in the form of her rosary and some images:

> I wisse quoth she, I love these better then the new Gospell,
> And for pure love unto them, she began to weepe.

The latter play shows that by this time the accusation of ignorance was also being turned on preachers of the new gospel. It would not be long before Protestant clergymen fell into the same comic stereotypes as their Catholic predecessors.

It is against this background of anticlerical satire that one can best understand Lindsay's play. In his own time he had the reputation of a daring reformer. Bullein's *Dialogue Against the Fever Pestilence* (1564) has a famous phrase describing him 'with a hammer of strong steele in his hande, breakyng a sonder the counterfeite crosse kaies of Rome, forged by Antichriste'.[2] His first editor, Henry Charteris, wondered how he had escaped burning. But the steel hammer was probably heard for the first time in 1540 as a short interlude given in the banqueting hall at Linlithgow, in the presence of James V and Marie of Lorraine. All we know about it, from an account which was sent to Cromwell shortly afterwards, is that, like other such interludes, it had comparatively little action. It consisted mainly of a poor man's complaint against the oppression of the church, interspersed with lighter episodes of drinking and singing. The king in the play was a

---

[1] *Actes and Monuments*, Vol. II, p. 639. Foxe was, however, thinking particularly of the Chaucer apocrypha, especially *The Testament of Love* and *The Ploughman's Tale*, which were printed as his in all sixteenth-century editions from 1532 and 1542 respectively.
[2] Ed. M. W. Bullen and A. H. Bullen, EETS (1888), p. 18.

silent figure and at one point it was made clear, by a graceful compliment to the king in the audience, that there was no connection between this stage figure and the 'other king in scotlande that hanged John Armestrang with his fellowes'.[1] James in fact knew the contents of the play beforehand, and, afterwards, called upon the Scottish bishops to reform their manner of living.

As the king's herald, Lindsay was in England in 1543, where he made a favourable personal impression despite the tense relations between the two countries, and he would have had an opportunity of describing in more detail the simple political interlude which had aroused such interest. In 1552 he rewrote and enlarged the piece extensively for outdoor production in Cupar in Fife, and in 1554, apparently at the request of the Queen Regent, it was put on in Edinburgh as well. *Respublica*, which might perhaps have been influenced by some details of the earlier *Three Estates*, was probably given during the Christmas season of 1553. The two dramatists were thus writing, virtually at the same time, two plays of completely opposite kinds: in one case, the last and best example of the medieval place-and-scaffold drama; in the other, the first English morality – perhaps the first English play – to use the five-act structure of classical comedy.

The atmosphere in which the longer *Satire of the Three Estates* was given was that of a jolly public occasion, with much emphasis on the need for actors and audience to have plenty of refreshment. The banns at Cupar were interrupted by actors pretending to be members of the public; their problems had to do with the usual farce topics – henpecking, cuckolding, cowardice – rather than with political or religious issues. And this set the tone for the play itself. The Queen Regent would hardly have asked for a public performance of the *Satire* if she had thought it a dangerous work. She might have been familiar already with the genre to which it belonged; it shares many elements with French farces and *sotties*, which also handled political and religious matters with great freedom. Lindsay may have been using the word 'satire' in one of its possible sixteenth-century meanings: gallimaufry. Certainly it is the most skilfully varied play that has survived from its period.

---

[1] See the letter from Sir William Eure, enclosing a summary of the play, in D. Hamer (ed.), *The Works of Sir David Lindsay of the Mount*, 4 vols – (Edinburgh and London, 1931), Vol. II, pp. 1–6. It is possible that this interlude may have been a different work altogether and even by a different author. Joanne S. Kantrowitz has shown that the date of *The Three Estates* as we know it cannot be earlier than 1549. See *Dramatic Allegory: Lindsay's Ane Satyre of the Thrie Estaitis* (Lincoln, Nebraska, 1975), pp. 17 ff.

For his main plot, Lindsay separated into the first and second parts of the play the two types of allegory which characterize *Magnificence* and *Respublica* respectively: the fall and repentance of the individual ruler and the fall and repentance of his kingdom. The player king in this version can hardly have been the one that James V saw, since his is a speaking part; young and naïve, he has to ask his courtiers' advice on how to behave when the courtesan Dame Sensuality arrives. As in the other life-of-man moralities, we are constantly reminded that there is a time for all sins: Flattery warns the other Vices that they must 'haist us quhill the King is young' (I, 994), particularly since they have heard a rumour that Divine Correction is on his way there. Good Counsel also recognizes that reformation is partly a matter of time:

> Bot, quhen youthheid hes blawin his wanton blast,
> Then sall Gude-counsall rewll him at the last. (I, 982–3)

His faults are not presented in a very serious light (there may have been a need for tact here, since the late James V had not been averse to Sensuality), but they do earn a solemn reproof from Verity, who makes what is probably the first of many speeches in drama about a king's responsibility to his subjects:

> Ye ar the lamps that sould schaw them the licht
> To leid them on this sliddrie rone [path] of yce. (I, 1047–50)

But the need for good example is still greater among the leaders of the three estates, especially the Spirituality, to whom the second part of the play is directed. Unlike the king, they have no intention of reforming (hence their famous entrance, walking backwards, led by their Vices). When the habits of the Spirituality are removed, revealing fools' clothing underneath, even Dame Sensuality refuses to know them. The clerical dress is not burnt, as it might have been in a thoroughgoing Reformation play; instead it is put on those who deserve to wear it, the worthy doctor of divinity and clerks who have proved their knowledge of Scripture and ability to preach. As F. P. Wilson puts it, Lindsay was 'for reformation rather than the Reformation'.[1] John o' the Commonweal, when asked to state his creed, includes Sanctam Ecclesiam but not the bishops or friars; Diligence's final speech includes (though only in the 1552 text of the play) a prayer that Christ, through the intercession of the Virgin, may preserve all the spectators.

Somewhere in the background there is danger. Lindsay's most

[1] Wilson, op. cit. p. 19.

remarkable creation, John o' the Commonweal, first appeared in his poem of
1528 or so, *The Dream*. He is not at all like his counterparts in the English
drama: Commonalty in *King John*, who is blind for want of spiritual
guidance and too poor to help his king, or People in *Respublica*, a lovable
but ignorant rustic. Despite his symbolic rags and lameness, he is full of
energy which sometimes suggests violence about to erupt. The Vices and
their followers in the Spirituality have power to do considerable damage.
At one point Spirituality 'fames [foams] and rages' (II, 2783) like Herod or
Caiaphas. The persecution of Chastity is a mainly comic episode, which has
as much to do with the problems of impotent craftsmen as with misconduct
among the clergy, but when Flattery discovers that the book Verity is carrying is an English New Testament his cry of 'Herisie, herisie, fire, fire,
incontinent' (I, 1147) shows what a different kind of play this could have
been. The hangings of the Vices at the end also have a tragicomic quality.
The counterpart of Bale's treatment of Sedition (probably based on Henry
VIII's treatment of Robert Aske) is Lindsay's evident belief that James V's
finest act had been his hanging of Johnny Armstrong. This in itself may be
enough to explain the numerous references to theft and hanging in the
second part of the play, but Common Theft also quotes (II, 3225–6) a line
from Villon, whose works were in print and well known by 1540. In the
style of the *Testament*, the scoundrels take a ludicrously sentimental farewell
of their innumerable followers – many of them no doubt members of the
audience – but the speech that Falsehood makes after the rope has been
tied round his neck is much stronger stuff:

> Cum follow me all catyfe covetous Kings
> Reavers but [without] richt of uthers Realmis and Rings [reigns],
> Togidder with all wrangous conquerours.
> And bring with yow all publick oppressours.
> With Pharao King of Egiptians,
> With him in hell salbe your recompence. (II, 4204–9)

Then he launches into an anti-feminist diatribe (one of many in the play); at
his hanging, his soul, in the form of a crow, is made to fly away. Then the
entrance of Folly turns everything to nonsense. He has heard about the
parliament where all grievances are to be settled by the king and Divine
Correction, and he wants to complain about his recent misadventure with a
sow. Seeing the pulpit which has been set up to symbolize the new
order that preaching shall be heard throughout the land, he preaches a

sermon on the text *Stultorum numerus infinitus*. It includes virtually every kind of character that has appeared in the play.

Despite the allegorical names of its dramatis personae, *The Three Estates* is not really allegorical. At one point, it is true, the familiar inability of vicious characters to understand allegorical language is used against them. The Doctor gives a sermon which ends with the moving image of love as a ladder with two steps (love of God and of one's neighbour):

> Be quhilk we may clim up to lyf againe,
> Out of this vaill of miserie and wa [woe] (II, 3493–4)

He is immediately ridiculed by the worldly parson and abbot, who say that heaven is too far to reach by so short a ladder. But Lindsay does not take the view that the spiritual is more real than the material. What he attacks in the Spirituality is not only their unspiritual character but the way in which they exploit the poor by taking material possessions from them in exchange for supposed spiritual benefits – as, on the simplest level, the Pardoner takes the Poor Man's last groat, assuring him that it has bought a thousand years of pardon. The play obviously endorses the Poor Man's reaction:

> Bot I can se[e] na thing sir be our Lady:
> Forsuith maister, I trow I be not wyse,
> To pay ere I have sene my marchandryse.
> That ye have gottin my groat full sair I rew.
> Sir, quhidder is your pardon black or blew? (II, 2251–5)

This insistence on seeing positive results in this world is one of the forces which were eventually to put an end to allegorical drama except as an intellectual exercise.

The constantly shifting tone of the play is perhaps best exemplified in the role of the presenter Diligence. He is not called 'Poeta', but it is hard not to see him as Lindsay's comic self-portrait, combining the poet's real-life functions of royal herald and deviser of court entertainments. There is a direct reference to one of his poems of half-serious complaint when, near the end of Part I, Diligence complains that he is being asked to do a great deal of work for no pay and the king graciously promises to reward him with a yearly grant of the tithe mussels of Ferny Mire – a place three miles from the nearest beach. The herald exists both inside and outside the world of the play, coping with emergencies, insulting the women in the audience, pretending to be indignant at interruptions, and acting as a 'feed' for each

new arrival. An example of the way in which he helps the theatrical illusion
even when he seems to be shattering it is his chasing the Poor Man and
Pardoner from the acting area with the command

> Into ane presoun put them sone,
> Syne hang them quhen the play is done. (II, 2292–3)

It is also characteristic of him that, when asked by Folly to identify Divine
Correction, he replies blandly, 'Yon with the wings. May thou nocht se[e]?'
(II, 4332), as if angelic visitations were an everyday occurrence in Cupar.
In its sheer variety of appeal, from the coarsest to the most sophisticated
kinds of humour, *The Three Estates* is the only play of its period which
one might compare with the best of Elizabethan and Jacobean comedy. It
is a great pity that it is also the only surviving example of sixteenth-
century Scottish drama.

Respublica is at least as much an academic comedy as it is an anti-
Reformation interlude, and its relation to the first of these categories will
be discussed later.[1] As the dramatist of the period most thoroughly soaked
in Latin comic authors, Nicholas Udall seems the obvious candidate for its
authorship; the difficulty is that he was also a well-known reformer. But
he knew Queen Mary well, and her declared policy at the beginning of her
reign was one to which he could hardly have objected: to favour the Roman
Catholic faith but not compel her subjects to adopt it. The persecution of
Protestants did not begin until 1555, the last year of his life. Specific
references to recent events are in any case very few in *Respublica*. The events
of the play cover a six-year period, which corresponds to the reign of
Edward VI, and Respublica's widowed state presumably symbolizes her
lack of an adult ruler rather than, as with 'England, a Widow', in Bale's
King John, the absence of her bridegroom Christ from the country. There is
a defence of the charitable work carried out by the monasteries and only one
brief insult is directed unmistakably at Protestantism: Avarice complains of
being pestered by beggars and is grateful that he has 'a speciall grace to saie
naie' (V. v). Yet this is Puritan cant, such as might have been ridiculed even
by a moderate Protestant.

Otherwise, the play is not so much an attack on the Reformation as on the
corrupt motives of the reformers. The prologue makes this clear:

> Oure meaninge is (I saie not, as by plaine storye,
> But as it were in figure by an allegorye)
> To shewe that all Commen weales Ruin and decaye

[1] See pp. 217–19.

> From tyme to tyme hath been, is, and shalbe alwaie,
> When Insolence, Flaterie, Opression,
> And Avarice have the Rewle in theire possession. . . .
> Yet time trieth all and time bringeth truth to light.

The implication is that the Protector and the King's Council have only been part of a cyclic historical pattern. The intrigue of the play is directed at making Insolence (under the name of Authority) ruler of the kingdom. Yet the actual 'vice of the plaie' is Avarice, both in his dramatic role and in the sense that he motivates the other three villains. As he says, when they start to tell him their plan,

> I understande all youre agreemente and accorde
> For I laie in your bosoms when ye spake the worde. (I. iii)

He is a universal motive. The Catholic bishops are also accused of covetousness and the only answer given is that those who confiscated their wealth were equally covetous. Respublica's first soliloquy also relates Reformation politics to a general sense of mutability:

> Lorde what yearethlye thinge is permanent or stable,
> Or what is all this worlde but a lumpe mutable?
> Who woulde have thowght that I from so florent estate
> Coulde have been browght so base as I am made of Late?
> But as the waving seas, doe flowe and ebbe by course,
> So all thinges els doe chaunge to better and to wurse.
> Greate Cyties and their fame in tyme dooe fade and passe;
> Nowe is a Champion [champaign] fielde where noble Troie was. (II. i)

However, as Willard Farnham points out, Respublica

> . . . does not draw the formerly inevitable lesson that the world is there-
> fore to be surrendered as incalculable and that man's gaze is to be fixed
> on Heaven. She concludes that the world is to some degree calculable
> and that states may be observed to fall for good reason, namely, lack of
> good government.[1]

Though this is true, it is also true that what saves Respublica is divine, not human help, working through Time, his daughter Truth, and Nemesis (which the prologue says is to be identified with Queen Mary).[2] It is Time

---

[1] *The Medieval Heritage of Elizabethan Tragedy* (Oxford, 1956), pp. 228–9.
[2] 'Veritas Filia Temporis' was the personal device of Mary Tudor. See D. J. Gordon, 'Veritas Filia Temporis: Hadrianus Junius and Geoffrey Whitney', *Journal of the Warburg and Courtauld Institutes*, III (1939–40).

which has brought Respublica to her wretched condition, but Time is also
an enemy to Avarice and his friends:

> Old tyme the evisdropper? I knowe hym pardee
> An Auncient turner of houses upside downe,
> And a comon consumer of Cytie and towne.
> Old tymes doughter (quod he?) I shrewe his naked harte,
> Manie of my frendes hathe he brought to paine and smarte. (V. ii)

Respublica refers in its prologue to some of the Vices of *Magnificence*,
and its emphasis on the role of 'People' and of Verity could be derived
either from *King John* or from *The Three Estates*. It is a more genuinely
political play than the other three. Unlike *Magnificence*, it shows the effects
as well as the process of court conspiracy; 'People', like Lindsay's
representatives of the commonwealth, judges the effectiveness of government in practical terms and cannot believe that Policy and Honesty are the
real names of rulers under whom he finds himself getting steadily poorer.
But Lindsay was writing about contemporary Scotland and Bale was
interpreting English history in the light of what he saw as an eternal
contest between Antichrist and the truth – which meant the true church.
Respublica is a more consistent, intellectual allegory (much of its humour
comes from giving abstractions the characteristics of real people) and consequently conveys a political message which 'from tyme to tyme hath been,
is, and shalbe alwaie' relevant. At the end, the four court Vices meet appropriate fates. Insolence and Oppression are imprisoned, to await trial;
Adulation repents – no morality play would be complete without a conversion – and is pardoned; Avarice is to be 'pressed, as men doo presse
a spounge' (V. x). It is Hamlet who points out the full implications of this
common emblem: 'But such officers do the King best service in the end. . . .
When he needs what you have glean'd, it is but squeezing you and, sponge,
you shall be dry again' (IV. ii).

(iii) Other late moral interludes

So the Reformation, with its emphasis on establishing the kingdom of God
on earth, jolted drama out of the world of allegorical time, bounded by the
Creation and the Last Judgement, into a sense of its place in human
history. For a while, the effect was to alter even the sense of history as a

steady process of degeneration since the loss of Eden, with Virtue always an elderly man and Vice always a youth in 'the new guise'. The reformers were inevitably representatives of the 'new learning' and 'new religion'; they thus had an obvious interest in demolishing the myth of a lost 'merry England' which seems to have grown up almost concurrently with the Reformation. Bale parodies the myth in his *Three Laws* by making Infidelity look back nostalgically on the 'good world' when sermons consisted of dirty stories and priests went about cuckolding all the parish (III. i). In *Lusty Juventus* (1547–53), Satan is outraged at the state of affairs in England:

> The olde people would beleve stil in my lawes,
> But the yonger sort leade them a contrary way.

Juventus is amazed at the doctrine given him by Good Counsel – 'My elders never taught me so before' – and has to be told that the parents he has been taught to respect were themselves misled by those they respected. Satan's son Hypocrisy later uses this traditional respect for authority to shake the faith of the newly converted young hero:

> I may say to you secretly,
> The world was never mery,
> Since children were so bolde:
> Now every boy wyl be a teacher
> The father a foole, and the chyld a preacher,
> This is preaty [pretty] gear
> The foule presumption of youth
> Wyl turne shortly to great ruth
> I fere, I feare, I feare.

There is an obvious reason why this Edwardian interlude should urge the young people in the audience not to be trapped into uncritical respect for their elders. The very imagery of Roman Catholicism – the Holy Father and the Mother Church – worked against the fifth commandment. 'If thy mother anger thee, call her whore',[1] was the classic lesson for the bad child – but, if Bale is right, young Edward VI had, figuratively speaking, done just that, in writing a polemic play called *The Whore of Babylon*. Moreover, it was impossible to pretend that the actions of the Protector and Council, in the name of the king, were following a course of which Henry VIII would have approved. One of the sermons which Latimer preached before the king found a scriptural parallel:

[1] E.g. in *The Longer Thou Livest the More Fool Thou Art.*

Josias, the best king that ever was in Jewry, reformed his father's ways, who walked in worldly policy. In his youth he took away all Idolatry, and purged his realm of it, and set a good order in all his dominions, and wrestled with idolatry.... Therefore you must not take it as a general rule, that the son must ever walk in his father's ways.[1]

The author of *New Custom* also appeals to youth in a way that suggests an original date in Edward VI's reign, although the play was evidently revised at a later time and is usually dated 1570–3. Perverse Doctrine and Ignorance complain of the 'new-fangled, prattling elves' who insist on reading the Bible instead of playing games suitable for their age:

> For since these Genevan doctors came so fast into this land,
> Since that time it was never merry with England. (II. ii)

Ironically, New Custom, the object of their hatred, turns out to be Primitive Constitution, and hence older than either of them.[2]

However, this defence of youth against age is essentially foreign to the spirit of the English Reformation. The reformers might see themselves as the defenders of a persecuted religion but in fact, except during the last years of Queen Mary's reign, they can more truly be seen – in the pattern set by Bale's *King John* – as the allies of the civil power against seditious and reactionary elements in the state. The obedience of children to their parents could thus be treated as a symbol of their need to obey all their superiors on earth. The numerous sixteenth-century education plays and variations on the prodigal son story will be discussed later.[3] All that needs to be said at present is that these too had a special relevance during the reigns of the three children of Henry VIII. One of Latimer's sermons hints at the possibility of the young king finding himself in the position of a morality play hero: 'when these flatterers and flibbergibs another day shall come, and claw you by the back, and say, "Sir, trouble not yourself: what should you study? Why should you do this or that?"'[4]

But a still more important form of obedience is emphasized in the

---

[1] 'The Fifth Sermon Preached Before King Edward VI', in *Sermons by Hugh Latimer*, ed. G. E. Corrie, Parker Society (Cambridge, 1844), pp. 176–7.

[2] Cf. Latimer's remarks in a sermon of 1536: 'But ye say, it is new learning. Now I tell you it is the old learning. Yea, ye say, it is old heresy new scoured. Nay, I tell you it is old truth, long rusted with your canker, and now new made bright and scoured.' (Ibid. p. 30.)

[3] See pp. 222–6.

[4] 'The Second Sermon Preached Before King Edward VI', *Sermons*, p. 124.

prologue to Lewis Wager's *The Life and Repentance of Mary Magdalene*
(1550–66), which defends the stage by asking 'Doth it not teache true
obedience to the kynge?' Everyman has become political man, liable to
fall from grace by disobedience to worldly as well as heavenly powers.
The protagonist in a fragment known as *The Four Cardinal Virtues* (1541–
1547) describes his career; he was originally called Adversity, but then

> Chaunged into prosperyte by crafte colorable
> Disobedience I was I feared no fall
> My myght and my myschefe was intollerable
> My purpose exalted to clymbe above all.

The story seems to be the same as that of the hero in *Impatient Poverty*
(1547–58), though here the allegorical meaning almost disappears under
the weight of satire on various forms of double-dealing and greed. The
presence of the chief virtue, Peace, allows Poverty to become Prosperity,
but he is then led astray by Misrule and suffers a well-deserved punishment. Even at the beginning of the play his predicament receives none
of the sympathy which Lindsay shows for that of John o' the Commonweal:

> POVERTY. For I am ever in greate necessyte,
> Meate and drinke with me is scarsite,
> No man will truste me of a peny,
> And also my clothes are but bare.
> Good syr what saye you therin?
> PEACE. I holde it punisshment for thi sinne.

This determination to make sense out of the apparent injustice of this
world also leads to an early expression of the 'scourge of God' idea. The
representative of 'People' in *The Longer Thou Livest the More Fool Thou
Art* (1559–68) complains of being ruled by the stupid and tyrannical Moros
but says that he will leave redress to God:

> Wee have offended him and his holy lawes,
> Therefore are wee worthy of this punishment.

Usually, popular drama prefers to show the justification of the righteous
in this world as well as the next. This is the theme which links the two
otherwise unrelated plots of *King Darius* (1565). To begin with a number
of Virtues meet a number of vaguely Catholic Vices in a series of undramatic
and inconclusive encounters consisting of sermons from one side and insults

from the other. Unlike the pre-Reformation Charity, who was put into the stocks by Youth and his companions, the Charity of this play is calmly assured of his immunity from evil:

> As for me, I trust, god hath geven me the grace
> All my enemies clerely to deface.

He is right. The chief Vice, Iniquity, is finally struck by divine fire. With a notable lack of the qualities they are supposed to represent, Charity, Constancy and Equity rejoice at his fate. Then follows the biblical part of the play: in a competition for the best answer to the question 'What is the strongest thing in the world?', the virtuous Zorababell wins by replying that it is truth. His reward is the position of King Darius's right-hand man, which he immediately uses to make the King keep his promise to restore the temple at Jerusalem – the author's way of symbolizing true religion.

The atmosphere of many of the later interludes is a disagreeable combination of self-righteousness and scapegoat-seeking which probably resulted from the disappointment of the belief that virtue would auto-matically transform Poverty to Prosperity. Comic and sinister foreigners appear or are mentioned in *Wealth and Health* (1554–5), *Impatient Poverty* (1547–58), *The Pedlar's Prophecy* (1561–3), *Like Will to Like* (1562–8) and *The Trial of Treasure* (1567). The most absurd accusation against them comes in *The Pedlar's Prophecy*, where they are blamed not only for the high prices of houses (a common accusation) but also for a father's unwillingness to let his daughter marry in case she should pollute her blood with some alien or alien's son. Elizabethan interludes look back on the Marian persecutions, drawing on Latimer and on the *Acts and Monuments* as Catholics had once drawn on the *Golden Legend*; Foxe's accounts of trials and burnings are used in *New Custom*, *The Trial of Treasure*, *Enough is as Good as a Feast* and *The Conflict of Conscience*. But those who had passed through the ordeal often seemed no better for it. In *Enough is as Good as a Feast* there is some sharp comment on the failure of Protestants to keep the promises they made during Mary's reign:

> If it please thee, good Lord (said they) thy word to us again send
> And then truly our covetous lives we will amend.
> But since it hath pleased God, them to wealth to restore,
> They are ten times more covetous than they were before.

Avarice remains the besetting sin in these plays, whereas Pride, once described as the chief of Vices, is hardly mentioned except in Lewis Wager's *Mary Magdalene*. There seem to have been a number of plays, now lost, on the story of Dives, the rich man who ended up in hell; Lupton's *All for Money* (1559–77) brings him on, with Judas, lamenting his greed.

Many of these plays are confusing because they are trying to attack too many targets at once. *Impatient Poverty*, for instance, seems to say that if men are poor it is their own fault. But it also attacks the vicious practices of the usurer Abundance, who behaves much worse than the hero but gets away with it because he has money to bribe the authorities.[1] During his brief period as Prosperity, moreover, the hero himself becomes the object of a different kind of satire, as a *nouveau riche* who dislikes being reminded that his name used to be Poverty and refuses to play at dice with a stranger until he is sure the latter is a gentleman. When Envy, pretending to be Charity, introduces himself as a poor relation, he gets a chilly welcome:

> PROSPERITY. Thou and I are not of one affynyte.
>
> ENVY. Yf I were a ryche man, ye wold not saye so by me.

The fact that Prosperity is perfectly right to be suspicious does not alter the effectiveness of Envy's retort.

A number of early Elizabethan plays show that the interest of morality writers had moved, as in *Impatient Poverty*, from the study of an Everyman hero to the depiction of a variety of social types. The craze of plays with proverbial titles may have been started by the publication in 1562 of the *Works* of old John Heywood, whose collections of proverbs and epigrams had been appearing since 1546. George Wapull is indebted to his *tour de force*, the *Dialogue of Proverbs*, for the episode of Wanton and her husband Wasteful in *The Tide Tarrieth No Man*, as well as for one bit of their dialogue.[2] The two plays by William Wager, *The Longer Thou Livest the More Fool Thou Art* (1559–68) and *Enough is as Good as a Feast* (1559–70), reflect the transition from one type of morality to the other.

---

[1] It is possible that, as McKerrow suggests, the scenes with Abundance are later than the rest of the play, post-dating the acts against usury in 1545 and 1550. But their discussion about making amends for ill-gotten gains by fasting, praying and alms-giving, as well as Abundance's feeble attempt to excuse his covetousness by blaming the bad example set by the clergy, sound more like the work of a pre-Reformation writer. See McKerrow's note to l. 253 in his edition of the play.

[2] See *The Dialogue Conteyning the Number of the Effectuall Proverbs in the Englishe Tounge*, II. v. 45–6, in *Works and Miscellaneous Short Poems*, ed. B. A. Milligan (Urbana, Ill., 1956), p. 71.

His heroes – Moros in the one play, Worldly Man in the other – are politically as well as personally evil; they oppress their tenants and favour Roman Catholicism. Inspired perhaps by *Respublica*, Wager shows in *Enough* that the effects of Avarice are both comic –

> But so couetouse, Lord! I think if he might chuse:
> The dropping of his nose he would not loose.
> Every week truely, nay then every day:
> He must have account how many Egges his hens lay.

– and, as one of the Vices tells Covetous, a political threat:

> You will not leaue til you have marred him clene.
> Not onely riches singuler and private:
> But also publicke weales you will spoyate [spoliate, despoil].
> For I perceiue by your former monition
> That through ghostly Ignorance you wil destroy deuotion,
> I meane true faith, in Gods loue and hope,
> And cause him in cleer Sun shine, for light to grope.

At the same time, both plays expound the familiar theme of the treachery and capriciousness of this world. Where they differ from pre-Reformation moralities is in the absence of choice in the lives of their heroes. Though *The Longer Thou Livest* looks superficially like an education play, it is significant that neither good nor bad teachers can make any impression on Moros; he mislearns the names of both. As the Prologue says,

> Bringing up is a great thing, so is dilligence,
> But nothing, God except, is so strong of [as?] Nature.

Similarly, in *Enough*, the Worldly Man's servant comments:

> Nay by gisse I thought he would not be heavenly long:
> For that to his nature were clene contrary and wrong.

Both heroes are in fact predestined to damnation from the beginning, and their wickedness is the proof, not the cause, of the fact.

Wager is an anti-intellectual writer. The teaching method of the virtuous characters in *The Longer Thou Livest* consists of trying to make Moros repeat precepts by rote under the threat of whipping if he refuses. Among the names which the Vices assume to hide their true natures are Philosophy (in this play) and Reason (in *Enough*) – because, as Covetous says, 'men nowadays to reason do trust.' It is Impiety, under the name of Philosophy, who offers to teach Moros the same kind of scientific knowledge which Rastell's *Four Elements* had been devoted to promulgating:

> I can teach you Heaven to know,
> Which they call a Sphericall figure,
> More perfight [perfect] than any other hye or lowe,
> Eternall forsoth in his owne nature,
> Also how that the worlde was made ...

The 'impiety' in this passage is, presumably, the speaker's failure to mention a Creator; Mephistophilis, thirty years later, would refuse to tell Faustus who made the world.[1] At first sight it might seem odd that Moros should be the object of a scientific lecture at all. He is such a stupid character that one of the Vices has already objected that there is no point in changing names for his benefit. Wager is, however, using the word 'fool' in two senses at once; his predominant meaning, the biblical one, is being made to cover a number of different targets – Catholicism, atheism, tyranny – for which he sometimes takes folly, in its lighter sense, as the symbol. This is the explanation for two of the most striking visual effects in the play. In the first, Moros is given a sword and flourishes it about; in the second, he is given a big red feather to wear in his hat and is so busy looking up at it that he falls over. Both episodes seem examples of mere stupidity. But in fact the business with the sword illustrates not only the natural quarrelsomeness of fools but also, as is pointed out at the end, a proverb which compares learning in the hands of an evil man to a sword in the hands of a madman. And the episode with the feather is paralleled by the well-known anti-intellectual anecdote about the philosopher who falls into a ditch while gazing up at the stars. Moros is not wicked because he is a fool; he is a fool because he is wicked.

Both Moros and Worldly Man achieve a moment of pathos at their end. Wager emphasizes the inevitability not of their damnation (this would raise all sorts of awkward issues) but of their deaths. Like the heroes of *The Castle of Perseverance* and *Everyman*, they have been cheated by the world; there is even the same emphasis in the role of 'I Wot Never Who':

> Straungers and those whome thou didst never knowe,
> Shall possesse that, which by frawd thou hast got.

---

[1] Impiety's speech may be based on the long scientific discourse of the Medicus, an obvious atheist, in Bullein's *Dialogue Against the Fever Pestilence*, (1564). His speech, at the deathbed of the rich man, is contrasted with the virtuous deathbed of a citizen who holds a dialogue with a theologian.

Worldly Man hears this in a dream from which he awakes, like Shake-speare's Duke of Clarence, full of terror:

> In deed Sir, I dreamed I had a great iourney to walke.
> O what great paines and torments I thought myself in.

The theatrical effectiveness of his death scene has been well analysed else-where.[1] That of Moros is equally poignant. His failure to understand what is happening – he calls for his servants to bring weapons to fend off God's Judgement – is a telling reversal of the usual comic inability to distinguish between spiritual and physical realities. Like Worldly Man, he seems to awake from sleep, but in this case it is his whole life which has been the sleep. The rich garments given him by Fortune are replaced by a fool's coat. For a moment this archetypal bad pupil has a glimpse of what he had failed to learn before: the illusory nature of human happiness:

> I see well that I was a sleepe indeede,
> What am I faine a fooles coate to weare?
> Wee must learne at Christ crosse me speede [i.e. the alphabet].
> Other I was a Gentleman and had servauntes,
> Or els I dreamed that I was a Gentleman.

But nothing can disturb him for long. Departing for hell on the back of the Devil, he shouts his parting words, 'An other while with the Devill I must go to schole'.

It is the proverbial title rather than the plot which gives unity to such revue-like plays as Ulpian Fulwell's *Like Will to Like* (1562–8), Thomas Lupton's *All for Money* (1559–77) and George Wapull's *The Tide Tarrieth No Man* (1576). *The Trial of Treasure* (1567), though not proverbial in its title, uses a similar technique of crystallizing familiar images – wrestling with lust, bridling inclination, watching pleasure and treasure rot away – through short, symbolic stage action which is then moralized, much as in Bunyan's House of the Interpreter. Since these playwrights knew and borrowed from each other's work, it is not surprising that they develop their action through similar processions of symbolic characters and tableau-like effects.

What the plays, like the proverbs, have in common is their emphasis on the deceptive nature of evil. Nichol Newfangle promises to match up the characters of *Like Will to Like* with suitable partners and rewards; all turn out to be disastrous. The characters who give *All for Money* are seeking

---

[1] See T. W. Craik, *The Tudor Interlude* (Leicester, 1958), pp. 106–10.

the fate of Judas and Dives. In *Tide Tarrieth*, where the ambivalently named Courage urges everyone to live up to the play's title, we are aware from the beginning that they are in fact being invited

> To the Barge of sinne:
> Wherein they doe wallow,
> Tyll hell doe them swallow,
> That is all they do win.

The dominance of the deceitful Vice character in these plays has received a good deal of critical attention. In part it is a necessary corollary of the breakdown of the formal allegorical plot in favour of an attack on society as a whole. Where there is no single protagonist, the Vice becomes an all-purpose character, both tempter and moralist, insulting both Virtue and Vice impartially. Catholic Vices speak no better of the Pope than they do of their Protestant enemies. Sin, in *All for Money*, insults his own son, Damnation –

> His face doth shine as bright as the buttocke of a beare.
> He hath a beautiful face in the night when the moone shines not clere

– and his father, the Devil:

> Is not here masters (thinke you) an amiable face?
> Happie may they be which with him shall dwell alwayes,
> But thrice happier then [them?] which godly end their dayes.

There is a slightly less naïve example of moralizing from a Vice in *The Tide Tarrieth No Man*, where Courage breaks off his moralistic advice and resumes his Vice role:

> Tush what meane I thus, of soule for to speake,
> In vayne with such talke, my braynes I doe breake.
> For soule there is none, when the body is dead,
> In such kind of doctrine, my schollers I leade.

Courage's double role is particularly necessary in this play, since no virtuous character appears in it until almost the end. But it also seems a survival of the folk aspect of the Vice, which is amoral rather than evil. The backchat between Devil and Vice is reminiscent of the relationship between the Fool and his Son in the mummers' plays; the frequent dagger fights between the Vice and his underlings may derive from the same source, and in *The Conflict of Conscience* the Vice Hypocrisy gives his confederates such a

convincing impersonation of a Protestant that they nearly behead him –
a situation which, again, has more affinities with folk drama than with
the Book of Martyrs.

The Vice's typical opening speech, an account of an imaginary or
nonsense journey, may have something to do with the patter of the much-
travelled quack doctor in the mummers' play. Covetous, in *Enough is as
Good as a Feast*, provides one of the best examples:

> It hapned between Peterborow and Pentecost,
> About such time as [ivy] was made of Wormwood:
> That Childes woork in Easilwood with fire was lost,
> And all through the treason of false *Robin Hood*.

If these speeches mean anything, they are presumably an expression of the
timelessness of the vice represented by the speaker; Inclination, in *The Trial
of Treasure*, reminds his followers that

> It was I that before you now doth appeare,
> Which brought to confusion both Hector and Alexander.

The recurrence of Robin Hood in Vice speeches is probably another link
with folk drama. Proverbially, tales of Robin Hood were good for fools,
and it is Rastell's Ignorance and Wager's Moros who sing snatches of Robin
Hood songs; Moros also persists, accidentally-on-purpose, in confusing
the outlaw's name with 'Manhood', the alias of one of his Vice-servants.

The hero's journey speech at the beginning of *The Pedlar's Prophecy*
(1561–3), and his appearance at the end in the disguise of a priest, suggest
that he is to be seen as a Vice figure, although he is never called one
and never involved in any allegorical action – nor, indeed, any action at
all. It has been suggested that this strange play is based on government
attempts at curbing would-be prophets at the beginning of Elizabeth's
reign,[1] and some such intention seems to be stated in the prologue; however,
the varied attitudes expressed towards the pedlar by other characters show
that the author, like his hero, is more interested in mystifying than in
enlightening his audience. A particularly curious effect occurs at the end,
when, after the prayer for the queen which marked the formal conclusion
of a play, the pedlar sneaks back to say a few words more – behind the
backs, as it were, not only of the other characters but of his fellow actors.

[1] See G. L. Kittredge, 'The Date of *The Pedlers Prophecie*', *Harvard Studies and Notes
in Philology and Literature*, XVI (1934), pp. 97–118; and cf. Keith Thomas, *Religion and
the Decline of Magic* (London, 1971), pp. 389–415.

The opening speech by the Vice Idleness in *The Marriage of Wit and Wisdom* (1570s?) combines the usual direct address to the spectators with a surprising awareness of dramatic convention: 'As for my properties I am sure you know them of old.' The audience certainly would have known Idleness of old, since this is an exceptionally derivative play. Even the buttonholing 'What, I wen [ween] all this company are come to se a play' can also be found in the short fragment of *Love Feigned and Unfeigned* (*c.* 1540–*c.* 1560). Apart from borrowing the plot of a recently printed school play called *The Marriage of Wit and Science* (1568), the supposed creator of Idleness, Francis Merbury, also drew comic material from plays which he could have seen as a student at Cambridge: *Gammer Gurton's Needle* and *Misogonus*. Like the other plays on the wit-and-science theme, the Merbury piece bears many resemblances to romance and shows, like romance, a tendency to split the Vice's fortunes from those of the hero, thus creating a comic subplot.

The development of the Vice's part beyond its strict function in the plot is probably the result of the increasing expertise of the professional actor which made it possible for the author to rely on him to supplement the dialogue with his own comic business. It may have been sheer desperation or incompetence that prompted the author of *Wealth and Health* to bring on his Vice with the stage direction '*Here entreth with some jest Ill Will*'. But in *The Trial of Treasure* the direction '*Looke in your spectacles*' clearly refers to a piece of business which, being part of the actors' stock routine, was not thought to need explanation. The ability to ad-lib was also being encouraged. The device of the misread proclamation – one character reads out the true wording in alternation with a mischievous dimwit who reduces it to nonsense – goes back to the mystery cycles. Both proclamation and parody are usually written out in full. But in *All for Money* the actor playing the Vice is allowed to use his own ingenuity to '*turne the proclamation to some contrarie sence*'. In *The Longer Thou Livest* Moros is to improvise his own asides during a moral lecture and to read aloud from his book '*as fondely* [i.e. foolishly] *as you can devise*'. The loosening of verse form in the middle of the century made it possible for a skilled performer to improvise in rhyme as well as prose. Nor was it only the Vice who was expected to deliver virtuoso speeches. When a company consisted of only five or six actors, there was no room for anyone who could not pull his weight.

The problem for the writer of moral allegorical drama is indicated by the remarks of one of the characters in *The Pedlar's Prophecy*:

I love none of these lying Poets indeed,
I marvell what favour to them, men can have;
For they do nothing els, but mens minds with vanities feed,
And hinder our faith, which should our soules save.

Poets 'hinder our faith', the speaker seems to say, because they feed the
mind instead of forcing it to believe by faith alone. Doubting Thomas
ought not to be pampered. The distinction between sermon and exemplum,
abstract and concrete, was also becoming a distinction between the words
on the page and the physical reality which the actor was expected to give
them. Few writers convey any sense of their characters except as the
speakers of words or, occasionally, participants in emblematic action. A
sense of physical reality is, however, sometimes found in the portrayal
of women. Thomas Garter's *The Most Virtuous and Godly Susanna* (1563–
1569) has a stage direction specifying that, while the heroine is talking
to her husband, the wicked elders are not to take their eyes off her. Lewis
Wager, in *The Life and Repentance of Mary Magdalene* (1550–66), gave
Mary an unusually long entrance during which the Vices have eight lines
of comment on her appearance and the audience is encouraged to share
their appreciation of the actor's performance:

I pray you behold how she trimmeth her geare!
She would have all well about her every where.

Since Wager's subject is justification by faith alone, his allegory is carefully worked out in terms of the contrast between Infidelity the Vice –
always talking to Mary of her appearance, her behaviour and her lovers
– and the abstractions of Faith and Love. When Infidelity tries to deflect
her from repentance, he does so by denying her spiritual nature ('Women
have no soules, – this saying is not newe') or showing its insubstantiality
beside the 'facts' of her life as a courtesan:

Prick of conscience, quod she? It pricketh you not so sore
As the yong man with the flaxen beard dyd, I thinke.

The detail about the flaxen beard shows the extent to which Wager was
able to enter imaginatively into the atmosphere of his play. Yet, though
he indicated the stages of Mary's sin and repentance with remarkable
clarity, he could not trust his audience to grasp the moral lesson from
action alone. The end of the play is given over to undiluted didacticism.
Mary asks Justification and Love to explain the meaning of her story,

which they do at great length, finally summing up with the conventional appeal to the previous action as proof:

> by Faith onely Marie was justified,
> Like as before it is playnly verified ...

Without more faith in its audience, the moral interlude could progress no further than this.

3 Rival traditions

(i) Romance

We have seen that many characteristics of the Tudor interlude were the necessary consequence of its brevity and the smallness of its cast. The advantage of the form was that it bred a generation of skilled and versatile professional actors; the disadvantage was that dramatists tended to rely on this very skill and versatility to do their job for them, with the result that the most interesting features of many plays are the stage directions. But some limitations were also inherent in their didactic purpose. The shape of the moral allegory was always that of the human life, or of the space between sin and repentance, which could be filled with as many incidents as the dramatist had room for. If virtue was always to be rewarded, the only suspense could arise from wondering whether a character would persevere in virtue; yet the Protestant emphasis on predestination largely removed this uncertainty from the drama. The only characters who suffered were those who deserved to suffer. Even when a story told of persecuted virtue – as in Garter's *Susanna* – opportunities for pathos and suspense were deliberately ignored. Susanna and her faithful servants are always certain that God will preserve her. Though Garter went out of his way to depict the affectionate relationship between Susanna and her husband, he did not show what effect was produced on Joachim by the false report about his wife and the danger she was in. It is possible that this was simply incompetent dramaturgy, but Garter's shaping of his material is perfectly consistent with two of the most important Protestant themes: the need for faith and the justification of the righteous on earth.

But there is evidence that the most popular plays of the period were characterized, on the contrary, by the long suffering inflicted on sympathetic characters and the many changes of fortune which preceded their final deserved reward. Perhaps because of their very popularity, few dramatic romances have survived from the early Tudor period. Some fascinating titles have been preserved, however – *Cloridon and Radiamanta*, *The Solitary Knight*, *The Knight in the Burning Rock* – and it is clear that, for intellectual critics like Sidney, such works typified the popular theatre.[1] There are also records of plays with what sound like romance titles nearly as far back as *The Castle of Perseverance*, which, we have seen, may itself be based on a romance theme. Saints' plays, like the Digby *Mary Magdalene*, were romantic not only in their settings but also in their scope, in terms of both time and place. Just as Mary Magdalene never grows old, despite her thirty years alone in the wilderness, so the heroes and heroines of romance struggle through enough adventures for a lifetime without ever ceasing to be young lovers. It is quite likely that some of the ridicule which this handling of time and place inspired in Sidney and others was the result of transferring romantic plays from the place-and-scaffold setting to which they would have been best suited. The spectators of *Mary Magdalene* could have watched the actors as they moved from one setting to another; now, as Sidney complained, each actor, on entering, had to explain where he was.

Bevington has pointed out that the romance pattern of 'separation, wandering and reunion' parallels the morality pattern of 'fall from grace, temporary prosperity of evil, and divine reconciliation'.[2] The traditional allegorical images of human life, as given in the anonymous fourteenth-century *Prick of Conscience*, are also the settings of romance: the sea, the wilderness full of wild beasts, the forest full of robbers, and the field of

---

[1] See C. R. Baskervill, 'Some Evidence for Early Romantic Plays in England', *MP* (1916–1917), pp. 229–51, 467–512, and the chapter on 'Medieval Stage Romances' in L. G. Salingar, *Shakespeare and the Traditions of Comedy* (Cambridge, 1974).

[2] *From Mankind to Marlowe: Growth of Structure in the Popular Drama of Tudor England* (Cambridge, Mass., 1962), p. 190.

battle.[1] Where romance differed from morality was in its purpose, which was frankly to play on the audience's feelings by offering as much suspense and surprise as possible. The two surviving plays generally thought to belong to the period before 1576 – *Common Conditions* (1576) and *Sir Clyomon and Sir Clamydes* (1570–83) – are so completely dedicated to this task as to be open to both aesthetic and moral objections. Far from displaying an edifying if unexciting faith throughout their trials, characters frequently succumb to despair. Lamphedon in *Common Conditions* and Neronis in *Sir Clyomon and Sir Clamydes* both come close to committing suicide (*twice*, in Lamphedon's case). The turn of events which saves them is completely arbitrary: in one scene an opportune entrance; in another, the actual descent of Providence. To some extent the plays justify such occurrences by their constant emphasis on the role of fortune, and by the large part played by the Vice as an agent of fortune, engaged in pointless malice and equally pointless good turns. In the background, moreover, is the ever-changing sea, constantly present in the imagery as in the action, which separates the characters and unites them again. The title character in *Common Conditions* (apparently played by either a child or a dwarf) actually describes himself as a kinsman of Fortune's; he himself does not understand why he feels impelled to cause so much trouble, and, though he talks like an intriguer in the morality tradition, seems actually no less a tool of fortune than anyone else.

Characters who are constantly the fools of fortune, however, tend after a while to seem simply fools. The initial separation of Sedmond from his sister Clarisia in *Common Conditions* is effected when they are attacked by robbers in a forest; he runs away, leaving her to face them alone. This unheroic behaviour can perhaps be justified as a plot necessity. But in *Sir Clyomon and Sir Clamydes* the heroes vie with each other not only in heroism but also in absurdity. Clyomon's first action is to take as his servant the obviously clownish and unreliable Subtle Shift, because 'endued with noble qualities, thy personage I see'; his next, which he considers a truly heroic exploit, is to get himself dubbed knight in place of the prince Clamydes, by dodging in front of him at the crucial point of the ceremony. The resulting rivalry between the two men takes up much of the play. Characteristically, neither of them turns up in time for their trial by combat; in Sir Clyomon's case, this is because he has become seasick on the way and had to be put ashore. They do meet, however, to fight in another cause. But by the time both challenger and champion are ready, the

[1] Quoted in Willard Farnham, op. cit. p. 108.

disputants have already settled their quarrel by arbitration. The feats of the title characters are parodied – as if they needed to be – by the antics of Sir Brian Sans Foy and Subtle Shift, each of whom is happy to confess himself 'Even the cowardlyest villaine ant shall please you that lives under the sun'. One can see why an early critic of this play argued that it was never meant to be taken seriously at all.[1]

Yet the female characters are treated with a great deal more sympathy, especially Neronis, daughter of the King of the Isle of the Strange Marshes. It is she who makes the first advances to her lover (by means of an extended simile); she also follows him in disguise and manages her reunion with him at the end in a teasing style that brings both of them, briefly, to life. Since plays of this type were frequently selected for performance at court, Queen Elizabeth's well-known antipathy to stories ending in marriage must not have extended to romances. Shadwell, a hundred years later, was to comment on the tendency of Restoration ladies to prefer heroic plays to comedies. He thought that they enjoyed the feeling of power which such plays gave them:

> poor frail woman's made a deity
> With senseless, amorous idolatry,
> And sniveling heroes sigh, and pine, and cry.[2]

Elizabeth may have shared these sentiments. The morality play was usually misogynistic; romance, by going to the other extreme, helped to clear the way for writers who could take a more humane and balanced view of relations between the sexes.

(ii) School plays

It is always necessary to bear in mind that the distinction between amateur and professional, in the sixteenth century, was not a qualitative one. If anything, it was the amateur production, often given on one special occasion only, that was likely to have more time and money lavished on it. The Passion play (1561) which Thomas Ashton produced with his pupils

---

[1] See E. Kellner, 'Sir Clyomon and Sir Clamydes, ein romantisches Schauspiel des 16. Jahrhunderts', Englische Studien, XIII (1889), pp. 187–229. Kellner thought the play later in date, attributed it to Peele, and took it to be a parody of The Faerie Queene, but the plot in fact comes from a French prose romance (see F. P. Wilson, op. cit. p. 123).
[2] Epilogue to The Virtuoso (1676).

at a quarry near his school in Shrewsbury was so much talked of that Elizabeth I twice tried unsuccessfully to make the journey to see it. *Jacob and Esau* (1550–7), another school play, is simple in setting but calls for 'Hebrew' costumes, hunting dogs and probably a live goat (its bleating is commented on). Students at the wealthy new colleges of Oxford and Cambridge had still more resources at their disposal. There were barking dogs again for Edwards's *Palamon and Arcite* (Oxford, 1566), also a tournament, a garden where the heroine gathered flowers, and a monster that appeared from under the stage. For Elizabeth's visit to Cambridge two years before, the authorities had turned King's College Chapel into a theatre; they used the side-chapels as 'Houses', creating what must have been an amazing flamboyant-classical setting for Plautus' *Aulularia*.[1] Oxbridge graduates, when they became schoolmasters themselves, were not likely to be modest in their theatrical ventures.

So it is not surprising that so many distinguished authors should have chosen to write for children. Like the private theatre dramatists of the early seventeenth century, they were probably attracted both by opportunities for visual and musical splendour and by the high quality of speaking that resulted from school emphasis on declamation. Moreover, they could be sure that their lines would be spoken accurately: children do not ad-lib. The schoolmasters and choirmasters who supervised the rehearsals may not all have been believers in corporal punishment, but they were undoubtedly able to impose more discipline on their actors than would have been possible in a professional company. The songs, for example, were not simply left to the actors to choose and rehearse; they were set pieces, carefully integrated into the action. Abra in *Jacob and Esau* sings while sweeping the floor; the maidservants in *Ralph Roister Doister* have to sew, spin and knit during their song; both the mock funeral service in *Roister Doister* and the shaving scene in *Damon and Pithias* depend for their effect on careful synchronization of speech, song and movement. The same sense of timing was demanded in the dialogue. The boy Mido comments in *Jacob and Esau*, after an exchange of stichomythia between Isaac and Rebecca,

Ye coulde not speake any thing unto hir so thicke,
But she had hir answere as ready and as quicke.

Was this what Rosencrantz meant when he told Hamlet of the child actors

[1] See F. S. Boas, *University Drama in the Tudor Age* (Oxford, 1914), *passim*.

'that cry out on the top of question and are most tyrannically clapp'd for't'? Certainly, the stage directions often suggest the importance of accurate timing. The author of *Jacob and Esau* specified: 'Here they knele doune to sing all foure, saving that Abra is slackest and Mido is quickest.' *Respublica* is full of stylized dialogue and business. The direction 'they goo foorthwarde one after other', followed by Avarice's whistle calling the three other Vices back, gives some idea of the almost balletic effect demanded.

Another pleasure offered by the children's plays may have been that of escape. It is evident, both from Hall's *Chronicle* and from the titles of some lost plays performed by children's companies at court, that writers then as later were not above using young actors to make comments on topical issues. But most of the plays that have survived – even *Respublica* – go out of their way to stress their harmlessness. The prologue to *Jack Juggler* warns the audience not to expect anything serious:

> For this maker told us that such maner things
> Doo never well besime little boyes handelings.

Most authors seem to have written with some awareness of what *did* become little boys. Parody, for instance, plays an important part in the school drama. *Thersites* (1537), which is based on a Latin school dialogue by Ravisius Textor and is thought to have been acted by young scholars or choirboys at Oxford,[1] would have been funny in the first place because of the small size of its hero. Moreover, schoolboys who had been wrestling with stories about the great classical heroes would certainly have enjoyed the way in which the play cuts them down to the size of the actors playing them. Thersites brags, on receiving a letter from Ulysses,

> Lo frendes ye maye see
> What great men wryte to mee.

But the letter turns out to be a request that Thersites' mother should use one of her charms on Ulysses' son Telemachus, who is suffering from worms. This scene is an addition of the translator, as is the Punch and Judy scene between mother and son which follows:

> MATER. Charme that charme wyll, he shal not be charmed of me.
> THERSITES. Charme or by the masse with my club I wil charme the.

Another feature of the children's plays is illustrated by the jingle which

[1] Boas, op. cit. p. 20.

the panic-stricken mother recites, presumably while being chased round
the stage by her son:

> He will kyll me
> He wyll spyll me
> He wyll brose me
> He wyll lose me
> He wyll pricke me
> He wyll stycke me ...

Jacob and Esau and *Wit and Science* are full of similar passages which
have something of the incantatory effect of children's singing games. Unlike
Magnificence, the most metrically inventive adult play of the period, the
school comedies seem to vary their rhyme schemes less for reasons of
decorum than out of a love of variety for its own sake.

Wit and Science is generally thought to be the work of one of the most
distinguished early Tudor composers, the organist and music teacher John
Redford, who died in 1547. It shows absolutely no sign of the troubled
period during which it was written. The world is present only as a distant
temptation. In a pretty little scene, Lady Science receives its emissaries
– four musicians called Fame, Favour, Riches and Worship, who play and
sing for her. But she sends them back to their master, and they recognize
that her lack of interest in them means that 'she careth not for the world'.
The hero, Wit, is less disinterested. When he thinks that his folly has
lost him the love of Science (Knowledge), he laments partly on her account
and partly because of the worldly gifts which he thinks he would have
won with her. The tension between intellectual idealism and the desire
to get on in material terms is only faintly sketched here; in later plays
it was to make the scholar the closest equivalent to the medieval Everyman
figure, torn between the claims of this world and the next.

Though *Wit and Science* has survived only in manuscript, its plot was
well enough known to be borrowed by at least two later dramatists: the
anonymous author of *The Marriage of Wit and Science* (1568) and the
Cambridge theology student, Francis Merbury, whose *Marriage of Wit
and Wisdom*, performed by a small adult company, has already been
mentioned. There may also have been a *Marriage of Mind and Measure*
(now lost). Critics have often preferred the Redford play to its successors
because of its skilful use of allegory. Whereas *The Marriage of Wit and
Science* contains a good deal of abstract discussion about the nature of
Wit, Will, Nature, and so on, *Wit and Science* embodies its theorizing

in its action. Both plays, however, share an essentially romantic plot, one which has many similarities to *Sir Clyomon and Sir Clamydes*.[1] Wit's wooing of Lady Science, who commands him to kill the giant Tediousness for her sake, and his unwitting exchange of clothes with Ignorance, can be compared with the episodes in the later play involving Sir Clyomon, Juliana and Sir Brian Sans Foy. However, the general nature of the story is more important than any particular analogy. Its suitability for child actors is obvious, though there would have been an element of parody in the spectacle of small boys waving their swords about and promising undying love. Indeed, Wit (in *The Marriage of Wit and Science*), though described as seventeen years old, says that he is not yet able to show a lady 'sport in bed' – a confession which may throw interesting light on the upper age limit for boy actors of women's parts in the later drama.

Every aspect of the 'Wit' plays suggests that the author thoroughly understood his actors. The allegorical message was a relevant and interesting one, with its reminder of the difficulty of distinguishing between Ignorance and Wit that has spent too long in the lap of Idleness. Reason, especially in Redford's play, is portrayed as a typical schoolmaster, slightly crotchety but likeable, who pretends to be angrier with Wit than he really is. When Wit, having made every possible mistake on the earlier part of his quest, bursts out penitently,

> Oh syr I am not woorthy to carye
> The dust out where your dowghter shoold syt,

Reason snaps, 'I wot well that', but makes the boy promise to reform, defers his threatened whipping, and hands him over with the sigh of the long-suffering teacher: 'Take him instruccion do what ye can'. In *The Marriage of Wit and Science* much of the fun comes from the relationship between the boys themselves: the young hero Wit and his still younger page Will. The difference in their heights and ages is one which Wit is always trying to remember and Will to forget:

> WIT. O my sweat [sweet] boy, how shall I recompence,
>   Thy faythfull hart and painfull diligence,
>   My hope, my stay, my wealth, the kaye [key] of all my joye.
> WILL. I praye you sir call me your man, and not your boye.

[1] *Perceforest*, the source of *Sir Clyomon*, was published in 1530. See Werner Habicht, 'The Wit Interludes and the Form of Pre-Shakespearean "Romantic Comedy"', *Renaissance Drama*, ed. S. Schoenbaum, VIII (1965).

The episodes involving Ignorance and Tediousness ('Ho ho') seem calculated to involve even the youngest actors; all the boys take part in the final combat, and little Will proves his value by tripping the giant from behind. Academic allegory remained popular well into the seventeenth century, but not in so zestful and boyish a form.

(iii) Foreign influences

Moralistic interpretations of Terence had been current since the Middle Ages, when his plays were often used as school texts. The influence of Plautus came later, after manuscripts of twelve of his plays had been discovered in fifteenth-century Italy. In the sixteenth century, he seems to have overtaken Terence in popularity, to judge from the number of performances that have been recorded of each dramatist.[1] English adaptations of both writers naturally reflected the moralistic approach which had been applied to them in the classroom. With their actors' special needs in view, the schoolmaster dramatists expanded the number of roles suitable for boys, especially those of women and children; *Jack Juggler*, indeed, has only one adult male character. Not all the Roman comic types could be used. Only one dramatist – the author of *July and Julian* (*c.* 1570) – attempted to retain, in an English setting, the essentially Roman type of household in which slaves could be sold at their owners' will.[2] But it must have struck the brighter child actors as ironic that the closest equivalent in sixteenth-century comedy to the Roman slave – constantly in danger of being tied up, beaten or sent to forced labour, dependent only on his wits for survival – should so often turn out to be the English schoolboy. The schoolboy also took over some of the characteristics of another 'un-English' comic type, the parasite. In *Jacob and Esau*, Ragau's relationship with his master Esau is more precarious than a parasite's but involves more flattery than a slave's, and the scene in which he is shut out of the tent while Esau is eating is reminiscent of what happens to the parasite in the *Menaechmi*. The play's constant stress on food and hunger is of course

[1] See Richard Hosley, 'The Formal Influence of Plautus and Terence', in J. R. Brown and B. Harris (eds), *Elizabethan Theatre*, Stratford-upon-Avon Studies (London, 1966), pp. 130–45.

[2] This recently discovered play also includes a song by Redford and an episode borrowed from the *Decameron* (Day seven, Story seven).

primarily intended to motivate the episode in which Esau sells his birthright for a mess of pottage, but it probably owes something both to the obsession with the subject in classical drama and to observation of schoolboy appetites. Sometimes the cook of Roman comedy is combined with the parasite; thus, in *Liberality and Prodigality*, Dandaline the hostess echoes a line spoken by the parasite in *The Supposes*, a play which derives, *via* its Italian original, from the Romans. Other female type-characters tend to be handled with great caution. While adult performers might represent Lechery or Mary Magdalene, schoolboys were not encouraged to imitate the manners of the classical courtesan. The heroine of *Ralph Roister Doister* could not have been allowed to act with the independence of her prototype in Terence, the courtesan Thais, if Udall had not made her a widow, free from parental authority.

The prologue to *Roister Doister* makes the usual pedagogical claim that Plautus and Terence 'under merrie Comedies secretes did declare' about 'very vertuous lore'. While the attempt to find moral messages in these stories of lies and cheating is often patently ridiculous, Roman comedies do have certain features in common with the morality. They sometimes use allegorical characters in the prologue – like Luxuria and his daughter Inopia in Plautus' *Trinummus* – and they contain some sententious, 'exemplary' speeches. Above all, their plots rely on an intriguer who, like the Vice, uses mistaken identity as a means to his ends and who implicates the audience in his schemes. Plautus goes beyond any of his successors in the sheer impudence of *Pseudolus*, where the slave refuses to explain the plot to his master because the audience has heard it already. And the typical comedy ending, where the audience is either invited to a feast within or told not to wait because the characters will be celebrating for some time, can be paralleled with the endings of *Godly Queen Hester* and *Nice Wanton*, where one of the actors, speaking in character, promises to join the others as soon as he has said a few words to the audience.

The greatest difference between the Roman comedy and the morality play lies not precisely in the five-act structure, whose origin in Terentian editions has been exhaustively traced by T. W. Baldwin, but in a development which is implied in that structure: the arrangement of dramatic events according to a principle of suspense and anticipation. Roman comedy shares with the morality its emphasis on intrigue, with the romance its use of suspense and uncertainty. Whereas the deception of the morality hero by the Vice (or by the world, or by fortune) is limited only by the length of his life or by the equally arbitrary moment of his conversion, that practised by the classical trickster involves a race against time: he must keep the slave girl from being sold that day, or finish his plots before the return of an absent master, or present his apparently irrefutable lie with such rapidity as to baffle the most suspicious listener. Another difference between morality and Roman comedy is that in the former our sympathies are with the victim, whereas in the latter they are with the trickster. We have already seen that in both *The Three Estates* and *Respublica* the Vices are aware that time is a threat to them. Part 1 of *The Three Estates* (the later of the two, probably, to be written) has the makings of a classical intrigue situation in the awareness of Flattery and his fellow Vices that they must do as much damage as possible before the king grows older and Divine Correction arrives. The plot is further complicated by the temporary defeat – when Chastity and Verity are put in the stocks – of forces which would otherwise have brought about a reformation earlier. However, this is only one of many incidents in Lindsay's complex play. In Part 2, the Poor Man and John o' the Commonweal are able to make their grievances heard almost immediately and there is no further suspense about the punishment of the criminals.

But in *Respublica* the same elements are combined in a plot with definite affinities to classical comedy. Avarice and his three followers are aware of the danger to them from Time and his daughter Truth, and they are further threatened by People, who begins to suspect them as early as Act III. On his first appearance, this naïve character is talked round by Adulation and by the well-meaning Respublica herself, but in Act IV he expresses himself more vehemently and the Vices have to drive him offstage with threats. When Avarice hears of the arrival of the Four Daughters of God, he tries to prevent them from meeting each other and, in particular, to keep Verity from meeting Respublica. The famous biblical lines about the meeting of Mercy and Truth and the kissing of Peace and Justice thus become a devastating revelation of his failure. The ending, with the gathering of the entire cast and awarding of rewards and punishment, recalls both the Doomsday play of the mystery cycles and the classical comedy dénouement. It is, of course, an effect that would be impossible for the small companies that performed the interludes.

The effect of this fusion of comedy and morality intrigues is to make the Vices of *Respublica* seem more precariously successful, and hence more sympathetic, than those of other moralities. Adulation and Avarice, at any rate, are comic rather than sinister. Adulation is primarily a comic simpleton but he is also something of a classical parasite (Avarice compares him to

Terence's Gnatho) and shares one piece of stage business – picking dust off the garments of the person he is flattering – with Matthew Merrygreek in *Ralph Roister Doister*.[1] Though Insolence and Oppression are more unpleasant characters, there is a touch of the smugness of the *miles gloriosus* in the complacent way Insolence accepts Adulation's flattery. As for Avarice, he establishes himself as one of the most distinctive comedy creations of the period, from the moment he breaks off his first soliloquy to rush home and make sure he has not been robbed in his absence. He is the victim as well as the embodiment of the vice he represents: in other words, a classical miser like the hero of the *Aulularia*. Along with the nervous absentmindedness which results from his constant unease about his wealth, he has a waspish sense of intellectual superiority ('What is your brainpan stufte withall? wull [wool] or sawe dust?') which perhaps suggests the schoolmaster. One of his most cutting bits of repartee, however, comes direct from the *Pseudolus*:

ADULATION. For wotte ye what?
AVARICE.   I shall whan ye have spake the
    woorde.[2]

(V. v)

He has an answer for everything. When Respublica, who has at last found out his identity, calls him 'mooste stinking Avarice', he pretends to be shocked at her language:

        well in gods name
I am sorie for yowe, een sorie, that I am. (V. vi)

His attempts to persuade the Four Daughters of God that his bag of ill-gotten gold is really a bag of rye result in something otherwise unheard of in a morality play: a virtuous character makes a joke.

VERITEE. Thou saiest even trueth: tis a bagg of Rye in dede,
    Usiree, perjuree, pitcheree, patcherie,
    Pilferie, briberee, snatcherie, catcherie ...

To all of which Avarice replies pathetically, 'The worlde is harde and the bag is but veraie smale' (V. ix).

    Except for the traditional uncasing of the disguised Vices at the end,

---

[1] See F. P. Wilson, op. cit. p. 106; also G. Scheurweghs's introduction to his edition of *Roister Doister* (Louvain, 1939; repr. 1963), pp. lxxii–lxxiii.
[2] The same repartee also occurs in Jeffere's *The Bugbears* (V. ix).

the action of *Respublica* is stylized rather than symbolic. It is easy to picture the rapid to-ing and fro-ing of Avarice as he keeps pretending to leave but darting back in case Respublica has changed her mind:

> AVARICE. Well than I see ye will none of mee.
> RESPUBLICA. No.
> AVARICE.   Than ye can be content I departe from yee.
> RESPUB. Yea.
> AVAR.   Well, yet and ye praie me I will tarrye still.
> RESPUB. No.
> AVAR.   Well, speake me faire and woo me yet and I will.
> RESPUB. No hens [hence], avaunt. (V. vi)

Other stylized devices may be noticed: the character who soliloquizes aloud while others try vainly to interrupt him (I. iii); the two parallel soliloquies by speakers unaware of each other's presence (II. ii); the scene (II. iii) where the Vices, under their borrowed names, have to stand poker-faced while Respublica urges them to destroy none other than Avarice, Oppression, Insolence and Adulation; and the re-entry of a character (People) just as the others are congratulating themselves on having got rid of him (IV. iv). Even the conventional Vices' habit of ending a scene with a song is transformed into a running gag. It is always Adulation who proposes a song, much to Avarice's disgust; at the end, when retribution is obviously at hand for all of them, it is Avarice who sarcastically urges Adulation to sing them a song *now*.

The other classical comedies of the mid-sixteenth century share the moral concerns of *Respublica*, if not its morality format. Udall's prologue to *Ralph Roister Doister*, as we have already seen, has the slightly defensive tone of a man determined to live down a disreputable past (which included heavy debts and the loss of the headship of Eton in 1541 on charges of theft and, perhaps, homosexual relations with one of the scholars).[1] 'Mirth', this excellent scholar assured his audience, is good for man, provided that it is 'mixed with vertue in decent comlynesse'. He claimed that in Roister Doister he was exposing a harmful social type, and another moral is incidentally drawn by Custance herself: comparing her situation to Susanna's, she notes the dangers which a braggart can offer to even the most discreet woman. However, the dangers are only temporary and trivial:

[1] See G. Scheurweghs's account in the introduction to his edition of *Roister Doister*, and, for a more recent defence of Udall (which argues that 'buggery' was a mistake for 'burglary'), W. L. Edgerton, *Nicholas Udall*, Twayne's English Authors (New York, 1965).

Custance's betrothed, Gavin Goodluck, is too sensible to suspect her long and Ralph is too ridiculous to be a real threat to anyone.

The mixture of mirth and virtue is particularly evident in Udall's contrast between the insatiable and ridiculous love of Ralph and the sober, sensible, but hardly romantic relationship of Gavin and Custance. Custance is as anxious for Gavin's approval as her maids are for hers; in this respect the play recalls its schoolroom origin. Other classical allusions are probably brought in as much for the pleasure of recognition as for any edification they might have to offer. In keeping with the Roman comedians' habit of parodying a tragic style, Udall makes Ralph address the delinquent scrivener in language which is probably meant to recall Seneca's tragedies, with their sense of unforgivable evil:

> All the stocke thou comest of later or rather,
> From thy fyrst fathers grandfathers fathers father,
> Nor all that shall come of thee to the worldes ende,
> Though to three score generations they descende,
> Can be able to make me a iust recompense,
> For this trespasse of thine and this one offense. (III. v)

A more obvious and more witty allusion is this exchange:

> MADGE MUMBLECRUST. I would take a gay riche husbande, and I were you.
> CHRISTIAN CUSTANCE. In good sooth Madge, een so would I, if I were thou. (I. v)

Udall had already translated a similar dialogue between Alexander the Great and Parmenio, quoted in the *Apophthegmata* of Erasmus.

As the limiting framework in *Respublica* is the absence of Truth, that of *Roister Doister* is the absence of Gavin Goodluck, which makes possible Ralph's self-deluded courtship. The spectacular comic climax of the play, the fight with kitchen implements between the men and the women, has the triple function of allowing Custance and her maids to revenge themselves for the trouble they have been caused, of punishing Ralph for his presumption, and of clearing up the suspicions which Ralph's behaviour has implanted in Gavin's mind. Udall had, in the two *miles gloriosus* plays which were his sources, a choice of endings, one much more moralistic than the other. In Plautus' *Miles Gloriosus*, the braggart is well beaten, learns of the deception that has been practised on him, and moralizes that all lechers deserve to be treated thus. Despite the obvious suitability of this ending for an exemplary comedy, Udall preferred to follow Terence's *Eunuchus*, in which Thraso is humoured and allowed to remain self-deceived – although, for the *ménage à trois* of the Latin play, he substituted an invitation to Ralph to join the feast within. Another neat touch is the reminder that some characters are still in the dark about the situation. Dobinet Doughty, Ralph's servant, who has last seen Custance and his master opposed in battle, is naturally astonished when he and his fellows are called on to 'Sing on sirs, for my frends sake'. 'Cal ye these your frends?' he gasps – but the explanation is deferred until after the play is over.

A more obvious example of the moralizing of a Latin comedy occurs in *Jack Juggler* (1553–8), which opens with the rascally Jack invoking a blessing on the audience in the names of God, St John, Christ and St Stephen. This kind of language does not necessarily stamp either character or author as Roman Catholic. In 1534 – at a time when he was certainly a Protestant – Udall recommended that the phrase 'dii deaeque' should be translated as 'God and all the saints of heaven'.[1] The epilogue to the play has sometimes been thought to be from another hand than that of the play itself, because it claims to find in the story a moral about how poor innocents can be made to believe anything (including, perhaps, the doctrine of transubstantiation) by sophistical arguments or brute force. It is possible, however, that this moral – leaving transubstantiation out of the question – might legitimately have been inferred by a Christian reader of *Amphitruo* and of other Plautine comedies where (as in *Miles Gloriosus* or, for that matter, as in *Respublica*) an honest servant is deceived and intimidated into denying the evidence of his own eyes. *Jack Juggler* can be seen as a parody of the *Amphitryon* when the heroic battle narration which Sosia rehearses is reduced to Jenkin Careaway's account of his day's activities. But it also introduces an element of poetic justice which was lacking in the original, since, whereas Sosia's narrative was true, Jenkin's is a lie. Though Jack Juggler himself is as heartless a deceiver as his prototype Mercury, and his protestations that he wants only to make sport for the audience link him with the morality Vice, he is also an agent of retribution. The story therefore, as is appropriate in an 'Enterlude for Chyldren to Playe', becomes a salutary lesson for bad boys like Jenkin who steal apples and play at dice when they ought to be running their master's errands. This was how the adapter coped with the contrasting Roman and Christian attitudes to deception.

---

[1] *Flowers for Latin Speaking* (1534), sigs 52–52v.

(iv) Prodigal son plays

A similar reversal of emphasis can be found in sixteenth-century treatments of the parent–child relationship in what is sometimes called the 'Christian Terence' tradition. Terence's comedies often deal with a conflict between father and son over the son's desire to marry, or simply to keep, an apparently unsuitable woman, and they usually end with reconciliation between the generations. They could thus be fairly easily assimilated to the prodigal son story, with the woman forming part of the rather vague 'riotous living' in which the hero is said to have indulged. But, as Ervin Beck has pointed out, there is a significant difference between Roman and Renaissance attitudes to the parent–child conflict. Whereas in Terence the comedy ends with the victory of the younger generation, the view of Renaissance writers is that the young man ought to repent and accept the values of his father's society.[1] Neither type of play comes very close to the actual meaning of the prodigal son parable, as exemplified in pre-Reformation drama: that forgiveness was always available, however unworthy the sinner might think himself to be.[2]

Naturally, the role of the prodigal's elder brother, which was meant as a reproof to the self-righteous, was one with which few Renaissance playwrights could come to terms; the best-known Latin prodigal play, *Acolastus*, omits the character altogether. Other writers treat the theme of the contrast between two brothers as evidence for predestination, without seeming to realize that this makes nonsense of the 'spare the rod' message. In *Nice Wanton* (1547–53) the virtuous son reproaches his mother for the excessive leniency which he thinks is responsible for the miserable fates of his wicked brother and sister. Then he adds,

> In that God preserved me, small thanke to you!
>   If God had not geven me speciall grace
> To avoyd evil and do good, – this is true –
>   I had lived and dyed in as wretched case
>   As they did, for I had both sufferaunce and space;
> But it is an olde proverbe, – you have herd it, I think, –
> That God wyl have se, shall not wynke.

[1] Terence Improved: The Paradigm of the Prodigal Son in English Renaissance Comedy', *Renaissance Drama*, N.S., VI (1973), pp. 107–22.

[2] From the twelfth century on, the parable had been interpreted as a story of the fall and redemption of man; previously, the elder brother and the Prodigal had been equated with the Jews and the Gentiles. See E. T. Schell and J. D. Schuchter (eds), *English Morality Plays and Moral Interludes* (New York etc., 1969), note to Introduction, p. xx.

Jacob and Esau quotes the same proverb as *Nice Wanton*, 'Early sharp that will be thorn' (that is, the child is father of the man). But the story of Jacob and Esau had been a classic argument for predestination since the time of St Paul, and the author who adapted it for the stage paraphrased Romans 9: 11–13 in his prologue:

> But before Jacob and Esau yet borne were,
> Or had eyther done good, or yll perpetrate:
> As the prophet Malachie and Paule witnesse beare,
> Jacob was chosen, and Esau reprobate.

We are also told that both Isaac and Rebecca have set good examples to their children but

> Esau hath ben nought ever since he was borne.
> And wherof commeth this, of Education?
> Nay it is of his owne yll inclination.

Nevertheless, the author of this play was determined to make the story acceptable in human terms. He stresses Esau's unworthiness to an extent for which there is no scriptural justification. Everyone loves Jacob and is delighted to see him usurp his brother's blessing and inheritance. Though the scheming of Jacob and his mother Rebecca – depending as it does on impersonation and mistaken identity – might seem to ally them with the intriguers of Roman comedy, the author does his best to represent them as mere instruments of Providence. The ostensible moral is the Protestant one that man's salvation is in the hands of God alone, but it also emphasizes the corollary: that the man who has received grace will prove it by doing gracious works. This belief is dramatized most effectively, not in the smug Jacob, but in the children, Mido and Abra, whose eagerness to please is positively comic. They can be compared with the good slaves of Roman comedy, who have an equally strong sense of their own exemplary nature.

Perhaps one ought to speak of a separate genre of 'elder brother' plays about good children, though in fact most of them are girls: the heroines of *Patient and Meek Grissil*, *Apius and Virginia* and *Virtuous and Godly Susanna* are all impeccably brought up and dutiful. The most obvious biblical example of a virtuous son to set against all these well-behaved daughters is to be found in the story of Abraham and Isaac. It has been suggested that the pathos of the episode in the mystery cycles may have inspired the authors of *Cambises* and *Apius and Virginia*, in both of which innocent children die in the presence of their parents.[1] The only surviving sixteenth-century play on the Abraham and Isaac story is Arthur Golding's translation in 1575 of the *Abraham sacrifiant* by the Calvinist theologian Théodore de Bèzé. In this version, the pathos of the situation moves Satan himself, 'Of God and nature enmie [enemy] though I bee', and what makes him depart, in shame, is the discovery that both father and son are prepared to do God's will. This, not the saving of Isaac's life, is the true happy ending of the play, because its theme, like that of *Jacob and Esau*, is the need for faith in God's providence.

Prodigal drama easily became school drama, with the schoolmaster replacing the father as symbol of authority. Italian dramatists often transformed the wild young men of Roman comedy into rebellious students and their dupes into elderly pedants. Though Gascoigne's *The Supposes* (1566) brought the figure of the student who plays truant for love from Italian into English comedy, the author may have felt uneasy about the sympathetic portrayal of such a character; his one significant expansion of Ariosto's dialogue comes in a passage where the heroine's father speaks of the reciprocal duties of parents and children. Moreover, in Jeffere's *The Bugbears* (1563–5), one of the translator's main departures from the original by Grazzini was his transformation of the play's arch-intriguer from a student and friend of the hero to a disreputable hanger-on in the Vice tradition. Since the translation was done with boy actors in view, it looks as if Jeffere was reluctant to offer them an example of rascally behaviour from a student.

The English school play, in fact, usually makes the 'spare the rod' theme all too explicit. T. W. Craik has noted the frequency with which references to beatings appear.[2] The subject may have been controversial, since even the author of *Nice Wanton* qualified his recommendation:

Salomon sobre correction doth meane,
Not to beate and bounce them to make them lame.

The school dialogues of Ravisius Textor, with their cool treatment of delinquency and its consequences, naturally appealed to English dramatists. One of them, *Juvenis, Pater, Uxor*, was adapted twice. Seen in the light of the prodigal son story, it is almost shocking in its reversal of the audience's

---

[1] See Rosemary Woolf, 'The Influence of the Mystery Plays upon the Popular Tragedies of the 1560s', *Renaissance Drama*, VI (1973), pp. 89–105. Cf. also the episodes in *Patient Grissil* where the heroine's children are carried off, supposedly to their death.
[2] *The Tudor Interlude*, pp. 43–4.

expectations. The schoolboy hero is eager for marriage, not for riotous living, but the former seems worse than the latter in the eyes of the author. When the bride turns out to be a shrew and the boy, now reduced to poverty, is forced to sell faggots in the street for a living, the father merely takes a grim satisfaction in seeing himself proved right. This is the story as it was first told in a translation of which only a fragment remains. *The Disobedient Child* (1559–70) by Thomas Ingelend expands the story further. The schoolboy refuses to follow his father's advice and get an education – he is terrified of beating and claims to have seen the funeral of a poor child who died 'throughe many strypes' – but he is equally reluctant to take up any profession or join the army. In fact, his only idea is to take advantage of his good looks and get married as soon as possible. The subsequent scene of preparations for the wedding feast (an addition by Ingelend) recalls Latin comedy as the cooks, Blanche Blab-It-Out and Long-Tongue, bustle about bandying Latin quotations and remarks about shrewish wives. The young couple exchange congratulations on their happy state:

> – Howe vehement, howe stronge a thynge love is!
> – Howe many smyrkes, and dulsome kysses!
> – What smylynge! What laughyng!
>   What sporte, pastyme, and playenge!
> – What ticklynge! What toyinge!
>   What dalyenge, what joyenge!

But the romantic tone is presented for ridicule, and the servant who describes the merriment at the feast strikes an ominous note when he adds that he hopes the boy will be able to pay for it. Happiness soon comes to an end, the father refuses to help his son, and Satan explains that everything has been his idea from the start. The play totally denies the possibility of forgiveness and salvation, which was the whole point of the original parable.

Gascoigne's *Glass of Government* (1575) is the English play most clearly in the continental prodigal son tradition set by the *Asotus* of Macropedius (1537) and the *Acolastus* of Gnaphaeus (1529). *Acolastus* was translated into English by John Palsgrave in 1540 and his edition, which offers alternative versions of every phrase in the dialogue along with explanations of rhetorical and grammatical devices, was used as a school text long afterwards. It is unreadable except as a crib, but it must have made the prodigal legend all too familiar to generations of boys. Its extraordinary repetitions –

> Thou art all ydel .i. thou art all togyther gyven to ydelnes, and
> therfore unworthy to whom lyvinge shuld be gyven .i. wherfore thou
> art not worthy, that men shuld gyve the[e] any lyvyng. (IV. vii)

– might have made a different sort of impact on any reader with a sense
of humour. Shakespeare's Holofernes ('to show, as it were, his inclination,
after his undressed, unpolished, uneducated, unpruned, untrained, or
rather, unlettered or ratherest, unconfirmed fashion') is obviously a product
of this tradition; so perhaps, is Touchstone ('abandon (which is in the
vulgar, leave) the society (which in the boorish is, company) of this
female (which in the common is, woman) . . .'). Gascoigne's play could not
even have inspired parody. Like the works of Macropedius and Gnaphaeus,
it depicts the prodigal's downfall in terms of the world of bawds and
courtesans, and emphasizes the role of bad servants in order to make his
conduct less reprehensible. Rather oddly, Gascoigne contrasted not one but
two pairs of brothers. Since each family produced one good and one bad son,
perhaps he was trying to give still more emphasis than his predecessors to
the arbitrariness of the Cain-and-Abel, Esau-and-Jacob relationship. He
may also have been influenced by Ascham's *Schoolmaster* (1570), the preface
of which describes an arrangement between the author and his friend for
educating their sons jointly, very like the one which takes place at the
beginning of *The Glass of Government*. The distinction between the quick,
clever, but careless elder brothers and their slower-witted but conscientious
younger brothers almost constitutes an intellectual predestination, corresponding very closely to what Ascham wrote:

> . . . commonlie men, very quicke of witte, be also, verie light of con-
> ditions: and thereby, very readie of disposition, to be carried over
> quicklie, by any light cumpanie, to any riot and unthriftiness when they
> be yong: and therfore seldome, either honest in life, or riche in
> living, when they be olde. . . . Hard wittes be hard to receive, but sure
> to keepe. . . . And theis be the men, that becum in the end, both
> most happie for themselves, and alwaies best estemed abrode in the
> worlde.[1]

Gascoigne takes this distinction to an extreme conclusion. The older sons
die miserably; the younger ones rise to dignity and wealth. Like the morality
play, the academic drama had come increasingly to expect tangible rewards
and punishments for its characters in this world instead of the next.

[1] Roger Ascham, *English Works*, ed. W. A. Wright (Cambridge, 1904), pp. 189–91.

(v) Plays from the Italian

It is possible that even the earliest English imitations of Roman comedy may also owe something to the secondhand influence of Italian Renaissance drama, which seems to have been known, at least in university circles, as early as the 1540s. What may have been still more important was the influence of Italian acting. In the 1540s, when the *commedia dell'arte* first established itself in Italy, Italian tumblers were already performing in the English provinces, and by the 1560s both plays and players were familiar sights. Queen Elizabeth could have seen an Italian comedy in its original language in 1565, if K. M. Lea is right in her dating of a letter from a foreign resident who was making arrangements for the performance.[1] It is evident from the cast list of *The Supposes* that the types of the *commedia* were already known by 1566, since characters are described as 'the young woman', 'the doctor', 'the parasite'. And if R. Warwick Bond is right in placing *The Bugbears* some time between 1563 and 1566, the time-lag between Italian and English productions could have been remarkably short, since the main source of Jeffere's play is Grazzini's *La Spiritata*, first produced in 1561.[2] The *commedia* style might therefore have inspired the kind of rapid, stylized dialogue and business which has already been noted in *Respublica*.

Like *Respublica*, *The Bugbears* is an interesting example of the adaptation of foreign dramaturgy to a native English tradition. Jeffere cannot help, for instance, seeing the old miser Amadeus as a morality figure like Avarice in *Respublica*. Describing a visit to his confessor, the old man indignantly reports that he was told to leave off his miserly behaviour,

> as thowgh that my Covetise
> (Which is cownted now good husbandrie) seemed ill in Gods eies.
>
> (III. ii)

The reference to the traditional name-changing of Vices is not to be found in the Italian original. Nor are the interpolated songs and the roles for boy servants. Another inserted scene shows the influence of romance, not only

---

[1] *Italian Popular Comedy*, 2 vols (Oxford, 1934), vol. II, pp. 362–9.

[2] His argument is based on the debatable assumption that if Jeffere had done his translation after *The Supposes* he would have used prose instead of verse. But the style of the play does seem to indicate a date some time in the 1560s. See R. Warwick Bond, Introduction to *Early Plays from the Italian* (Oxford, 1911), pp. 82–3.

in its use of the fourteener but in the heroine's alliterative references to fortune in terms of the sea: 'So pitiously in waves of woe my balefull bark was tost' (III. iv). Though Jeffere's main source was a prose comedy, he was also influenced by Terence's *Andria*, which was in verse, and by *Gl'Ingannati*; he therefore stuck to doggerel (perhaps 'as fittest for discourse, and nearest prose') as his basic metre. For this reason, and also because it survives only in a somewhat mutilated manuscript,[1] *The Bugbears* has received less attention than *The Supposes*. It has definite faults of plotting. Though the *in medias res* opening is excellent, Jeffere pays for it by needing a long exposition in the second scene. Moreover, the clever scheme of his young lovers, once devised, proceeds smoothly on without any of the dangers and counterplots that make *The Supposes* so much more interesting. Jeffere also had difficulty with the final unravelling of a plot involving so many characters. His time-consuming method of bringing each one on separately to explain the point at which he has arrived can only increase one's admiration for the way Shakespeare handled the final scene of *Cymbeline*.

Gascoigne's *The Supposes* is a translation of an excellently constructed play and he follows it very closely, apart from a few anglicizations and expansions. His marginal notes drawing attention to the various 'supposes' are an interesting indication of the kind of pleasure the play was meant to give: that of increasing intricacy and confusion, finally resolved by a single, all-explaining discovery. The notes were probably needed by many readers, since the dialogue at cross-purposes, common enough in Latin comedy, would have been largely unfamiliar in English. Gascoigne also introduced another device which belongs to Italian acting rather than writing. His use of prose enabled him to insert the symbol '&c' at a few points, meaning that the actors were free to improvise, in the Italian manner, if they wished.

(vi) Two Cambridge plays: *Gammer Gurton* and *Misogonus*

Whatever its original date of production (perhaps *c.* 1552–63), *Gammer Gurton's Needle* was not printed until 1575. Its anonymous author was thus enabled to take a hint from *The Supposes* (printed 1573) and draw attention in the margin to some of his own 'supposes'. For instance, when Hodge

---

[1] It is one of the few manuscripts belonging to Warburton *not* to have been destroyed, unwittingly, by his cook. At least, so the legend goes.

complains to Diccon that the cat has stolen the bacon (II. i), the margin[1]
provides the equivalent of something which must surely have happened in
performance: a glance of complicity from Diccon to the audience, remind-
ing them that he himself had already told them of his theft. This is only
one of many intellectual subtleties in the play which indicate that neither
author nor audience could have had much in common with the simple
rustics involved in the plot. As the title-page says, *Gammer Gurton* was acted
at Christ's College, Cambridge, and was the work of a Master of Arts.
Misogonus is connected with the names of three Cambridge men, two
from Trinity and one from Christ's, and the manuscript in which it survives
seems to have been copied shortly after the publication of *Gammer Gurton*.
Both plays make use of rustic settings and speech; both depict incompetent
clergymen, though without making them the object of Reformation propaganda; both ridicule stupidity and superstition (Diccon's 'conjuring',
Cacurgus's quack doctor impersonation); both also, interestingly, have a
streak of anti-intellectual humour, which may explain the choice of the
'Bedlam' Diccon and the supposed 'natural' Cacurgus as plot-movers in
their respective plays. In each case there is also some ridicule of the false
intellectual pride of other characters. 'Alas poore fole,' sighs Philogonus
(*Misogonus*, I. i), little guessing how thoroughly his fool despises and
deceives him. And in *Gammer Gurton* the sensible Baily easily exposes the
false logic and conceit of Dr Rat, who agrees that he himself would have
stopped a thief from entering his house, but insists that his own attempt
to break into Dame Chat's cottage was different:

> DR RAT. But I am no theefe sir but an honest learned Clarke.
> BAILY. Yea but who knoweth that, when he meets you in the darke?

And one can imagine the reaction of a Cambridge audience to the scene
between Cacurgus and two village gossips, in which he pretends to be a
learned doctor whose fool's coat and nightcap are the national costume of his
native Egypt:

> My heade is so full of the supermundall science
> That I am faint [fain] to bynde it least my braynes should crowe.
> This nitcape was given me when doctor I did commense.
> Good Lord, good Lord, what thinges do I knowe. (III. iii)

Awestruck, the women agree that this great genius must have been at
Cambridge.

[1] 'Which bacon Diccon stole, as is declared before.'

Of the two plays, *Gammer Gurton* has the advantage of being complete (there are some gaps, especially at the end, in the manuscript of *Misogonus*), of a consistent comic tone, and of considerable skill in versification and plotting. It has a double framework: one, which might pompously be called the work of fortune, is the loss and finding of the needle; the other is the work of the intriguer, Diccon, who uses this chance event to set half the village at odds. Like Jack Juggler, he promises to make the audience 'sport'; like characters in both *The Supposes* and *The Bugbears*, he compares the antics of the others to a play. His status as a 'Bedlam' is puzzling, since there is nothing mad about him. He seems well known in the village but does not speak dialect. His neat dovetailing of the gulling of Hodge, about his supposed raising of the Devil, with his lies to Gammer Gurton and Dame Chat, leads to an ingenious situation where each gulling is used to corroborate the other. There are two 'mistaken identity' situations: one is the dialogue at cross-purposes between the two old women, where one talks of a needle and the other of a cock (cf. Plautus' *Aulularia*); the other is the device by which Dr Rat gets beaten in mistake for Hodge. The final scene between all the injured parties and the tolerant Baily might well have given Jonson the hint for his handling of the dénouement in *Every Man in His Humour*; there is the same fellow feeling between the Baily and Diccon, the only two intelligent men in the place, as between Justice Clement and Brainworm. What keeps the progressive revelation of lie after lie from becoming boring, since the audience already knows the truth, is the very complexity of the plot. The leisurely unravelling allows the audience time to understand exactly how skilfully everything has been woven together. Also, of course, there is the suspense, as Diccon's exposure becomes increasingly imminent, about whether he will be allowed to get away with so much roguery. A final twist is that his mock-punishment – taking an oath of good behaviour on Hodge's breech – becomes the instrument by which the needle is found. Diccon thus acts as an agent for good, however much against his will. Perhaps the loss and finding of the needle may have been intended as a parody of the discovery of long-lost children in classical comedy. Messenio in *Menaechmi* compares his master's search for his twin brother to the search for a lost needle. It also recalls the end of the prodigal son parable, whose hero 'was lost, and is found'.

Misogonus (1560–77), however, is a fully developed English version of the prodigal son story. Its author, who obviously knew the continental Latin plays on the subject, combines several of their motifs to good effect, particularly the use of the servants (including the supposed fool Cacurgus) as good and bad influences. His most original contribution is his treatment of the older brother. Like the author of *Acolastus*, he obviously realized that this character was likely to be an embarrassment to the plot. He therefore kept him out of the story until the end, when, borrowing a device of Roman comedy, he produced him as the long-lost heir to the family fortune. Misogonus's discovery that he has been disinherited (reminiscent of the situation of Esau) provides a credible motive for his repentance which, presumably, would have concluded the play. The handling of the discovery is also very skilful. The father, who is pathetically eager to hear the news, has to learn it from a peasant husband and wife who are, respectively, too inarticulate and too garrulous to communicate except in fragments. Even the elder brother, when he finally arrives, turns out to be a comic simpleton: his most memorable contribution to the reunion scene is the suggestion that, if they want to identify him by the extra toe on one foot, they ought to rip his stocking rather than make him take down his trousers.

The serious side of *Misogonus* is less well handled than the comic. Philogonus rightly describes as an 'oration' the speech in which his friend takes twenty lines to say that he will be glad to give his advice if he is asked (I. i). Luckily, there is not a great deal of this sort of thing, even in connection with religion. On this theme, the play gives fascinating glimpses of a society in transition. There is a comic priest who drinks, gambles, dances, and will not leave his sport for evensong; needless to say, he is 'none of this new start up rables' (II. iv). The prodigals who consort with him use Reformation doctrine as an excuse for their behaviour, arguing that '[Its] poperye to use fastinge' (II. ii). And an exchange between the prodigal's father Philogonus and the rustic couple shows that religious differences were beginning to be accommodated with tolerance. The old man politely but firmly reproves them for praying for his dead wife 'accordinge toth olde rate'; 'Low yow Alison,' says Codrus, 'wer [our] Moster is oth new larninge; did not I tell yow before?' Philogonus simply tells them to discuss the subject among themselves some other time (III. i). The relationship between Codrus and his wife – 'She is not bookish but sheil place hir wordes as scretly [i.e. discreetly] as some of those that be' (III. i) – is beautifully handled. Many of Codrus's lines, out of context, could be mistaken for those of a Shakespearian clown – e.g. 'Voole? I was the wisest that my mother had and we were nintene / I have bin lected for my scretion five tymes constable' (III. i). The play thus comes even closer than *Gammer Gurton* to what we think of as fully fledged Elizabethan comedy, complete with the important element of forgiveness at the end. What both plays lack, of course, is romantic love. Perhaps undergraduates were particularly reluctant to play serious love scenes. As in *The Disobedient Child* and *Ralph Roister Doister*, love is treated only as an object of parody. The hero's mistress Melissa is a sort of Doll Tearsheet who, offered more wine, replies daintily that 'I have dronke so muche that my bellie ene grones' and refuses to go out in the meadows to 'heare the birdes singe and smell the swete floure' because she prefers to play cards indoors (II. iv). On the evidence of these two plays, it seems that interest in the classics, at Cambridge, went hand in hand with a strong urge towards social realism.

4 Elizabethan experiments

(i) Varieties of dramatic verse

What exactly happened to English verse in the mid-sixteenth century has never been fully explained. It cannot have been a simple matter of writers suddenly discovering how to scan. Yet a good deal of what they wrote sounds strange to our ears. For example, there is the opening speech of Jupiter in Heywood's *Play of the Weather*:

> Ryght farre to[o] longe as now were to recyte
> The auncyent estate wherin our selfe hath reyned
> What honour what laude gyven us of very ryght
> What glory we have had dewly unfayned
> Of eche creature whych dewty hath constrayned
> For above all goddes syns our fathers fale [fall]
> We Jupiter were ever pryncypale.

This can be scanned, according to modern notions of verse rhythm, only by contracting or eliding as many syllables as possible. In this respect it is like much of the non-dramatic verse of the same period – for instance, Wyatt's sonnets. The best explanation that has been offered for its apparent irregularity is that Heywood, like his contemporaries, was working simultaneously with two different metrical concepts: one, which derived from the Old English tradition of alliterative verse, used 'balanced' lines with a fixed number of stresses rather than syllables, and a strong break in the middle; the other, under the influence of French and Italian poetry, was what we still know as iambic pentameter. If the stanza is read with natural speech stresses and a sharp break after 'longe', 'estate', 'laude', and so on, with no attempt to force the lines into an iambic pattern, it ceases to sound hurried and awkward. The caesura does not necessarily have to fall in the middle of the line; in the fourth line it would seem equally appropriate after 'glory' or 'had'. Or, indeed, the line could be read as an iambic pentameter.

Probably one reason why the earlier sixteenth-century dramatists use the stanzaic forms for serious speech and the couplet for comic characters is that rhyme is the most insistent reminder of the fact that one is listening to verse. The greater the frequency of the rhyme words, the more likely the listener is to be conscious of the form of the verse rather than its content. Skeltonics, for instance, though they may not always be funny, are better suited to nag the ear than to inform it:

> But and you wolde me permyt
> To schewe parte of my wyt,
> Somwhat I coulde enferre
> Your Consayte to debarre,
> Under supportacyon
> Of pacyent tolleracyon. (*Magnificence*, ll. 57–62)

There is at least no difficulty about how to read these. It is when the lines get longer that the trouble starts. Some dramatists and some printers, indicate a caesura by a line or comma. The most recent editor of *King John* has noted that Bale's markings in the manuscript consistently demand a break after the second stress in a five-stress line, even when this comes in an awkward place for sense or rhythm; he is even capable of separating adjective from noun.[1] The lines have a large number of unstressed syllables, which means a high proportion of dactylic or anapaestic feet, although it is difficult to say that one or the other is the metrical basis of the line. The term doggerel is usually given to lines of irregular scansion, but the modern, pejorative sense of the word hardly does justice to some of the effects which the better dramatists obtain with it. Even F. P. Wilson, despite his

[1] Barry B. Adams (ed.), *King Johan* (San Marino, 1969), pp. 48–51.

admiration for *Jacob and Esau*, complains that it lacks poetry and is handi-capped by its verse form. But the variety of pace within the doggerel couplets shows a genuine dramatic sense on the part of the author. He can move from the briskness of

> I must to the gardine as fast as I can trotte,
> As I was commaunded to fet [fetch] hearbes for the potte.
> But in the meane time, I pray you nourse [nurse] looke about
> And see well to the fyre that it go not out.
> I will aumble so fast, that I will soone be there,
> And here again I trow, ere an horse licke his eare. (IV. iv)

to his leisurely versifying of Isaac's biblical blessing of his son (accentuated by the use of an unrhymed line – though this may be an accident):

> What swete flavour my sonnes raiment dooth yelde,
> Even the fragrant smell that commeth from a fielde
> Which the Lord hath blessed, and the same lord blesse thee:
> With the dewe of heaven, the Lorde thy ground encrease
> That the fatnesse of the earth may never cease.
> The Lorde send thee abundaunce of corne and wine,
> And prosper continually all thing that is thine. (IV. xi)

The play departs from this basic verse form only for the special effect of the children's mocking of Esau, which is obviously a set piece:

> MIDO. Here is good meate Jacob.
> RAGAU. As ere was eate Jacob.
> MIDO. As ere I sawe Jacob.
> RAGAU. Esau a dawe Jacob.
> MIDO. Swete rice pottage Jacob.
> RAGAU. By Esaus dotage Jacob.

What happens in drama of the 1560s and 1570s is that the basic verse line becomes a good deal longer and its stresses become more insistent. There is suddenly a much clearer distinction between iambic and 'balanced' verse, which now corresponds to the distinction between serious and comic characters. The reasons for the popularity of the iambic 'fourteener' have been much discussed. It is usually associated with the publication in 1557 of Tottel's *Miscellany*, which contains many examples of this metre in non-dramatic poetry, but this still requires one to explain why so many poets chose to write in the form. The fourteener does not seem a particularly

appropriate equivalent for the metres of Latin poetry. It is possible,
however, that the adoption of iambic verse can be related to the influence
of the Reformation on the church liturgy. John Stevens has pointed out the
implications for music of the reformers' insistence that words ought to be
clearly audible at all times, with only one note per syllable.[1] The psalms of
Sternhold and Hopkins, used on the Continent by Protestant exiles during
the reign of Queen Mary and published in their complete text in 1562, were
written in 'eight and six' (which is simply a fourteener couplet printed
as a quatrain). It has been suggested that this metre was considered
especially easy to memorize,[2] which might have made it attractive to actors
as well as to the writers of works designed for congregational singing.
However, the fourteener was also the metre chosen by the Jesuit, Jasper
Heywood, for his translation of Seneca's *Troas* (1559), which set a kind of
precedent for other translators of the plays over the next decade.

The young men who turned their hands to the translation and adaptation
of classical tragedy during this period seem to have aimed at a greater
uniformity of tone and versification than could be found in most English
drama of the time, or even in Seneca himself. Most of them used only two
kinds of verse, fourteener couplets for the dialogue and quatrains or some
other distinctive form for the choruses. Later dramatists were indebted to
them for this metre, but not for other 'Senecan' qualities, which the
translations notably fail to convey. No one would ever guess from them,
for example, that Seneca was capable of dignity and understatement as well
as ranting. But some Elizabethan dramatists may have been taken with the
experiments with onomatopoeia and alliteration which produced such
amazing phrases as Studley's description of Medea's 'slibber slabbar sosse
[sauce?] of chauntments' (*Medea*, III. i) and 'threatening thunders thump-
ing thicke doe bounce out all the day' (*Hercules Oetaeus*, II. i). A combination of this 'tyrant's vein', as Bottom calls it, with the style of the tyrants
in the biblical mysteries produces the language of characters like Apius in
Apius and Virginia:

> I finde it, I minde it, I sweare that I will,
> Though shame, or defame, do happen no skill.

[1] *Music and Poetry in the Early Tudor Court*, pp. 74–97.
[2] An abridgement of the Old Testament in 'Sternhold's metre' (1569) includes a system
which enables anyone who memorizes the book to tell, 'by counting upon the joints of
his fingers, in exactly what book and chapter of the Bible any given story or parable is
to be found' (Hallett Smith, 'English Metrical Psalms in the Sixteenth Century and their
literary significance', *HLQ*, IX (1945–6), pp. 249–71).

The sheer badness of the verse given to serious characters in this period is partly the result of lack of experience with the new metres. To make his lines scan, the writer is now forced to pad them out, to subtract definite articles, and to use an excessive number of inversions; the result is the style of *Cambises* and *Horestes*. But the comic characters continue to use doggerel, which is much more fluent and speakable. The lines of this doggerel get longer and longer, to the point where the rhyme scheme is lost altogether. In *Sir Clyomon and Sir Clamydes*, the fourteener line of the romantic hero is made to rhyme with an exceptionally long doggerel reply from the Vice:

CLAMYDES. My Ladies charge for to fulfill, behold I do entend.
SHIFT. Your Lady ant shall please you, why who is your Lady, may a man be so bold as aske and not offend?

Common Conditions is a similar jumble. The following couplet, for instance, is 'balanced' in the first line but the second could be read as iambic:

And when they thinke them selves in the wood moste surest to bee,
Their purses wee will bee so bolde as share betwixt us three.

The author is capable of writing smoother fourteeners than most of the Seneca translators could manage:

You see the Nightingall also, with sweete and pleasant lay,
Sounds forthe her voice in cherping wise, to banish care awaie.

This is the style of the 'serious' characters. Yet they are also capable of falling into what, to our ears, sounds like pantomime rhythm:

CARDOLUS. O stay sir knight, end not through fight my daies, but graunt me grace.
LAMPHEDON. A wretch I denaye thee, for I intend to slay thee, or I from hence trace.

These plays, then, indicate a shift in the dramatists' way of differentiating comic from serious characters. In the early sixteenth century it was the comic speakers who used insistent, highly rhythmic verse while the 'high style' was characterized by an expansive stanza form which, although more formal and elaborate in versification, actually *sounded* less like verse because the rhyme words fell less frequently on the ear. But the adoption, for serious dialogue, of the sing-song fourteener seems to have led to the development of an alternative comic style which can best be described as 'rhymed prose'.[1]

[1] A term applied to the verse of *Damon and Pithias* in Leicester Bradner, *The Life and Poems of Richard Edwards* (New Haven, Conn., 1927), p. 70.

We are thus on the way to the verse–prose distinction as it is usually understood in later Elizabethan drama. Plays like *Damon and Pithias* and *The Bugbears* – both contemporaries of *The Supposes* – can best be appreciated, perhaps, as attempts to achieve something of the flexibility of prose without forgoing rhyme altogether. Their verse offers an interesting example of a form specifically devised for drama rather than carried over from non-dramatic poetry.

Blank verse, on the other hand, had already been used by Surrey in his translation of part of the *Aeneid* and by Nicholas Grimald in two narrative poems published in Tottel's *Miscellany*. Unrhymed verse of a similar type was also used for some Italian comedy, but it is more likely that the epic qualities of the English experiments were what attracted Sackville and Norton. Their own style is not specifically Senecan, but its terseness is more Latin than English:

> When fathers cease to know that they should rule,
> The children cease to know they should obey.

The sheer clarity of this writing is a relief after the turgid fourteeners. But the weakness of *Gorboduc* is a tendency to make the sentences nearly as long as the speeches (Sackville and Norton do not use stichomythia, which first appears in the translation of *Jocasta*), and to fall too frequently into the same balanced cadences; a favourite one is 'For you, for yours, and for our native land'. Gascoigne's part of *Jocasta*, which he translated from the Italian, with Francis Kinwelmershe, in 1566, shows a considerable advance in flexibility:

> O carefull caytife, howe am I nowe changd
> From that I was? I am that *Oedipus*,
> That whylome had triumphant victorie
> And was bothe dread and honored eke in Thebes:
> But nowe (so pleaseth you my forwarde starres)
> Down headlong hurlde in depth of myserie,
> So that remaynes of *Oedipus* no more
> As nowe in mee, but even the naked name,
> And lo, this image, that resembles more
> Shadowes of death, than shape of *Oedipus*. (V. v)

Blank verse, however, had not yet established itself as the only suitable form for serious drama. The five authors of *Gismond of Salerne* (1566?) seem to have been determined to achieve as much variety of style as was consistent with the dignity of their tragedy. They wrote it chiefly in decasyllabic quatrains, with one explosion of fourteeners at the most obviously emotional, and Senecan, moment: Tancred's speech after he has learned of his daughter's illicit love. There is also some alternation of couplets with quatrains. Though the flowing quatrains are generally musical and pleasant, they are not a particularly suitable form for dialogue and tend to sound too calm for the expression of feeling. The authors of Acts III and IV went almost to extremes of irregularity in their attempt to avoid this monotony. The phrasing fights against the verse form, producing a sort of rhymed blank verse, as in this passage by Christopher Hatton:

> I think you know,
> That whilom was this palace builded strong
> For warr, where dredlesse peace hath planted now
> A weaker court, where we long time have reigned,
> And ruled in rest. But of that palace old,
> Against the force of time one vaut remained,
> That secret way under the dolven mold
> Conveyeth streight unto the place where lyes
> Gismond my daughter. (IV. ii)

The full stops after 'rest' and 'daughter' allow the actor to indicate suppressed emotion, while the enjambment and overriding of the breaks between quatrains prevent him from indulging in a sing-song delivery. It is unlikely that this could ever have become a feasible alternative to blank verse; it is, rather, a tacit acknowledgement of the unsuitability of rhyme to English tragic drama. The natural tendency of the language is to sound much more heavily stressed than either French or Italian, and this, combined with rhyme, nearly always works against that direct contact with the speaker's emotions which tragedy demands. Woodes's *Conflict of Conscience* has sometimes been compared with Marlowe's *Dr Faustus* because of its emphasis on the psychology of despair and damnation. But even when the thoughts of the two plays come closest to one another, Woodes's heavy fourteeners and alliterative repetitions virtually obscure the accents of genuine despair which he found in his source, described by Calvin as a 'pageaunt of desperation' and 'tragicall motion'.[1] Where the prose pamphlet made Francis Spira say, 'I would I were in the place of any damned person', the verse play forced him into:

[1] From the introduction to Edward Aglionby (trans.), *A Notable and Marveilous Epistle of the Famous Doctour, Matthewe Gribalde, Professor of the Lawe, in the Universitie of Padua* (1570?), sigs. A2-v to A3-v.

> I would most gladly chuse to lyve, a thousand, thousand yeare
> In all the torments and the griefe that damned soules sustaine,
> So that at lengthe I might have ease, it would me greatly cheare.
> But I alas, shall in this lyfe, in torments still remaine.

And yet this is relatively straightforward compared to Woodes's obviously serious attempt to pull all the stops out for his hero's great outburst:

> O painfull paine of deepe disdaine, oh griping greefe of hell,
> Oh horror huge, oh soule supprest, and slaine with desperation,
> Oh heape of sinnes, the sum wherof, no man can number well:
> Oh death, oh furious flames of hell, my iust recompensation,
> Oh wretched wight, oh creature curst, oh childe of condempnation.
> Oh angrie God, and mercilesse, most fearefull to beholde,
> Oh Christ thou art no Lambe to mee, but Lion fearce and boulde.

The Reformation had given drama a potentially tragic subject; what it needed now was the language in which to express it.

(ii) Seneca and the Inns of Court tragedies

We have already seen that the language of the translations of Seneca's tragedies did most dramatists nothing but harm. The influence of their subject matter has been much debated. It is perfectly true that the Elizabethan dramatists needed no Senecan ghost come from the grave to tell them that ordinary men are often happier than princes, that life is transitory and that ambition is evil. The stories told by Seneca were also told by other Latin writers, and had long since passed into English poetry. But the same was true of the philosophy of Seneca; as has been pointed out, it was itself one of the sources of medieval *contemptus mundi* literature, either directly or via Boethius.[1] It was against a background of respect for Seneca the Stoic philosopher that the Elizabethans read the works of Seneca the tragedian. The philosophy and the tragedy are in fact complementary. The constant Senecan emphasis on the power of the human mind to surmount any kind of suffering inevitably led to a horrified fascination with the kinds

---

[1] See Willard Farnham, *The Medieval Heritage of Elizabethan Tragedy*, ch. 2, and Paul Bacquet, 'L'Imitation de Séneque dans "Gorboduc" de Sackville et Norton', in Jean Jacquot (ed.), *Les Tragédies de Sénèque et le théâtre de la Renaissance* (Paris, 1973), p. 156.

of suffering which it might be asked to surmount. In the epistles which offer consolation for various sorts of pain and loss, the consolation is much less vividly imagined than the pain. The savage world of the tragedies is thus a counterpart of the world which the Christian had been taught to despise.

Shortly after the accession of Elizabeth – the last survivor of the royal house of Henry Tudor – there was a revival of *contemptus mundi* literature. The two most obvious examples of it were the Seneca translations and the *Mirror for Magistrates*, both of which began to appear in 1559. But Tottel's *Miscellany* had already given a wider currency to the theme of the superiority of 'the Meane Estate' in a number of poems by different authors, as well as to the bitter complaints of both Wyatt and Surrey about the treachery of life at court compared to a quiet country retreat. They wrote, of course, from experience, as well as out of a literary tradition, and if we look for a cause of the revival of interest in Stoicism in the sixteenth century, the answer may well be that it was the philosophy that best met the needs of the time. Montaigne's essay on 'the Institution and Education of Children' (1580) indicates something of the atmosphere which decades of religious conflict had created; the child, he says, should be inured to pain and sickness, and also, 'if need require, patiently to beare imprisonment, and other tortures . . . for according to time and place, the good as well as the bad man may haply fall into them; we have seen it by experience.' Faced with the third major change of religious policy in just over ten years, many Englishmen may have had to ask themselves the question which Sartre describes as having been constantly on the minds of members of the French Resistance: 'If they torture me, will I keep silent?' Jasper Heywood, a Roman Catholic, chose the *Troas* for his first translation from Seneca, because, he says, it was his favourite among the plays. More than any other Latin tragedy, it is about the decline and fall of kingdoms as well as kings. Troy, already referred to in *Respublica* as a symbol of the revolution of fate, occupies a similar role here, when Agamemnon uses its fall as a mirror to the victorious Greeks:

> Troy made me fierce and proude of mynde, Troy makes me frayd withal:
> The Grekes now stand wher Troy late fel, ech thing may have his fal.
> (II. iii)

Sackville would soon take up the theme of Troy as well, in *Gorboduc* and in his Induction (first published in 1563) to *The Mirror for Magistrates*. This was evidently the tone which the translators admired most in

Seneca. Their alterations and interpolations all seem directed either to accentuating the horrors of his plots or to underlining the theme of the inevitability of death:

> Lyfe seemes the bayte to sight that lyeth brim,
> Death is the hooke that underlies the same.

The Chorus in which these lines occur was added by Studley to his version of the *Medea* (1566). And the Nuntius in the *Hippolytus* (1567) reminds the audience that the fate of the young man shows what happens to all earthly beauty. Queen Elizabeth herself tried to make a translation of the Chorus from *Hercules Oetaeus* on the theme of human misery, especially that of the great; the best she could do was:

> A man full rarely happye is and olde.
> Moe surer sleepes thee downie turfes procure.

She put the same idea much better in 1601 in one of her most famous speeches: 'To be a king and wear a crown is more glorious to them that see it than it is pleasure to them that wear it.'

The opposite attitude – 'A kingly Crowne is never deare, what ever price it cost' (the *Thebais*, trans. Newton, 1581) – is an example of what Newton, in his dedication to *The Ten Tragedies*, described as Seneca's 'many Phrases and sentences, literally tending (at the first sight) sometime to the prayse of Ambition'. But of course Elizabethan readers were accustomed to discounting such sentences, since the tyrant was also a medieval dramatic figure; indeed, the first so-called neo-Senecan tragedy, the *Ecerinis* of Albertino Mussato (1315), was an Antichrist play. Other aspects of the tragedies also recall traditional English drama. Seneca's is a guilt-haunted world. His characters do not merely recognize their crimes, however; they wallow in them, trying to find as many ingenious ways as possible of describing the horror of their actions or the greatness of their sufferings. It is characteristic that Hippolytus, on hearing of Phaedra's guilty passion, should wish a thunderbolt to fall not on her but on him:

> For guilty (Jove) I guilty am, deserved death I have,
> My stepdames Fancy I have fed. (II. ii)

The translators of these plays were determined to see the sufferings and crimes as brought about 'by the deepe hidden secret Judgements of God', as Neville said about the fate of Oedipus. And this is typical of the way in which the sixteenth century approached tragedy. The difference between

Christian and Senecan attitudes can perhaps best be seen in the final song
from *The Disobedient Child* (*c.* 1569), which belongs to the *Ubi sunt* and
contemptus mundi traditions:

> Howe shorte a Feaste is this worldly joyenge!
> Even as a shadowe it passeth awaye,
> Depryvynge a man of Gyftes everlastynge,
> Leadynge to darkenes and not to daye.
> O meate of wormes, O heape of duste,
> O lyke to dewe, clyme not to[o] hye:
> To lyve to morrowe, thou canst not truste,
> Therfore now betyme helpe the nedye.

The theme of transitoriness is common to both kinds of drama, but
Ingelend's play offers an alternative to its picture of 'the worlde that is so
vayne', both in the prospect of 'Gyftes everlastynge' and in the need for
virtuous action before it is too late.

In this respect the young men of the Inns of Court, who wrote and acted
in the first English tragedies, were more like Seneca the philosopher, who
took an active part in political life, than like the tragedian whose characters
all recognize, too late, that they should have stayed away from the world
of aspiration and action. Revels had an important place at the Inns; students
were taught music and dancing in order to take part in them to the full.
The plays written for these occasions were intellectual, experimental, and
obviously the product of a close acquaintance and fascination with the court.
The very sumptuousness with which they were produced and the festive
occasion with which they were associated worked against the negative tone
of Senecan tragedy. Only one of them is strongly influenced by Seneca
– *The Misfortunes of Arthur*, an ingenious collage of quotations from his
works, which came too late (1588) to be discussed here. The authors of the
other three surviving plays look not only backwards, to their sources in
Latin, Italian and English, but outwards to their courtly audience. *Gorboduc*
(1562) discusses the importance of an assured succession, the best way to put
down rebellion, and what the role of parliament should be at times when the
royal power is weak. *Jocasta* (1566) is a translation from an Italian version
twice removed from Euripides, but was perhaps chosen because, like *Gorboduc*, it deals with the theme of warring heirs to a throne and the
importance of patriotism. Even *Gismond of Salerne* (1566), a romantic
tragedy based on a story from *The Decameron*, was directed at the queen's
maids of honour, and preaches a moral which she would certainly have

found satisfactory: that Cupid is a cruel god and that nothing but harm can come of his influence.

The message of *Jocasta*, as interpreted by Christopher Yelverton in his epilogue, was familiar and Senecan:

> Cease to aspire then, cease to soare so hie,
> And shunne the plague that pierceth noble breastes.
> To glittring courtes what fondnesse is to flie,
> When better state in baser Towers rests?

But neither *Gorboduc* nor *Gismond* follows this advice. *Gorboduc* begins and ends *in medias res*, with characters making plans for the future. The king whose decision sets the play in motion is not a tyrant; he is guilty not of ignoring good advice but of making the wrong decision between alternatives offered by his advisers. These have been compared to the good and bad angels of the morality, but the description applies more appropriately to the two counsellors who accompany each of the princes. All of Gorboduc's advisers – three in number – seem to be well-meaning. Their speeches, like those of an academic debate, are well thought out and well argued even when they are wrong. Like King John in Bale's play, which may have been revived at about the same time,[1] Gorboduc puts his country's interests before his own, praying that the gods may inflict their wrath

> on me
> And on my sonnes, not on this giltlesse realme. (III. i)

Even his sons are not wholly wicked; each takes arms for supposedly defensive reasons, so that we may be shown how suspicion escalates into war. Though there are several Senecan dialogues between king and counsellor (the one between Nero and Seneca himself, in the pseudo-Senecan *Octavia*, was especially popular in the Renaissance), their purpose is ethical, not practical as in *Gorboduc*. The relation of king and counsellor, for the Inns of Court men, had an obviously personal relevance. By the end, Eubulus and his hard-pressed companions have become the real heroes of the play, still coping with the problems of life after the royal family has been wiped out by the results of its own mistakes and crimes.

The classical structure of the play, with its messengers entering at crucial points with news that changes the course of action, needs no comment. The

---

[1] S. F. Johnson discusses the two plays together in 'The Tragic Hero in Early Elizabethan Drama', in Josephine Bennett, O. Cargill, Vernon Hall, Jr (eds), in *Studies in English Renaissance Drama* (London, 1959), pp. 157–71.

handling of the opening dialogue between the passionate Videna and her son
Ferrex is, however, more unusual. It is probably the first example in English
drama of information conveyed to an audience through dialogue rather than
direct address. Step by step, with dramatic effect taking precedence over
the obvious need for rapid communication between mother and son,
Ferrex's questions draw from Videna the information that (1) she is
depressed (2) about a wrong being done (3) to both of them (4) by the king
himself (5) who is planning to give away half his kingdom (6) to her younger
son, Porrex.

In other respects, the play is curiously unclassical. There are more
characters than are strictly needed for the action, and new ones tend to
appear in each scene, only to be dropped. There is no preparation for the
sudden emergence of Fergus, the aspiring Duke of Albany, as a threat in the
last act. It is possible that Sackville and Norton decided to make him a
complete nonentity so as to reinforce the point already made in Act I about
the universality of ambition. Linked, conventionally enough, to the actor
image, it suggests that the most ordinary man, in seeking power, is trying
to usurp a role that does not belong to him:

> Such is in man the gredy minde to reigne,
> So great is his desire to climbe alofte,
> In worldly stage the stateliest partes to beare ... (I. ii)

Fergus comes to stand for all the factions that will create fifty years of
civil war for Britain. This is the prospect to which Eubulus looks forward
at the end of the play. Yet his final words are optimistic:

> For right will alwayes live, and rise at length,
> But wrong can never take deepe roote to last. (V. ii)

This conviction, obviously, belongs more to the Christian morality play
than to Senecan tragedy.

A much odder example of unexpected optimism comes at the end of
Gismond of Salerne. The heroine, having been sent her lover's torn-out heart
in a golden goblet, has committed suicide; her father plans to die himself
once he has laid her and her lover in their graves. Then, in a device borrowed
from comedy, the speaker of the epilogue enters and tells the spectators
not to wait in hopes of seeing the funeral, or to fear the reappearance of the
vengeful Cupid or the fury Megaera: the women of Britain, unlike those of
Italy, are virtuous. Perhaps the fact that it was played directly at the ladies in

the audience accounts for its resemblance to the end of a Restoration comedy.

In 1565 the gentlemen of Gray's Inn had offended the queen by presenting *Juno and Diana*, a play which she took as an attack on her refusal to marry. This *faux pas* probably explains the seemingly perverse way in which the five authors of *Gismond* treated their Italian source. Like Painter's translation of this and other Italian tales in *The Palace of Pleasure* (which, however, they seem not to have used), the Inner Temple's attempt to make amends for Gray's Inn adopted a moral tone not found in the source. The play emphasizes the connection of lust with idleness and luxury and juxtaposes the portrayal of Gismond's passion with a choric lament for the general decline of female chastity since the days of the Roman matrons. In his extensive revisions of 1591, Robert Wilmot (author of the fifth act of the original version) added to this chorus a reminder that there was one exception to this gloomy picture – 'a virgin, one without compare', whose identity no reader could fail to guess. Apart from flattering the queen, the young authors may have thought they were being gallant in omitting the two most original features of Boccaccio's story: the widowed Gismond's frank assertion of her need to fulfil her sexual nature despite her father's refusal to let her remarry, and her choice of a man of lower birth as her lover. These two facts, and her brave defiance of her conduct, were later to inspire Webster's superb portrayal of the Duchess of Malfi, whose story is found in another chapter of Painter's book. Antonio's reaction to the Duchess's courtship of him ('Ambition (Madam) is a great mans madnes', I. ix) and his dying words ('And let my Sonne, flie the Courts of Princes', V. iv) have struck critics as incongruous, coming as they do from the hero of a tragedy of love. What they show is the power, even for a Jacobean dramatist, of the Senecan inheritance: the tragedy of passion was inseparable from the tragedy of ambition.

(iii) Plays of the court

The Senecan reinterpretation of the conflict between the world and God in terms of court versus retirement probably helped to create an interesting group of plays, dating from the 1560s, which seem for the most part to have been designed for court performance by children. One of them, *Horestes*, appeared only a year after Studley's translation of the *Agamemnon* of Seneca

(1566), but shows no direct influence of the play to which it is, in a sense, a sequel. The effect of the translations, elsewhere, can be seen chiefly in the use of the fourteener for serious passages and in the development of the soliloquy in place of the externalization of inner conflict which the morality had depicted.[1] Each of these works might be called, as Pickering called *Horestes*, an 'Interlude of Vice', since the Vice character is not simply a link with the values and conventions of the morality but an embodiment of the evil principle which informs the entire play.[2] If the Vices of the romance served as symbols of fortune, Ambidexter and the rest represent the way of the world. In *Cambises* (1558–69) ambidexterity is the quality of the tyrant as well as the Vice, who also reminds us that it is present in the audience:

> Thereby you may perceiue I use to play with eche hand.
> But how now Cousin cutpurse with whom play you?
> Take heed for his hand is groping even now.

Playing with both hands means not only treachery but arbitrariness. Politic Persuasion in *Patient and Meek Grissil* (1558–61) can be seen either as a villain or as a neutral quality (though the word 'politic' was beginning to take on pejorative connotations) which works on Gautier (without, apparently, making him evil) when he decides to test his wife's patience. Haphazard in *Apius and Virginia* (1559–67) represents the spirit of taking a chance, or fatalism, which has tragic consequences in the main plot and comic ones in the subplot about the Vice's corrupting of the servants. The two plots come together briefly, when Virginius, reckoning up the ill omens that have troubled him, includes the puzzling fact that his once-willing servants are no longer reliable. In the biblical play about the calumniated *Susanna* (1563–9) the Vice is, appropriately, Ill Report. The treatment of the Vice in *Horestes* is more complex. It is not until the end that he gives his real name, but his quality, Revenge, spreads, thanks to his influence, from high to low characters.

It has often been pointed out that the evil characters in these plays are sufficiently motivated not to need the temptation of a Vice to set them on their course. It is true that his function often seems to be only the practical one of supplying his victims – Sisamnes in *Cambises*, the two elders in *Susanna*, the Judge Apius – with the means of gratifying their desires. But

---

[1] See Catherine Belsey, 'Senecan Vacillation and Elizabethan Deliberation: Influence or Confluence?', *Renaissance Drama*, N.S., VI (1973), pp. 65–88.

[2] Cf. the role of Avarice in *Respublica*, and the reformation of Adulation, which suggests possible ambidexterity in vice.

his utility as a plot device is unquestionable, in a period when writers were still learning how to transform narrative subject-matter into drama. His activities relieve them from having to explain the motivations of their characters. With other abstractions, like Shame in *Cambises* and Rumour in *Apius*, he compresses the passage of time, informs us that Cambises has, for some reason, become evil, and supplies Virginius with information (about the motives behind Apius's conduct) which could hardly have been obtained from any other source.

Above all, the Vice keeps the audience in touch with familiar moral standards. The exotic world of the cruel Cambises is brought nearer home when the Queen's death is linked to those of the Protestant martyrs; she sings a psalm before departing and Ambidexter compares the King to Bishop Bonner. In *Horestes*, Revenge presents himself to the hero as a messenger of the gods called Courage, but his speech would have been recognized as the imaginary journey of the typical Vice. Nevertheless, Pickering seems to have gone out of his way to keep the atmosphere of this play a pagan one. Revenge is opposed not by Forgiveness but by Nature (Horestes' filial instincts) and Fame (his concern for his reputation); it is finally banished by Amity (Horestes' reconciliation with Menelaus and the final picture of a happy, well-ordered kingdom). Such comments of the Vice as 'Se, se, I praye you, how he joyse, that he must war begin!' suggest that the audience is meant to remember the Christian attitude to war and vengeance, yet King Idumeus and his counsellor, who are presented as wise and good men, decide to give Horestes their aid because crimes cannot go unpunished. Horestes himself, in his formal debate with Nature, appeals to both 'Law of God' and 'Law of Man'. Pickering seems to have regarded the rightfulness of revenge as a genuine subject for debate, with truth on both sides. However, one should not make too much of the intellectual aspect of the play, since its main attraction, for most spectators, was probably the spectacle of boy actors marching and fighting in proper military style. The detailed stage directions make it clear that this part of the action was taken very seriously and that it was sometimes necessary to remind the performers to stop the battle noises before a character began to speak. Concentration on the spectacular side of the play may have led to some confusion in the writing: one would expect Revenge's disclosure of his true name to serve some dramatic purpose, as is usual with Vices, but it is simply thrown away.

Plays of the 1560s mostly share with *Horestes* both king-and-counsellor scenes and spectacular episodes of conflict and violence. Good kings consult their counsellors, bad ones refuse to listen and even punish them, as Cambises does. In *Apius and Virginia*, the judge's refusal to listen to his Conscience actually leads to the death of that abstraction. The violence may derive from Seneca, from the Italian *novella*, or from the gory martyrdoms of saints' plays; it includes flaying, stoning to death, beheading, hanging and the cutting out of a child's heart with the arrow still in it. The contrast betweeen rational debate and violent action is thus taken still further than in the earlier plays of this period. It becomes part of the double view of the court as the centre of power, the potential reward for virtue but also the source of unlimited evil if that power falls into the hands of a ruler like Cambises, a false judge like Apius, or the wicked elders in *Susanna*. Divine intervention finally punishes the villain in each of these plays, but not always in time to prevent tragedy.

Marion Jones has pointed out a passage in *Virtuous and Godly Susanna* which, she suggests, reflects the glamorous legends which had gathered about the Elizabethan court by the 1560s:

I heard once in my fathers house, a Gentleman declare,
The worthy customes of the court, and eake the Princely fare,
The gorgeous Garments of eche Dame, their fyne and famous lyfe,
The noble workes of amorous Knights, their stoute and loving stryfe,
The pleasure of eche worthy Dame, how they doe hunt and hawke,
And wearyed with eche pastyme thus, the streates how they did walk;
The noble maskes that were showed forth in every winters night,
The Revels and the reveling cheare that did eche harte delight,
Musitions how they did devyse with songes to please the eare,
And Musickes arte by instrument that gladded hartes to heare,
And sometyme the pore mans chylde, that there is plaste to be,
To honour clymes for vertues sake, and brought to hye degree.[1]

Even in *Susanna*, a play of virtue rewarded, there is a darker side to the court. The servant girl who gives this glowing description admits that she has not found court life as pleasant as she expected. The heroine of *Patient and Meek Grissil*, whose fate is an obvious illustration of the last two lines of the speech, experiences both the cruelty of the court and, at last, its capacity for rewarding virtue. The contrast between her life there and the humble contentment of her parents' cottage does not have to be made explicit. But in *Cambises* there is a suggestion of the Senecan 'retirement' theme when the tyrant's virtuous younger brother soliloquizes,

---

[1] 'The Court and the Dramatists', in J. R. Brown and B. Harris (eds), op. cit. p. 174.

> I am wandring alone heere and there to walke.
> The Court is so unquiet, in it I take no joy:
> Solitary to my selfe now I may talke,
> If I could rule I wist what to say.

Cambises' court certainly seems a place of horror, yet the vision of glamour is evoked, touchingly if incongruously, just before the Queen's death:

> Farwell you Ladies of the Court, with all your masking hue:
> I doo forsake these brodered gardes, and all the fashions new.
> The Court and all the courtly train wherin I had delight;
> I banished am from happy sporte and all by spitefull spite.

Cambises' court can never have been so delightful as this; the Queen is describing the world which came into being at the accession of Elizabeth.

A few plays of the period are more obviously directed at the Elizabethan court, both by statement and by implication. *Damon and Pithias* was probably performed before the queen by the Children of the Chapel Royal in the Christmas week of 1564; *Liberality and Prodigality* was given at court in 1602, but was probably a revival, with some alterations, of an earlier play – perhaps the one called *Prodigality* which children played at the court in 1567–8. Both plays have prologues which show the author's awareness of the occasion and his audience. Both deal with courts and courtiers, and the resolution of their conflicts depends on the decision of an absolute monarch. Both likewise direct their conclusions to the queen in the audience. And both make a moral point, highly flattering to her, which could only have been made through the medium of drama.

Richard Edwards, whose one surviving play is *Damon and Pithias*, was highly esteemed in his own time not only as a poet and playwright but as a musician, theatrical producer and – to judge from some of his poems – a courtier as well. As Master of the Children of the Chapel Royal from 1561 until his early death in 1566, he must often have been called upon to present plays at court. It is possible to guess what sort these were from a poem of Barnaby Googe's in 1563 which describes him as surpassing even Plautus and Terence. The prologue to *Damon and Pithias* refers to the character types of Latin comedy as if these had also been used by the author in earlier works, and draws on Horace's concept of decorum to justify what he had done. Presumably he had been criticized for these 'toying Playes' because 'he seemed too muche, in yonge desires to range'. Had Queen Elizabeth disliked his emphasis on love and marriage? At any rate, he promises that the new piece will be quite different; it is about friendship rather than love, and it is based on a true story, 'no Legend lie'. It is a great pity that his later work, *Palamon and Arcite* (1566), is lost; it would have been interesting to see how he handled the conflict between love and friendship on which *The Knight's Tale* is based.

The title-page of *Damon and Pithias* points out that the printed text is the same one played before the queen, 'except the Prologue that is somewhat altered for the proper use of them that hereafter shall have occasion to plaie it, either in private, or open audience'. Perhaps, for the court performance, Edwards had introduced some topical references, or a compliment to the queen to amplify his caution that,

> talking of Courtly toyes, wee doo protest this flat,
> Wee talke of *Dionisius* Courte, wee meane no Courte but that.

The play does, indeed, make sufficiently clear that the tyranny of Dionysius has left him friendless, unlike the royal spectator; the final prayer is that she may have friends who, like Damon and Pithias, would die for her. The Elizabethan court is always present in the play as an ideal, contrasted with the frightened, suspicious world which Dionysius has made for himself. The distinction between true and false courtiers, directed at the parasite Carisophus, is one of many passages which bring the audience into the play:

> A right courtier is vertuous, gentill, and full of urbanitie,
> Hurting no man, good to all, devoid of all villanie:
> But suche as thou art, fountaines of squirilitie, and vayne delightes,
> Though you hange by the courtes, you are but flatring Parasites,
> As well deserving the right name of courtesie,
> As the coward Knight, the true praise of chevalrie.

As soon as Damon and Pithias have arrived in Syracuse, their servant Stephano recognizes that there is something wrong with the place. What he describes is reminiscent of the court scenes in *Magnificence*:

> I lyke not this Soyle: for as I go ploddynge,
> I marke there two, there three, their heades alwayes noddinge,
> In close secret wise, styll whisperyng together:
> If I ask any question, no man doth answer:
> But shakyng their heads, they go their wayes speakynge ...

This is the worst side of the court, the whispering in corners which Jonson, Chapman and Webster also use to create an atmosphere of plotting and insecurity. It is parodied by the comic scene in which the pages Jack and Will shave Grim the Collier. As Werner Habicht has pointed out, the idea of shaving probably came from an earlier reference to Dionysius' terror of assassination which forces him to rely on his daughters as barbers and to have them singe, rather than shave, his hairs.[1] It is also a pun – shaving and polling can also, equally, mean cheating and pillaging, which happens both to the Collier and to Damon: each of them suffers for being too outspoken.

The play shows a number of ways in which characters attempt to keep their heads above the troubled waters of the court. Carisophus, the bad courtier, is Edwards's own creation, funny yet sinister. Eubulus, the good counsellor, recalls the character of the same name in *Gorboduc*, and his advice to Dionysius derives from Seneca's *Octavia*. Aristippus is the most interesting of the three. More may well have been thinking of his career, as told by Diogenes Laertius in his *Lives of the Philosophers*, when he described the kind of philosophy suitable for princes' courts.[2] His attempt to combine the roles of intellectual and courtier did not, however, always provide a good example. Erasmus's *Apophthegmata* includes a number of anecdotes in which he is shown putting his intelligence to no better purpose than the witty defence of immoral or cowardly behaviour; to one of them, the translator Udall added the comment: 'it was the saying of a corrupte Gentile . . . and not of a Christian manne.'[3] Edwards portrays the character with a similar ambivalence. In his first speech, the philosopher reasons, 'I can helpe one [i.e. himself], is not that a good poinct of Philosophy?' What the play reveals, however, is that he cannot help anyone else. When Pithias tries to enlist his services on behalf of Damon, all Aristippus can do is sympathize:

> I dare not gainsay the kynge, be it right or wrong:
> I am sory, and that is all I may or can doo in this case,
> Nought avayleth perswasion, where frowarde opinion taketh place.

Though he never does as much harm as a Vice, this comment recalls the attitude of Ambidexter in *Cambises* after the Queen has been condemned to death:

---

[1] *Studien zur Dramenform vor Shakespeare* (Heidelberg, 1968), p. 61.
[2] See above, p. 160.
[3] Erasmus, *Apophthegmes* (trans. Nicholas Udall), sig. 46-r. Edwards's biographer suggests that Aristippus may have been a self-portrait; if so, it was a very critical one (Leicester Bradner, *Life and Poems of Richard Edwards*, p. 67).

If that I durst, I would mourn your case;
But, alas! I dare not, for fear of his grace.

Against tyranny, the play seems to say, no amount of persuasion can take effect. The virtuous counsel of Eubulus accomplishes no more than the moral cowardice of Aristippus. Even the detached attitude of Damon is shown not to work:

Pithagoras said, that this world was like a Stage,
Wheron many play their partes: the lookers on the sage
Phylosophers are saith he, whose parte is to learne
The maners of all Nations, and the good from the bad to discerne.

But the answer to that famous analogy was given by Bacon, who declared that in the theatre of man's life only God and the angels were allowed to be lookers-on. Damon's attempt to be in the city but not of it leads to his arrest – admittedly, on false evidence – as a spy, and even those most sympathetic to him agree that his behaviour was 'more curious then wise'. Thus he and Pithias are forced to become actors in spite of themselves. As Anne Righter notes, 'Edwards actually presents the central plot of his tragi-comedy . . . as a kind of play within the play.' When Damon rushes in to stop the execution, he refers to the scaffold as a stage and declares that it is he who must 'play' on it.[1] Ironically, this exemplary 'performance' of the duties of friendship turns out to be the one thing which has any effect on Dionysius; it effects a sudden conversion, whose nature he himself defines:

this sight hath brought this aboute:
Which thy grave counsell Eubulus, and learned perswasion could never
    doo.
O noble gentlemen, the immortall Gods above,
Hath made you play this Tragidie, I thinke for my behove.

This is not only a statement of the superiority of examples to precepts; it is also a defence of the role of drama at a prince's court.[2]

Liberality and Prodigality is a less intellectual play and its ending seems rushed, perhaps as the result of revision, but it nevertheless offers many points of comparison with *Damon and Pithias*. In this case, Elizabeth's court is symbolized onstage as the court of Virtue, whose steward,

[1] *Shakespeare and the Idea of the Play*, (London, 1962), pp. 74–5.
[2] See J. E. Kramer, '*Damon and Pithias*, an Apology for Art', *ELH*, XXXV (1968).

Liberality, is shown distributing rewards and punishments according to desert; Craik has suggested that the recipients may have bowed to the queen in the audience.[1] Contrasted to it is the court of Fortune, a capricious ruler, with her steward Vanity. There is also a subordinate contrast between two of Fortune's suitors, Prodigality and Tenacity, each of whom has his turn at being rewarded by her. The career of Prodigality seems intended to parallel that of the prodigal son, and it is likely that at an earlier stage the scenes with the Hostess Dandaline and the gamblers Dick Dicer and Tom Toss may have been more fully developed than in the text as we have it. Still more than in Edwards's play, visual effects dominate language. Vanity's first speech indicates its emphasis (he is dressed in feathers):

> In words, to make description of my name,
> My nature or conditions, were but vaine,
> Sith this attire so plainely shewes the same,
> As shewed cannot be in words more plaine.

It is full of other visually symbolic actions: the various appearances of Money, now thin and ragged because he has been exhausted by Prodigality, now fat and sluggish because Tenacity never lets him out of doors; Fortune in her chariot drawn by kings; Prodigality's attempt to climb up to Fortune – a classic symbol of aspiration, which leads to his being nearly hanged. The murder of Tenacity by Prodigality, which takes place offstage, is allegorically less satisfactory, but it makes possible the trial scene at the end where he announces his intention of reforming and is given a reprieve – a compliment to the mercy of the queen. Liberality claims that

> what account, how sleight regard, is had of vertue here,
> By actions on this worldly stage, most plainely doth appeare.

As in *Gorboduc*, we find the phrase 'worldly stage'. But here it is ambivalent, meaning not only the world-as-stage but also the stage-as-world. The speaker goes on to distinguish between the two courts: that of Fortune, which destroys men, and that of Virtue (Elizabeth), which rescues and rewards them according to their desert. By dividing the glamorous and sinister aspects of court life between two separate rulers, the author was able to avoid raising the awkward questions of *Damon and Pithias*. Eternal, perfect, all-seeing, the queen as God on earth had become the only refuge for the victims of worldly aspiration.

---

[1] *The Tudor Interlude*, p. 117.

Queen Elizabeth's talent for inspiring ceremony and pageantry had its most impressive consequence in the Kenilworth entertainment of 1575. A reminiscence of the occasion may lie behind Wapull's *The Tide Tarrieth No Man* (1576), in which the courtier, Willing-to-Win-Worship, is described as selling his jewels and borrowing money at extortionate rates of interest in order to make a gallant show at some court celebration. Dressing up and play-acting were the essence of Leicester's entertainment. Some of the 'devices' which would have required the most direct participation from her majesty were not in the end presented – for instance, the elaborate nocturnal battle on the water, where Elizabeth was to have been invited to go out in her barge and put an end to the tyranny of Sir Bruce Sans Pitié over the Lady of the Lake. Leicester himself did his best to use the occasion to argue the case for marriage over chastity. But Gascoigne, who wrote many of the speeches for the occasion, was still more assiduous in acting out his own persona, a combination of prodigal son and 'salvage man'. His manner since 1574 had been that of the repentant sinner, after a career which included imprisonment for debt and accusations (apparently not unfounded) of ruffianly conduct, bankruptcy, spying and manslaughter. In a scene which also served to explain the meaning of the devices used at the queen's arrival (evidently many spectators needed to be told what they had seen), Gascoigne, 'all in Ivie', conducted a long conversation with Echo in which he was able to ask the reason for such a concourse of spectators and other pertinent questions. Having established the identity of the royal visitor, the Salvage Man then fell to his knees, converted at once from his rude way of life, and expressed his desire to serve such a beautiful woman. The queen apparently remarked that he must be blind to make such remarks, because Gascoigne followed his little play with a sequel, though it was left unperformed. On a later day, he intended to have the 'son' of the Salvage Man appear to the queen and tell her that his father was languishing in a wretched state which required her healing presence,

> For sure he is nor blinde,
>   Nor lame of any limme:
> But yet because you tolde him so,
>   He doubts his eyes are dimme.

Gascoigne's flirtation with the queen – for that is obviously what it was – was partly a plea for a post at court; he was appealing to her as the symbol both of fortune, which could reinstate him in this world, and of virtue, which had converted his misspent youth. *The Glass of Government*, similarly, sees fortune and virtue as complementary. The other works which Gascoigne published before his death in 1577 include a translation of the *De Contemptu Mundi* of Innocent III.

Amid all the pageantry at Kenilworth, with its sophisticated use of British and classical mythology, we find one interesting offering from the past. A group of Coventry citizens asked the queen's permission to revive what was described as 'their old storiall sheaw' – a Hock Tuesday play. It seems to have been essentially a folk combat with rhymed speeches, involving the fighting and beating of men by women that can also be found in *Cambises*, *Horestes* and some versions of the mystery play about the Slaughter of the Innocents. To the Coventry men, however, it was the commemoration of a historical event and an occasion for local pride. Their comments on it, as described by Robert Laneham in his extraordinary phonetic spelling, record what must have been a widespread sixteenth-century wistfulness about the passing of pre-Reformation dramatic traditions, even on the part of men who otherwise accepted the new order:

> This thing, said they, is grounded on story [i.e. history], and for pastime woont to bee plaid in oour Citee yeerely: without ill exampl of mannerz, papistry, or ony superstition: and elz did so occupy the heads of a number, that likely inoough woold have had woorz meditationz: had an auncient beginning, and a long continuauns: tyll noow of late laid dooun, they knu no cauz why, onless it wear by the zeal of certain theyr Preacherz: men very commendabl for their behaviour and learning, and sweet in their sermons, but sumwhat too sour in preaching awey theyr pastime.[1]

The continuity between medieval and Elizabethan dramatic methods was not seriously disturbed by the zeal of the preachers. The dramatists who wrote later for the professional playhouses were naturally concerned above all to emphasize their difference from their predecessors; they ridiculed the small size of the companies, the frantic doubling, the doggerel verse, the crude humour of the Vice, and, as always in this kind of theatrical joke, the sheer number of things that kept going wrong. But a fifteenth-century spectator who suddenly found himself transported to a performance of *Tamburlaine* or the *Henry VI* plays would have seen little to surprise him.

---

[1] *Robert Laneham's Letter*, ed. F. J. Furnivall, New Shakespere Society (1890), pp. 26–7. It is also quoted in E. K. Chambers, *The Mediaeval Stage*, 2 vols (Oxford, 1903), and its origins are discussed in vol. I, pp. 154–5.

He would have been familiar with the king surrounded by counsellors, the battles and sieges, the circular space symbolizing the world. It is the language of the drama that would have been new to him. Yet even this could not have developed its densely metaphorical qualities without a long dramatic tradition which had acted out the very images which audiences were now being asked to visualize. It was Everyman's departure on his journey to heaven with Good Deeds which made it possible for Webster to write his macabre reversal of the allegory. In *The White Devil*, Flamineo, pretending to be dying, cries out, like Everyman, for a companion on his journey:

FLAMINEO.   O the waies darke and horrid! I cannot see,
            Shall I have no company?
VITTORIA.   O yes thy sinnes,
            Do runne before thee to fetch fire from hell,
            To light thee thither. (V.6. 139–42)

The audience's familiarity with visual symbolism also made it possible for dramatists to play off contrasting effects of sight and sound. One of the greatest poetic moments in *Tamburlaine* is the hero's speech on man's aspiring mind and its natural goal, 'The sweet fruition of an earthly crown'. At the foot of the speaker, however, lies the dying king Cosroe, whose image speaks, in its way, as loudly as Tamburlaine's:

Take hede of this caytyfe that lyeth here on grounde;
Beholde how Fortune on hym hath frounde....
Today a lorde, to morowe ly in the duste:
Thus in this worlde there is no erthly truste.
                    (*Magnificence*, ll. 1946–7, 2538–9)

Bibliography

Abbreviations

AUMLA	*Journal of the Australian Universities Modern Language and Literature Association*
CBEL	*Cambridge Bibliography of English Literature*
DNB	*Dictionary of National Biography*
EETS	Early English Text Society
ELH	*Journal of English Literary History*
ELN	*English Language Notes*
HLQ	*Huntington Library Quarterly*
JEGP	*Journal of English and Germanic Philology*
MLN	*Modern Language Notes*
MLQ	*Modern Language Quarterly*
MLR	*Modern Language Review*
MP	*Modern Philology*
MSC	Malone Society Collections
MSR	Malone Society Reprints
N & Q	*Notes and Queries*

PMLA	Publications of the Modern Language
	Association of America
PQ	Philological Quarterly
RES	Review of English Studies
Sh.Q.	Shakespeare Quarterly
Sh.S.	Shakespeare Survey
SP	Studies in Philology
STS	Scottish Text Society
TFT	Tudor Facsimile Texts
TLS	Times Literary Supplement

I The social and historical context

The most complete accounts of the medieval stage are to be found in E. K. Chambers's *The Mediaeval Stage*, 2 vols (Oxford, 1903), K. Young's *The Drama of the Mediaeval Church*, 2 vols (Oxford, 1933), and H. Craig's *English Religious Drama of the Middle Ages* (Oxford, 1955). However, several works have caused a modification of some of the interpretations of evidence found in these books, particularly O. B. Hardison's *Christian Rite and Christian Drama in the Middle Ages* (Baltimore, Md, 1965), H. C. Gardiner's *Mysteries' End* (New Haven, Conn., 1946), F. M. Salter's *Mediaeval Drama in Chester* (Toronto, 1955), and G. Wickham's *Early English Stages 1300–1660*, Vol. I (London, 1959). Recent works on the Corpus Christi plays, such as R. Woolf's *The English Mystery Play* (Berkeley, Cal., 1972) and V. A. Kolve's *The Play Called Corpus Christi* (London, 1966), incorporate much of this new research.

Tabulation of the factual evidence about all plays of the period can be found in A. Harbage's *Annals of English Drama 975–1700*, rev. S. Schoenbaum (London, 1964), and full documentation of printing and publication is available in W. W. Greg's *A Bibliography of English Printed Drama to the Restoration*, 4 vols (London, 1939–59). Information about performances comes from various sources. Contemporary accounts of court festivities are included by E. Hall in his *The Union of the Two Noble and Illustre Famelies of Lancastre and Yorke* (1548; London, 1809) and in the *State Papers Foreign and Domestic*. There are special studies of royal entertainments by S. Anglo, 'The Court Festivals of Henry VII', *Bulletin of the John Rylands Library*, Vol. XLIII (1960), pp. 12–45; E. Welsford, *The Court Masque* (Cambridge, 1927); M. S. Steele, *Plays and Masques at Court During the Reigns of Elizabeth, James, and Charles* (New Haven, Conn., 1926); and G. M. Sibley, *The Lost Plays and Masques 1500–1642*

(Ithaca, NY, 1933). The court Revels Office and its operations have been extensively studied. E. K. Chambers published his *Notes on the History of the Revels Office under the Tudors* (Oxford, 1906) and has an essay on the same topic in *The Elizabethan Stage*, Vol. I. Transcriptions of the Office's records are in A. Feuillerat's *Documents Relating to the Revels at Court in the Time of King Edward VI and Queen Mary* (Louvain, 1914) and *Documents Relating to the Office of the Revels in the Time of Queen Elizabeth* (Louvain, 1908), published as part of W. Bang's *Materialien zur Kunde des älteren englischen Dramas*. A. Edinborough has an important note in *Sh.Q.*, II (1951) on 'The Early Tudor Revels Office', and Sir Thomas Benger's tenure of the mastership is dealt with in F. B. Benger's *A Calendar of References to Sir Thomas Benger, Master of the Revels and Masques to Queen Elizabeth, 1560–72* (printed privately, 1946).

The extensive theatrical activity outside the court is less well documented. F. S. Boas's *University Drama in the Tudor Age* (Oxford, 1914) is still the standard work in its field, and there is a useful survey by T. H. V. Motter in *The School Drama in England* (London, 1929). Records of college performances in Cambridge are available in G. C. Moore Smith's *College Plays Performed in the University of Cambridge* (Cambridge, 1923) and in MSC, II, 2 (1924); and R. E. Alton has transcribed the play entries from the account books of four Oxford colleges in MSC, V (1959). Playing at the Inns of Court is covered in A. W. Green's *The Inns of Court and Early English Drama* (New Haven, Conn., 1931) and R. J. Schoeck's 'Early Tudor Drama and the Inns of Court', *American Society for Theatre Research Newsletter* (November 1957); while the most thorough treatments of juvenile acting are in H. N. Hillebrand's *The Child Actors* (Urbana, Ill., 1926) and Vol. II of E. K. Chambers's *The Elizabethan Stage*. Records of other sponsored theatre are printed in various volumes of Malone Society Collections. Those for the City of London are in Vols I, 1 (1908), and II, 3 (1931); and for the Livery Companies in Vols III (1954) and V (1959). Public performances by itinerant entertainers in Kent between 1450 and 1642 and in Lincolnshire between 1300 and 1585 can be found in MSC, VII (1965) and VIII (1969–74). These volumes are part of a continuing series to supplement the records of provincial theatre activity which appear in J. T. Murray's *English Dramatic Companies 1558–1642*, 2 vols (London, 1910), and in E. K. Chambers's work.

There are a number of special studies of the relationship between the drama and historical events and social conditions. The best surveys of official efforts to control the stage are V. C. Gildersleeve's *Government*

Regulation of the Elizabethan Drama (New York, 1908), chapter 3 of G. Wickham's *Early English Stages 1300–1660*, Vol. II, Pt 1 (London, 1963), and E. K. Chambers's studies of the Revels Office. Most of the key documents of control can be found excerpted in Vol. IV of *The Elizabethan Stage*. D. M. Bevington's two books, *From 'Mankind' to Marlowe* (Cambridge, Mass., 1962) and *Tudor Drama and Politics* (Cambridge, Mass., 1968), have much information on the ways in which the drama was affected by contemporary social conditions; and H. C. White has a wide-ranging study of *Social Criticism in Popular Religious Literature of the Sixteenth Century* (New York, 1944). John Bale's dramatic propagandizing is fully treated by W. T. Davies in *Oxford Bibliographical Society Proceedings*, V (1940), and by J. W. Harris in *John Bale* (Urbana, Ill., 1940); and the relationships between Medwall, Rastell, Heywood and the Sir Thomas More family are dealt with in A. W. Reed's *Early Tudor Drama* (London, 1926) and P. Hogrefe's *The Sir Thomas More Circle* (Urbana, Ill., 1959).

It is possible to make only a very small selection from the enormous number of historical studies of the Tudor period. Surveys can be found in S. T. Bindoff's *England under the Tudors* (London, 1969), G. R. Elton's book of the same title (Cambridge, 1955), W. G. Zeeveld's *Foundations of Tudor Policy* (Cambridge, Mass., 1948), G. R. Elton's *The Tudor Revolution in Government* (Cambridge, 1959) and J. D. Mackie's *The Early Tudors 1485–1558* (Oxford, 1952). Good studies of the lives and reigns of the monarchs are G. Temperley's *Henry VII* (New York, 1918), J. J. Scarisbrick's *Henry VIII* (Berkeley, Cal., 1968), G. R. Elton's *Henry VIII: An Essay in Revision* (London, 1962), W. K. Jordan's *Edward VI: The Threshold of Power* (London, 1970), H. M. F. Prescott's *Mary Tudor* (London, 1934), P. Johnson's *Elizabeth I* (New York, 1974) and J. B. Black's *The Reign of Elizabeth* (Oxford, 1959). Detailed discussion of the religious changes of the time are J. Gairdner's *The English Church in the Sixteenth Century*, Vol. IV in W. R. W. Stephens and W. Hunt (eds), *A History of the English Church* (London, 1902), M. Powicke's *Reformation in England* (Oxford, 1941), A. G. Dickens's *The English Reformation* (London, 1964) and H. N. Birt's *The Elizabethan Religious Settlement* (London, 1907).

The intellectual and religious currents of the age are provocatively discussed by C. S. Lewis in his Introduction to *English Literature in the Sixteenth Century, Excluding Drama* (Oxford, 1954) and by G. Wickham in chapter 2 of his *Early English Stages 1300–1660*, Vol. II, Pt 1. Excellent working bibliographies on the topics of philosophy, travel, daily life, education and the arts during the period can also be found in pages 613–25 of Lewis's volume. However, the following studies, which make use of literary and dramatic evidence to depict the ideas, beliefs and social conditions of the time, may be of particular interest to the student of drama: E. M. W. Tillyard's *Elizabethan World Picture* (London, 1943), H. Craig's *The Enchanted Glass* (New York, 1936), H. Haydn's *The Counter-Renaissance* (New York, 1950), J. M. Bamborough's *The Little World of Man* (London, 1952), chapters 1–3 of M. M. Reese's *The Cease of Majesty* (London, 1961), I. Ribner's *The English History Play in the Age of Shakespeare* (London, 1965), F. Caspari's *Humanism and Social Order in Tudor England* (Chicago, Ill., 1954) and G. M. Trevelyan's *English Social History* (London, 1944).

II The technique of play presentation

Allardyce Nicoll's *The Development of the Theatre* (London, 1927) is a useful and well-illustrated general survey from the Greeks to the moderns. For the present period the later part of E. K. Chambers's *Mediaeval Stage*, 2 vols (Oxford, 1903), and the same author's *Elizabethan Stage*, 4 vols (Oxford, 1923), are indispensable. They are supplemented by the first two volumes of G. Wickham's *Early English Stages* (London, 1959, 1963). The influence of symmetrical design is well brought out in G. R. Kernodle's *From Art to Theater* (Chicago, Ill., 1944) and that of *English Pageantry* in R. Withington's study, 2 vols (Cambridge, Mass., 1918–20). The stage requirements and conventions of the interludes are a main subject of T. W. Craik's *The Tudor Interlude* (Leicester, 1958), of R. Southern's 'The Contribution of the Interludes to Elizabethan Staging', in *Essays on the Elizabethan Drama in Honour of Hardin Craig* (London, 1962), and of his *Staging of Plays before Shakespeare* (London, 1973).

III The companies and the repertory

The indispensable statement of the history of the Elizabethan companies and of their individual members is given by E. K. Chambers, *The*

Elizabethan Stage, 4 vols (Oxford, 1923): Book III, 'The Companies' (in Vol. II, pp. 1–350), is a detailed and specific account, but the whole work should be consulted, as should the same author's *The Mediaeval Stage*, 2 vols (London, 1903), for the pre-Elizabethan companies. J. T. Murray, *English Dramatic Companies 1558–1642*, 2 vols (London, 1910), records the travelling companies' tours. Giles E. Dawson (ed.), *Records of Plays and Players in Kent 1450–1642*, MSC, VII (1965), and Stanley J. Kahrl (ed.), *Records of Plays and Players in Lincolnshire 1300–1585*, MSC, VIII (1974), supersede the corresponding parts of Murray's work. Individual actors' brief biographies are collected in E. Nungezer's *A Dictionary of Actors and Other Persons associated with the Public Representation of Plays in England before 1642* (New Haven, Conn., and London, 1929); the careers of some representative ones are discussed in M. C. Bradbrook's *The Rise of the Common Player* (London, 1962), which deals with the social status of the Elizabethan actor in general. G. Wickham's *Early English Stages 1300–1660*, Vol. I (London, 1959) and Vol. II, (London 1, 1963), is also relevant to this latter aspect: see, in particular, Vol. I, ch. 8 ('Players and Commerce'), and Vol. II, Pt 1, chs 3 and 4 ('State Control of British Drama, 1530–1642'; 'Actors, Playmakers and Theatres under State Control'). State control has had a special study, V. C. Gildersleeve's *Government Regulation of the Elizabethan Drama* (New York, 1908). On all these matters Chambers's *Elizabethan Stage* is fundamental reading (Vol. I, chs 8–11: 'Humanism and Puritanism'; 'The Struggle of Court and City'; 'The Actor's Quality'; 'The Actor's Economics').

The best short introduction to the subject is in F. P. Wilson's *The English Drama 1485–1642* (Oxford, 1969). See also *Shakespeare's England*, 2 vols (Oxford, 1916), Vol. II (P. Simpson, 'Actors and Acting'); H. Granville-Barker and G. B. Harrison (eds), *A Companion to Shakespeare Studies* (Cambridge, 1934), ch. 2 (C. J. Sisson, 'The Theatres and Companies'); and K. Muir and S. Schoenbaum (eds), *A New Companion to Shakespeare Studies* (Cambridge, 1971), ch. 3 (Daniel Seltzer, 'The Actors and Staging'). See also A. W. Ward and A. R. Waller (eds), *The Cambridge History of English Literature*, 15 vols (Cambridge, 1932), Vol. VI, ch. 10 (H. Child, 'The Elizabethan Theatre') and ch. 11 (J. M. Manly, 'The Children of the Chapel Royal and their Masters').

On the boys' companies the standard work is H. N. Hillebrand's *The Child Actors* (Urbana, Ill., 1926). Detail has since been added by A. Brown's articles on John Redford, *MLR*, XLIII (1948), and on Sebastian Westcott, *MLR*, XLIV (1949); *MLQ*, XII (1951); *MLR*, XLVII (1952); Trevor Lennam gives much information about Westcott before and during his master-ship in his *Sebastian Westcott, the Children of Paul's, and 'The Marriage of Wit and Science'* (Toronto and Buffalo, 1975); and C. C. Stopes has a book-length study of 'William Hunnis and the Revels of the Chapel Royal', in W. Bang's *Materialien zur Kunde des älteren englischen Dramas*, Vol. XXIX (Louvain, 1910). T. H. V. Motter, *The School Drama in England* (London, 1929), includes grammar school performance. F. S. Boas, *University Drama in the Tudor Age* (Oxford, 1914), deals generally with university acting; see also G. C. Moore Smith, *College Plays performed in the University of Cambridge* (Cambridge, 1923). Michael Shapiro's *Children of the Revels* (New York, 1977) is chiefly concerned with performances after 1575.

T. W. Craik, *The Tudor Interlude* (Leicester, 1958), and D. M. Bevington, *From 'Mankind' to Marlowe* (Cambridge, Mass., 1962), indicate how a company's size and constitution were related to the plays it could perform. C. W. Wallace, *The Evolution of the English Drama up to Shakespeare* (Berlin, 1912), though in general superseded by Chambers and Hillebrand, is full of detail and still worth consulting. A. Feuillerat, *Documents Relating to the Office of the Revels* (in Bang's *Materialien*, Vol. XXI (1908), Elizabeth I; Vol. XXIV (1914), Edward VI and Mary), contains important editorial commentary. A. W. Reed, *Early Tudor Drama* (London, 1926), discusses the theatrical connections of Heywood, Rastell and Medwall.

IV The plays and the playwrights

Only post-1500 morality plays are included here. The first edition cited is normally the one from which quotations in the text have been taken.

(a) GENERAL

(i) *Bibliography*
Plays are listed and described in W. W. Greg, *A Bibliography of the English Printed Drama to the Restoration*, 4 vols (London, 1939–59), and Alfred Harbage (ed.), *Annals of English Drama 975–1700*, rev. Samuel Schoenbaum (London and Philadelphia, Pa., 1964). See also E. K. Chambers, *The*

Mediaeval Stage, 2 vols (Oxford, 1903), and *The Elizabethan Stage*, 4 vols (Oxford, 1923).

There is an excellent bibliography by G. K. Hunter in F. P. Wilson, *The English Drama 1485–1585* (Oxford, 1969), and a useful shorter one by T. W. Craik, 'Tudor and Early Elizabethan Drama', in *English Drama (Excluding Shakespeare)*, Select Bibliographical Guides, ed. Stanley Wells (Oxford, 1975). Carl J. Stratman's *Bibliography of Medieval Drama* (Berkeley and Los Angeles, Cal., 1954; rev. ed. New York, 1972) offers quantity rather than quality. A useful specialized bibliography is D. M. Bergeron, *Twentieth-Century Criticism of English Masques, Pageants, and Entertainments* (San Antonio, Texas, 1972), which includes a supplement on folk plays and related forms.

(ii) *Critical histories*

There are a number of good collections of essays on this period: the Stratford-upon-Avon Studies volumes on *Medieval Drama*, ed. Neville Denny (London, 1973), and *Elizabethan Theatre*, ed. J. R. Brown and Bernard Harris (London, 1966); Jerome Taylor and Alan H. Nelson (eds), *Medieval English Drama, Essays Contextual and Critical* (Chicago, Ill., and London, 1972); a special number of *Comparative Drama*, VIII (1974), is devoted to the medieval period. Most numbers of the periodical *Renaissance Drama* are also worth consulting.

For the period as a whole, see E. K. Chambers, *English Literature at the Close of the Middle Ages* (Oxford, 1945), and C. S. Lewis, *English Literature in the Sixteenth Century, Excluding Drama* (Oxford, 1954). There is a brief history of 'Stage and Drama till 1660' by Glynne Wickham in Christopher Ricks (ed.), *English Drama to 1710*, Vol. III of the Sphere History of Literature in the English Language (London, 1971). Good critical histories are A. P. Rossiter, *English Drama from Early Times to the Elizabethans* (London, 1950), and F. P. Wilson, *English Drama 1485–1585* (Oxford, 1969). The medieval background is well covered in Richard Axton, *European Drama of the Early Middle Ages* (London, 1974), Stanley J. Kahrl, *Traditions of Medieval English Drama* (London, 1974), and Anna J. Mill, *Mediaeval Plays in Scotland* (Edinburgh and London, 1927); while H. C. Gardiner, *Mysteries' End: An Investigation of the Last Days of the Medieval Religious Stage* (New Haven, Conn., 1946), traces the process by which the religious cycles were finally suppressed. See also Glynne Wickham, *Shakespeare's Dramatic Heritage: Collected Studies in Mediaeval, Tudor and Shakespearean Drama* (London, 1969). A. W. Reed, *Early Tudor*

Drama (London, 1926), is still the best source of information on dramatists of the 'More circle', who are also discussed in Pearl Hogrefe, *The Sir Thomas More Circle: A Program of Ideas and their Impact on Secular Drama* (Urbana, Ill., 1955).

Studies of the continental background include Leicester Bradner, 'The Rise of Secular Drama in the Renaissance', *Studies in the Renaissance*, III (1956); Merle Fifield, 'The Community of Morality Plays', *Comparative Drama*, IX (1975); C. H. Herford, *Studies in the Literary Relations of England and Germany in the Sixteenth Century* (Cambridge, 1886); and Grace Frank, *The Medieval French Drama* (Oxford, 1954).

(iii) *Dramaturgy*
The only full-length study of the verse of Tudor drama is J. E. Bernard, Jr, *The Prosody of the Tudor Interlude* (New Haven, Conn., 1936). R. Warwick Bond also discusses verse form in his Introduction to *Early Plays from the Italian* (Oxford, 1911). The analysis of the plays in terms of structure has been well done by David Bevington, *From 'Mankind' to Marlowe: Growth of Structure in the Popular Drama of Tudor England* (Cambridge, Mass., 1962), and, over a somewhat larger area, by Werner Habicht, *Studien zur Dramenform vor Shakespeare: Moralität, Interlude, romaneskes Drama* (Heidelberg, 1968). David Bevington has also investigated the controversial area of possible dramatic allusions to contemporary political events in *Tudor Drama and Politics* (Cambridge, Mass., 1968); a useful survey of one aspect of political thought is N. W. Bawcutt, '"Policy", Machiavellianism, and the Earlier Tudor Drama', *English Literary Review*, I (1971). T. W. Craik, *The Tudor Interlude: Stage, Costume, and Acting* (Leicester, 1958), is particularly good on theatrical and comic qualities of the plays. Staging is also discussed in several useful articles in *The Elizabethan Theatre*, Vol. V, ed. G. R. Hibbard (Toronto, 1975), and in Richard Southern, *The Staging of Plays Before Shakespeare* (London, 1973). On critical theory, see Madeleine Doran, *Endeavors of Art: A Study of Form in Elizabethan Drama* (Madison, Wisc., 1954). Two works which deal extensively with this period as part of their study of relations between the world and the stage are Anne Righter, *Shakespeare and the Idea of the Play* (London, 1962), and Jackson I. Cope, *The Theatre and the Dream: From Metaphor to Form in Renaissance Drama* (Baltimore and London, 1973). T. W. Baldwin, *William Shakespeare's Five-Act Structure* (Urbana, Ill., 1947), traces the development of classical ideas of plot and act division in the

sixteenth century. A number of early Elizabethan plays are discussed in Dieter Mehl, *The Elizabethan Dumb Show: The History of a Dramatic Convention* (Heidelberg, 1964; London, 1965), and in Marie Axton, 'The Tudor Mask and Elizabethan Court Drama' in Marie Axton and Raymond Williams (eds), *English Drama, Forms and Development* (Cambridge, 1977). A useful summary of 'Shakespeare's Allusions to the Older Drama' is given by Katherine H. Gatch in *PQ*, VII (1928).

(iv) *The morality play*

For the sermon background to some of the most popular allegorical themes, see G. R. Owst, *Literature and Pulpit in Medieval England: A Neglected Chapter in the History of English Letters and of the English People* (Oxford, 1933 and 1961). Important surveys of the field are those of E. N. S. Thompson, *The English Moral Plays*, Transactions of the Connecticut Academy of Arts and Sciences (New Haven, Conn., 1910); W. Roy Mackenzie, *The English Moralities from the Point of View of Allegory* (Boston and London, 1914); and Robert Potter, *The English Morality Play: Origins, History and Influence of a Dramatic Tradition* (London and Boston, 1975).

More attention has been paid to the Vice figure than to any other aspect of the morality. See, especially, Bernard Spivack, *Shakespeare and the Allegory of Evil: The History of a Metaphor in Relation to his Major Villains* (New York and London, 1958). A different view of the character is taken in F. H. Mares, 'The Origin of the Figure Called "The Vice" in Tudor Drama', *HLQ*, XXII (1958–9). See also Robert C. Jones, 'Dangerous Sport: The Audience's Engagement with Vice in the Moral Interludes', *Renaissance Drama*, N.S., VI (1973).

(v) *Comedy, romance and folk drama*

An excellent and very wide-ranging study is L. G. Salingar, *Shakespeare and the Traditions of Comedy* (Cambridge, 1974). For Continental and critical background, see Marvin T. Herrick, *Comic Theory in the Sixteenth Century* (Urbana, Ill., 1950) and *Tragicomedy: Its Origin and Development in Italy, France, and England* (Urbana, Ill., 1955); K. M. Lea, *Italian Popular Comedy*, 2 vols (Oxford, 1934); R. Warwick Bond, *Early Plays from the Italian* (Oxford, 1911). On Latin comedy, see Richard Hosley, 'The Formal Influence of Plautus and Terence', in J. R. Brown and Bernard Harris (eds), *Elizabethan Theatre* (London, 1966); B. R. Smith, 'Sir Amorous Knight and the Indecorous Romans; or, Plautus and Terence in the Renaissance', *Renaissance Drama*, N.S., VI (1973); and, in the same issue of *Renaissance Drama*, Ervin Beck, 'Terence Improved: The Paradigm of the Prodigal Son in English Renaissance Comedy'. F. H. Mares, 'The Treatment of Classical Materials in Some English Plays of the Sixteenth Century', *AUMLA*, XV–XVI (1961), is particularly concerned with the transition from Vice to Fool.

On romance, see C. R. Baskervill, 'Some Evidence for Early Romantic Plays in England', *MP*, XIV (1916–17), and Patricia Russell, 'Romantic Narrative Plays: 1570–1590', in J. R. Brown and Bernard Harris (eds), *Elizabethan Theatre* (London, 1966). Folk drama is discussed in Chambers, *The Mediaeval Stage* and *The English Folk Play* (Oxford, 1933; New York, 1966); C. R. Baskervill, 'Mummers' Wooing Plays in England', *MP*, XXI (1924); Alan Brody, *The English Mummers and Their Plays: Traces of Ancient Mystery* (n.d.); and Richard Axton, 'Folk Play in Tudor Interludes', in Marie Axton and Raymond Williams (eds), *English Drama, Forms and Development* (Cambridge, 1977). Special character types are covered in Enid Welsford, *The Fool: His Social and Literary History* (London, 1935; London and New York, 1961), and D. C. Boughner, *The Braggart in Renaissance Comedy: A Study in Comparative Drama from Aristophanes to Shakespeare* (Minneapolis, 1954).

(vi) *Tragedy*

Willard Farnham, *The Medieval Heritage of Elizabethan Tragedy* (Oxford, 1956), explores the origins and variations of the *contemptus mundi* theme. See also J. M. R. Margeson, *The Origins of English Tragedy* (Oxford, 1967); S. F. Johnson, 'The Tragic Hero in Early Elizabethan Drama', in Josephine W. Bennett, O. Cargill, Vernon Hall, Jr (eds), *Studies in English Renaissance Drama* (London, 1959); P. Happé, 'Tragic Themes in Three Tudor Moralities', *Studies in English Literature 1500–1900*, V (1965); W. Clemen, *English Tragedy Before Shakespeare: The Development of Dramatic Speech* (London, 1961).

The influence of Seneca is debated by J. W. Cunliffe in his introduction to *Early English Classical Tragedies* (Oxford, 1912); F. L. Lucas, *Seneca and Elizabethan Tragedy* (Cambridge, 1922); Howard Baker, *Induction to Tragedy: A Study of the Development of Form in 'Gorboduc', 'The Spanish Tragedy', and 'Titus Andronicus'* (Baton Rouge, La., 1939; New York, 1965); G. K. Hunter, 'Seneca and The Elizabethans: A Case-Study in "Influence"', *Sh.S.*, XXII (1967); R. J. Kaufmann, 'The Senecan Perspective and the Shakespearean Poetic', *Comparative Drama*, I (1967); Catherine Belsey, 'Senecan Vacillation and Elizabethan Deliberation: Influence or Confluence?', *Renaissance Drama*, N.S., VI (1973); and Jean Jacquot (ed.), *Les Tragédies de Sénèque et le théâtre de la Renaissance* (Paris, 1973). Ronald Broude, in '*Vindicta Filia Temporis*: Three English Forerunners of the Elizabethan Revenge Play', *JEGP*, LXXII (1973), derives the idea of revenge from Reformation emphasis on divine judgement. Glynne Wickham has also noted the connection between 'Neo-Classical Drama and the Reformation in England', in M. J. Anderson (ed.), *Classical Drama and Its Influence* (London, 1965). The most recent study is Renate Stamm's *The Mirror Technique in Senecan and pre-Shakespearean Tragedy*, Cooper Monographs, Vol. XXIII (Berne, 1975).

(vii) *Academic drama and the Inns of Court*
The standard works on school, university and Inns of Court, respectively, are T. H. V. Motter, *The School Drama in England* (London, 1929); F. S. Boas, *University Drama in the Tudor Age* (Oxford, 1914); and A. W. Green, *The Inns of Court and Early English Drama* (New Haven, Conn., 1931). More specialized information on children's companies is given in J. P. Brawner, 'Early Classical Narrative Plays by Sebastian Westcott and Richard Mulcaster', *MLQ*, IV (1943), corrected by Arthur Brown's 'Note on Sebastian Westcott and the Plays Performed by the Children of Paul's', *MLQ*, XI–XII (1951); and R. L. De Molen, 'Richard Mulcaster and the Elizabethan Theatre', *Theatre Survey*, XIII (1972).

(b) THE INDIVIDUAL PLAYS AND PLAYWRIGHTS

Many of these plays have been issued individually in Malone Society Reprints (MSR) or Tudor Facsimile Texts (TFT), which preserve the original spelling and punctuation. Useful anthologies include J. M. Manly, *Specimens of the Pre-Shakespearean Drama*, 2 vols (Boston, 1897–8; New York, 1967) – which is, however, slightly expurgated; Alois Brandl, *Quellen des weltlichen Dramas in England vor Shakespeare* (Strasbourg, 1898); R. Warwick Bond, *Early Plays from the Italian* (Oxford, 1911); J. W. Cunliffe, *Early English Classical Tragedies* (Oxford, 1912); J. Q. Adams, *Chief Pre-Shakespearean Dramas* (London, 1924); F. S. Boas, *Five Pre-Shakespearean Comedies* (Oxford, 1934); A. K. McIlwraith, *Five Elizabethan Tragedies* (Oxford, 1938); E. T. Schell and J. D. Schuchter, *English Morality Plays and Moral Interludes* (New York, etc., 1969); Peter Happé, *Tudor Interludes* (Harmondsworth, 1972); T. W. Craik, *Minor Elizabethan Tragedies* (London, 1974); J. A. B. Somerset, *Four Tudor Interludes* (London, 1974);

D. M. Bevington, *Medieval Drama* (Boston, etc., 1975), which is intended as a replacement of the Adams collection; and Glynne Wickham, *English Moral Interludes* (London, 1976). These will be cited below under the names of their editors. Translations of four continental interludes, along with a modernized text of Heywood's *Johan Johan*, are available in N. Denny, *Medieval Interludes* (London, 1972).

A number of dramatic fragments have been edited in Malone Society Collections (MSC). These include *Albion Knight*, MSC, I (iii), *Four Cardinal Virtues*, MSC, IV; *Love Feigned and Unfeigned*, MSC, I (i); *Pater, Filius, Uxor, or, The Prodigal Son*, MSC, I (i); *Processus Satanae*, MSC, II (iii); *Somebody and Others, or the Spoiling of Lady Verity*, MSC, II (iii); *Temperance and Humility*, MSC, I (iii); and two fragments of *The Cruel Debtor*, entered in the Stationers' Register as by 'Wager', MSC, I (iv and v) and MSC, II (ii).

R. B. [Richard Bower?], *Apius and Virginia*
Editions: MSR, Adams, Happé.
Criticism: See above, Section IV (a) (vi), especially the articles of Catherine Belsey and Peter Happé.

John Bale
Editions: All the plays are available in TFT and, modernized, in J. S. Farmer, *The Dramatic Writings of John Bale* (London, 1907). Wickham reprints *The Temptation of Our Lord*. A transcript of the manuscript of *King John* was made for the MSR by J. H. P. Pafford (1931), but the play is available in many modernized editions and can be read most easily in that of Barry B. Adams (San Marino, Cal., 1969).
Biography and criticism: Both Honor McCusker, *John Bale: Dramatist and Antiquary* (Bryn Mawr, 1942), and Jesse W. Harris, *John Bale: A Study in the Minor Literature of the Reformation* (Urbana, Ill., 1942), contain a good deal of useful information, but the best critical study is Thora B. Blatt, *The Plays of John Bale: A Study of Ideas, Technique and Style* (Copenhagen, 1968). See also E. S. Miller, 'The Antiphons in Bale's Cycle of Christ', *SP*, XL (1951); Irving Ribner, *The English History Play in the Age of Shakespeare* (Princeton, NJ, 1957); and S. F. Johnson, 'The Tragic Hero in Elizabethan Drama', in Bennett *et al.* (eds), *Studies in English Renaissance Drama* (London, 1959).

Calisto and Melebea
Editions: MSR, TFT. H. Warner Allen's edition of *The Celestina* (Broad-

way Translations, n.d.) prints the interlude along with Mabbe's 1631 translation of the Spanish novel, which unfortunately is too free to be used for purposes of comparison. The introduction of this edition is extremely informative.

Criticism: A. S. W. Rosenbach, 'The Influence of "The Celestina" in the Early English Drama', *Jahrbuch der deutschen Shakespeare-Gesellschaft*, XXXIX (1903), has recently been supplemented by a closer comparison of the novel and the interlude in H. D. Purcell, 'The *Celestina* and the Interlude of *Calisto and Melebea*', *Bulletin of Hispanic Studies*, XLIV (1967). See also A. W. Reed, *Early Tudor Drama*, for a discussion of authorship.

Clyomon and Clamydes
Editions: MSR, TFT, also the edition by B. J. Littleton (The Hague, 1968).

Criticism: The play's authorship and parallels with other works of the period are discussed by E. Kellner, '*Sir Clyomon and Sir Clamydes*: Ein romantisches Schauspiel des 16. Jahrhunderts', *Englische Studien*, XIII (1889), and G. L. Kittredge, 'Notes on Elizabethan Plays', *JEGP*, I (1898). The source is identified in Lucy Mary Ellison, *The Early Romantic Drama at the English Court* (London, 1917).

Common Conditions
Editions: C. F. Tucker Brooke (New Haven, Conn., 1915) gives the most complete text.

Criticism: C. F. Tucker Brooke, 'The Source of *Common Conditions*', *MLN*, XXXI (1916). See also above, Section IV (a) (v).

Richard Edwards, *Damon and Pithias*
Editions: MSR, TFT, Adams. A song for his lost play, *Palamon and Arcite*, is printed in Hyder E. Rollins, 'A Note on Richard Edwards', *RES*, IV (1928).

Biography: See Leicester Bradner, *The Life and Poems of Richard Edwards* (New Haven, Conn., etc., 1927). The Oxford performance of *Palamon and Arcite* is described in F. S. Boas, *University Drama in the Tudor Age*, and contemporary accounts are reprinted by W. Y. Durand in *PMLA*, N.S., XIII (1905).

Criticism: W. A. Armstrong discusses 'The Sources of *Damon and Pithias*', *N & Q*, CCI (1956). See also L. J. Mills, 'Some Aspects of *Damon and Pithias*', *Indiana University Studies*, LXXV (1927); J. L. Jackson, 'Three Notes on Richard Edwards' *Damon and Pithias*', *PQ*, XXIX (1950); A. Holaday, 'Shakespeare, Richard Edwards, and the Virtues Reconciled', *JEGP*, LXVI (1967); and J. E. Kramer, '*Damon and Pithias*: An Apology for Art', *ELH*, XXXV (1968).

Ulpian Fulwell, *Like Will to Like*
Editions: TFT, Happé and Somerset.
 Biography: See Irving Ribner, 'Ulpian Fulwell and His Family', *N & Q*, CXCV (1950), and 'Ulpian Fulwell and the Court of High Commission', *N & Q*, CXCVI (1951). Robert C. Jones, in the *Yearbook of English Studies*, III (1973), suggests that Jonson may have known and used the play's Vice hero in *The Staple of News*.

Thomas Garter, *The Comedy of the Most Virtuous and Godly Susanna*
Editions: MSR.
 Criticism: M. T. Herrick, 'Susanna and the Elders in Sixteenth-Century Drama', *Studies in Honour of T. W. Baldwin* (Urbana, Ill., 1958).

George Gascoigne
Editions: The plays and his account of *The Princely Pleasures at Kenilworth Castle* are printed in J. W. Cunliffe (ed.), *The Works of George Gascoigne* (Cambridge, 1907–10). Cunliffe also edited *The Supposes* and *Jocasta* for the Belles Lettres Series (Boston, 1906), with the Italian and English texts on facing pages. *Jocasta* can also be found in Cunliffe's *Early English Classical Tragedies*, and *The Supposes* in Boas.
 Biography and criticism: C. T. Prouty, *George Gascoigne: Elizabethan Courtier, Soldier and Poet* (New York, 1942), and R. C. Johnson, *George Gascoigne* (New York, 1972). Linda B. Salamon, 'A Face in *the Glasse*: Gascoigne's *Glasse of Government* Re-Examined', *SP*, LXXI (1974), points out the influence of Ascham and Elyot.

Gentleness and Nobility
Editions: MSR, TFT. The edition by K. W. Cameron, *Authorship and Sources of Gentleness and Nobility: A Study in Early Tudor Drama* (Raleigh, NC, 1941), is also the most thorough critique of the play.
 Criticism: See under Heywood and Rastell, the two most frequently suggested authors.

Godly Queen Hester
Editions: The best is still W. W. Greg's in Bang, *Materialien zur Kunde des älteren englischen Dramas* (Louvain, 1904).

John Heywood
Editions: The six plays attributed to Heywood are printed in TFT and in a modernized edition by J. S. Farmer, *The Dramatic Works of John Heywood* (London, 1905). There are many editions of individual plays. For *Love*, see Somerset; for *Weather*, Happé or Bevington; for *The Four PP*, Boas; for *Johan Johan*, Manly, Adams or Bevington. *Witty and Witless* is printed in R. de la Bere's *John Heywood, Entertainer* (London, 1937) and, with a full discussion of sources, by K. W. Cameron, *The Background of John Heywood's Witty and Witless: A Study in Early Tudor Drama, together with a Specialized Bibliography of Heywood Scholarship* (Raleigh, NC, 1941). Cameron is also responsible for a source study of *Weather* (Raleigh, NC, 1941).

   Biography and bibliography: A more recent bibliography than Cameron's, above, was compiled by S. A. and D. R. Tannenbaum in 1946. See also the most recent biography, R. C. Johnson, *John Heywood* (New York, 1970).

   Criticism: For the context of the 'More circle', see A. W. Reed, *Early Tudor Drama*, and Pearl Hogrefe, *The Sir Thomas More Circle* (Urbana, Ill., 1955). Elizabeth Merrill, *The Dialogue in English Literature*, Yale Studies in English (New Haven, Conn., 1911; repr. 1969), gives a useful survey of the form. The link between French farce and Wolsey's foreign policy was pointed out in a letter to the *TLS* by Sidney Thomas (7 December 1935); Ian Maxwell discusses *French Farce and John Heywood* (Melbourne and London, 1946), but the publication of Gustave Cohen, *Recueil de farces françaises inédites du XVe siècle*, Medieval Academy of America (Cambridge, Mass., 1949), enabled one of his parallels to be corrected by T. W. Craik, 'The True Source of John Heywood's *Johan Johan*', *MLR*, XLV (1950), and by W. Elton in a letter to the *TLS* (1950). Two brief studies of Heywood are D. M. Bevington, 'Is John Heywood's *Play of the Weather* really about the Weather?', and T. W. Craik, 'Experiment and Variety in John Heywood's Plays', both in *Renaissance Drama*, N.S., VII (1964).

Hickscorner
Editions: TFT, Manly.
   Criticism: The play has attracted attention mainly because of its close verbal parallels with *Youth*. See E. T. Schell, '*Youth* and *Hickscorner*:

Which Came First?' *PQ*, XLV (1966), and Ian Lancashire, 'The Sources of *Hickscorner*', *RES*, N.S., XXII (1971).

Impatient Poverty
Editions: R. B. McKerrow in Bang, *Materialien zur Kunde des älteren englischen Dramas* (Louvain, 1911), which contains a discussion of the play's date and background; also TFT.

Thomas Ingelend, *The Disobedient Child*
Editions: TFT. The play's source, Textor's dialogue *Juvenis, Pater, Uxor*, is printed by F. Holthausen in *Englische Studien* (1902), with some discussion of parallels and differences.

Jack Juggler
Editions: MSR.
    Criticism: The source of the play and its 'identity crisis' are discussed in R. Marienstras, '*Jack Juggler*, aspects de la conscience individuelle dans une farce du 16e siècle', *Études anglaises*, XVI (1963); further sources are suggested by Jacques Voisine, 'A propos de *Jack Juggler*', *Études anglaises*, XVIII (1965), with a brief reply by Marienstras. See also under Udall.

Jacob and Esau
Editions: MSR, TFT.
    Criticism: The date, and parallels with Calvin's *Institutes*, are discussed in G. Scheurweghs, 'The Date of "The History of Jacob and Esau"', *English Studies*, XV (1933). A modification of this view is proposed in Helen Thomas, '*Jacob and Esau* – "rigidly Calvinistic"?', *Studies in English Literature*, IX (1969).

John Jeffere (Jeffrey?), *The Bugbears*
Editions: R. Warwick Bond.

John the Evangelist
Editions: MSR.
    Criticism: H. Bradley, in *MLR*, II (1906–7), and W. H. Williams, in *MLR*, III (1907–8), propose textual emendations of this badly printed play.

July and Julian
Editions: MSR

King Darius
Editions: TFT and Brandl.

Liberality and Prodigality
Editions: MSR, TFT.

Sir David Lindsay (or Lyndsay), *A Satire of the Three Estates*
Editions: The standard edition of Lindsay's works, ed. Douglas Hamer, 4 vols, Scottish Text Society (Edinburgh, 1931–6), prints the two extant texts of the play (that of the Bannatyne MS, and the 1602 printed edition) on facing pages, with some rearrangement of the MS to achieve the parallel. James Kinsley has edited the play on the basis of the 1602 text, with a critical introduction by Agnes Muir Mackenzie and an essay by Ivor Brown on the version performed at the Edinburgh Festival (London, 1954).
    Criticism: W. Murison, *Sir David Lyndsay: Poet and Satirist of the Old Church in Scotland* (Cambridge, 1938), is primarily concerned to show that the play's anticlerical satire is historically justified. Textual problems have absorbed a good deal of critical attention: see R. A. Houk, 'Versions of Lindsay's *Satire of the Three Estates*', *PMLA*, LV (1940). Anna J. Mill reviews the evidence for 'The Influence of the Continental Drama on Lyndsay's "Satyre of the Thrie Estaitis"', *MLR*, XXV (1930). The date of the play's first performance is discussed by John MacQueen, Anna J. Mill, Vernon Harward and Joanne S. Kantrowitz in *Studies in Scottish Literature*, Nos 3 (1966), 6 (1968), 7 (1970) and 10 (1972) respectively. Joanne Kantrowitz has since published *Dramatic Allegory: Lindsay's Ane Satyre of the Thrie Estaitis* (Lincoln, Neb., 1975).

Thomas Lupton, *All for Money*
Editions: TFT, Schell and Schuchter.
    Criticism: T. W. Craik, 'Some Notes on Thomas Lupton's *All for Money*', *N & Q*, CXCIX (1954).

The Marriage of Wit and Science
Editions: MSR, TFT and the edition by Trevor Lennam, in *Sebastian Westcott, The Children of Paul's, and 'The Marriage of Wit and Science'* (Toronto, 1975).
    Criticism: See the introduction to Lennam's edition, also the review of it by T. W. Craik, *N & Q*, CCXXI (1976). The three 'Wit' plays are often discussed together: e.g. in Werner Habicht, 'The Wit Interludes and

the Form of Pre-Shakespearean "Romantic Comedy"', *Renaissance Drama*, VIII (1965). See also R. S. Varma, 'Philosophical and Moral Ideas in *The Marriage of Wit and Science*', *PQ*, XLIV (1965).

Henry Medwall
Editions: *Nature* can be found in TFT and Brandl; *Fulgens and Lucrece* is edited by F. L. Boas and A. W. Reed (London, 1926) and in the anthologies of Boas, Wickham and (extracts only) Happé.
   Biography and criticism: A. W. Reed, *Early Tudor Drama*, tells what little is known of this author. C. R. Baskervill, 'Conventional Features of Medwall's *Fulgens and Lucrece*', *MP*, XXIV (1926–7), points out resemblances to folk drama, while A. W. Reed compares it with a continental play based on the same source in 'Sixt Birck and Henry Medwall', *RES*, II (1926). The debate background is discussed in E. M. Waith, '*Controversia* in the English Drama: Medwall and Massinger', *PMLA*, XXXV (1953). Robert C. Jones, 'The Stage World and the "Real" World in Medwall's *Fulgens and Lucrece*', *MLQ*, XXXII (1971), finds sophisticated theatricality in the relation between the English and Roman aspects of the play.

Francis Merbury, *The Marriage of Wit and Wisdom*
Editions: MSR, TFT, Wickham.
   Biography and criticism: See above, under *The Marriage of Wit and Science*. Trevor Lennam has compiled the facts about 'Francis Merbury, 1555–1611' in *SP*, LXV (1968). M. P. Tilley analyses the play's use of proverbs in *The Shakespeare Association Bulletin*, X (1935). S. A. Tannenbaum and W. W. Greg argue about disputed readings of the MS in *PQ*, IX (1930), X (1931) and XII (1933).

Misogonus
Editions: R. Warwick Bond, TFT.
   Criticism: See Bond's introduction. Several scholars since Bond have puzzled over its enigmatic indications of authorship; the latest is D. M. Bevington in *ELN*, II (1964).

New Custom
Editions: TFT.
   Criticism: L. M. Oliver, 'John Foxe and the Drama *New Custom*', *HLQ* , X (1946–7), gives the source of a story told in the play.

Nice Wanton
Editions: Manly, TFT, Wickham.

Thomas Norton and Thomas Sackville, *Gorboduc*
Editions: TFT, Cunliffe, McIlwraith, Craik, etc.
   Criticism: The fullest account of the play comes in Normand Berlin's recent biography, *Thomas Sackville*, Twayne's English Authors (New York, 1974). S. A. Small, 'The Political Import of the Norton Half of *Gorboduc*', *PMLA*, XLVI (1931), and S. R. Watson, '*Gorboduc* and the Theory of Tyrannicide', *MLR*, XXXIV (1939), argue that the Norton and Sackville portions of the play represent different political ideologies. See also R. Y. Turner, 'Pathos and the *Gorboduc* Tradition', *HLQ*, XXVI (1962), and above, Section IV (a)(vi).

The Pedlar's Prophecy
Editions: MSR and TFT.
   Criticism: The only real attempt to make sense of this play is G. L. Kittredge, 'The Date of *The Pedler's Prophecie*', *Harvard Studies and Notes in Philology*, XVI (1934).

John Phillip, *The Comedy of Patient and Meek Grissil*
Editions: MSR.
   Criticism: Louis B. Wright, 'A Political Reflection in Phillip's *Patient Grissil*', *RES*, IV (1928), thinks the advice given to Gautier about marriage may have been intended also for Elizabeth I.

John Pickering, *Horestes*
Editions: MSR, Brandl, TFT.
   Criticism: See above, Section IV (a)(vi). The most up-to-date account of the play's source is by Karen M. Merritt in *RES*, N.S., XXIII (1972). Political allusions are discussed by J. E. Phillips, *HLQ*, XVIII (1954), and R. S. Knapp, *ELH*, XL (1973). E. B. de Chickera, 'Horestes' Revenge – Another Interpretation?', *N & Q* (1959), argues that the play never questions the rightness of the hero's action.

Thomas Preston, *Cambises*
Editions: TFT, Manly, Craik. R. C. Johnson's *Critical Edition of Thomas Preston's Cambises* (Salzburg, 1975) reprints the source passage from Taverner.

Criticism: See above, Section IV (a)(vi); also, Don Cameron Allen, 'A Source for *Cambyses*', *MLN*, XLIX (1934); W. A. Armstrong, 'The Background and Sources of Preston's *Cambises*', *English Studies*, XXI (1950), and 'The Authorship and Political Meaning of *Cambises*', *English Studies*, XXXVI (1955). J. P. Myers, 'The Heart of King Cambises', *SP*, LXX (1973), argues that the play is thematically unified by the image of the heart.

John Rastell, *The Interlude of the Four Elements*
Editions: TFT.
   Criticism: Studies of this play have been confined mainly to the tracing of Rastell's scientific sources. See Johnstone Parr, 'More Sources of Rastell's *Interlude of the Four Elements*', *PMLA*, LX (1945), which gives references to earlier work in the field; also Pearl Hogrefe, *The Sir Thomas More Circle* (Urbana, Ill., 1955). The best biographical information on Rastell is to be found in A. W. Reed, *Early Tudor Drama*.

John Redford, *Wit and Science*
Editions: MSR (with some fragments also attributed to Redford), Schell and Schuchter, Happé, Bevington.
   Biography and criticism: See *The Marriage of Wit and Science*. Redford as a musician is discussed in W. H. Grattan Flood, *Early Tudor Composers* (London, 1925). Arthur Brown's 'Two Notes on John Redford', *MLR*, XLIII (1948), add some biographical information. See also J. W. Velz and C. P. Dow, Jr, 'Tradition and Originality in *Wyt and Science*', *SP*, LXV (1968).

Respublica
Editions: W. W. Greg in EETS (1952), TFT, Brandl, Happé (extracts).
   Criticism: Textual suggestions are made in T. W. Craik, 'The Text of *Respublica*: A Conjecture', *N & Q*, CXCVIII (1953), and G. A. Starr, 'Notes on *Respublica*', *N & Q*, CCVI (1961). See also under Udall.

Robin Hood and the Sheriff of Nottingham and *A Play of Robin Hood for May Games*
Editions: Manly, F. J. Child, *English and Scottish Popular Ballads*, Vol. III (Boston, Mass., 1888–9, often reprinted), and B. Dobson and J. Taylor, *Rymes of Robin Hood* (London, 1976).

'Mr S', *Gammer Gurton's Needle*
Editions: TFT, Boas, and many other editions.
   Criticism: Authorship is discussed in F. S. Boas, *University Drama in the Tudor Age*, which is also the best analysis of the play. J. C. Maxwell gives a useful textual emendation in *N & Q*, CXCVIII (1953).

Thomas Sackville; *see* Norton

John Skelton, *Magnificence*
Editions: R. L. Ramsay's edition for the EETS (London, 1908 and 1925) includes an important introduction.
   Criticism: Ramsay's view of the play has been a starting point for most subsequent criticism. His claim that *Magnificence* advocates an Aristotelian concept of the golden mean has been disputed by W. O. Harris, *Skelton's Magnificence and the Cardinal Virtue Tradition* (Chapel Hill, NC, 1965); his view of it as a satire on Cardinal Wolsey has also been questioned by recent scholars; see especially A. R. Heiserman, *Skelton and Satire* (Chicago, Ill., 1961). Skelton's use of *Piers Plowman* and *The Ship of Fools* is pointed out by Norma Phillips, 'Observations on the Derivative Method of Skelton's Realism', *JEGP*, LXV (1966). His use of proverbs and sentences is discussed in R. S. Kinsman, 'Skelton's *Magnyfycence*: The Strategy of the "Olde Sayde Sawe"', *SP*, LXIII (1966).

Thersites
Editions: TFT.
   Criticism: See under Ingelend for original Textor dialogue. Most of what has been written on this play is concerned with its authorship; see under Udall.

Tom Tyler and His Wife
Editions: MSR, TFT.

The Trial of Treasure
Editions: TFT.
   Criticism: Sources and parallels are discussed by E. Beatrice Daw, 'Two Notes on *The Trial of Treasure*', *MP*, XV (1917–18), and L. M. Oliver, 'William Wager and *The Trial of Treasure*', *HLQ*, IX (1946).

Nicholas Udall, *Ralph Roister Doister*
Editions: Adams, MSR, Boas.

  Biography and criticism: W. L. Edgerton, *Nicholas Udall* (New York, 1965), questions traditional interpretations of the facts known about this author; in particular, he defends Udall against the charges of apostasy. See also A. W. Reed, 'Nicholas Udall and Thomas Wilson', *RES*, I (1925). The sources of *Ralph Roister Doister* are discussed by J. Hinton in *MP*, II (1913–14), and the evidence for the play's date has most recently been reviewed by W. L. Edgerton in *PQ*, XLIV (1965). E. S. Miller, 'Roister Doister's "Funeralls"', *SP*, XLIII (1946), notes the implications of Udall's parody of the Roman liturgy.

Lewis Wager, *The Life and Repentance of Mary Magdalene*
Editions: TFT and F. I. Carpenter (Chicago, Ill., 1902 and 1904).

William Wager
Editions: *Enough is as Good as a Feast* is available in a reprint by S. de Ricci (San Marino, Cal., 1920) and in Schell and Schuchter. *The Longer Thou Livest the More Fool Thou Art* is in TFT. Both are also edited by R. M. Benbow in the Regents' Renaissance Drama Series (Lincoln, Neb., 1968).

George Wapull, *The Tide Tarrieth No Man*
Editions: TFT and Schell and Schuchter.

Wealth and Health
Editions: TFT and MSR.

  Criticism: T. W. Craik, 'The Political Interpretation of Two Tudor Interludes', *RES*, XIV (1953), and Rainer Pineas, 'The Revision of *Wealth and Health*', *PQ*, XLIV (1965), relate the play to its Reformation background.

Richard Wever, *Lusty Juventus*
Editions: TFT, MSR and Somerset.

Robert Wilmot and others, *Gismond of Salerne*
Editions: TFT and Cunliffe. Wilmot, the author of Act V, later revised the entire play under the title *Tancred and Gismund* (1591); this version is published in TFT and MSR.

Criticism: Apart from Cunliffe's introduction, see J. Murray, '*Tancred and Gismund*', *RES*, XIV (1938), and D. Klein, 'The Decorum of These Days', *PMLA*, XXXIII (1918), for a comparison of the two versions. Werner Habicht compares the two treatments of the Senecan nurse-scene in *Anglia*, LXXXI (1963).

Nathaniel Woodes, The Conflict of Conscience
Editions: TFT, MSR, Schell and Schuchter.
   Biography and criticism: For Woodes's life, see Celesta Wine, 'Nathaniel Woodes, Author of the Morality Play *The Conflict of Conscience*', *RES*, XV (1939). L. M. Oliver, 'John Foxe and *The Conflict of Conscience*', *RES*, XXV (1949), finds material from the *Acts and Monuments* in Philologus's interrogation. L. B. Campbell gives the full background of the Spira story in 'Doctor Faustus: A Case of Conscience', *PMLA*, LXVII (1952).

The World and the Child (*Mundus et Infans*)
Editions: Manly, TFT, Schell and Schuchter.
   Criticism: See H. N. MacCracken, 'A Source of *Mundus et Infans*', *PMLA*, N.S., XVI (1908).

Youth
Editions: TFT, Happé, Schell and Schuchter.
   Criticism: See *Hickscorner*.

Index

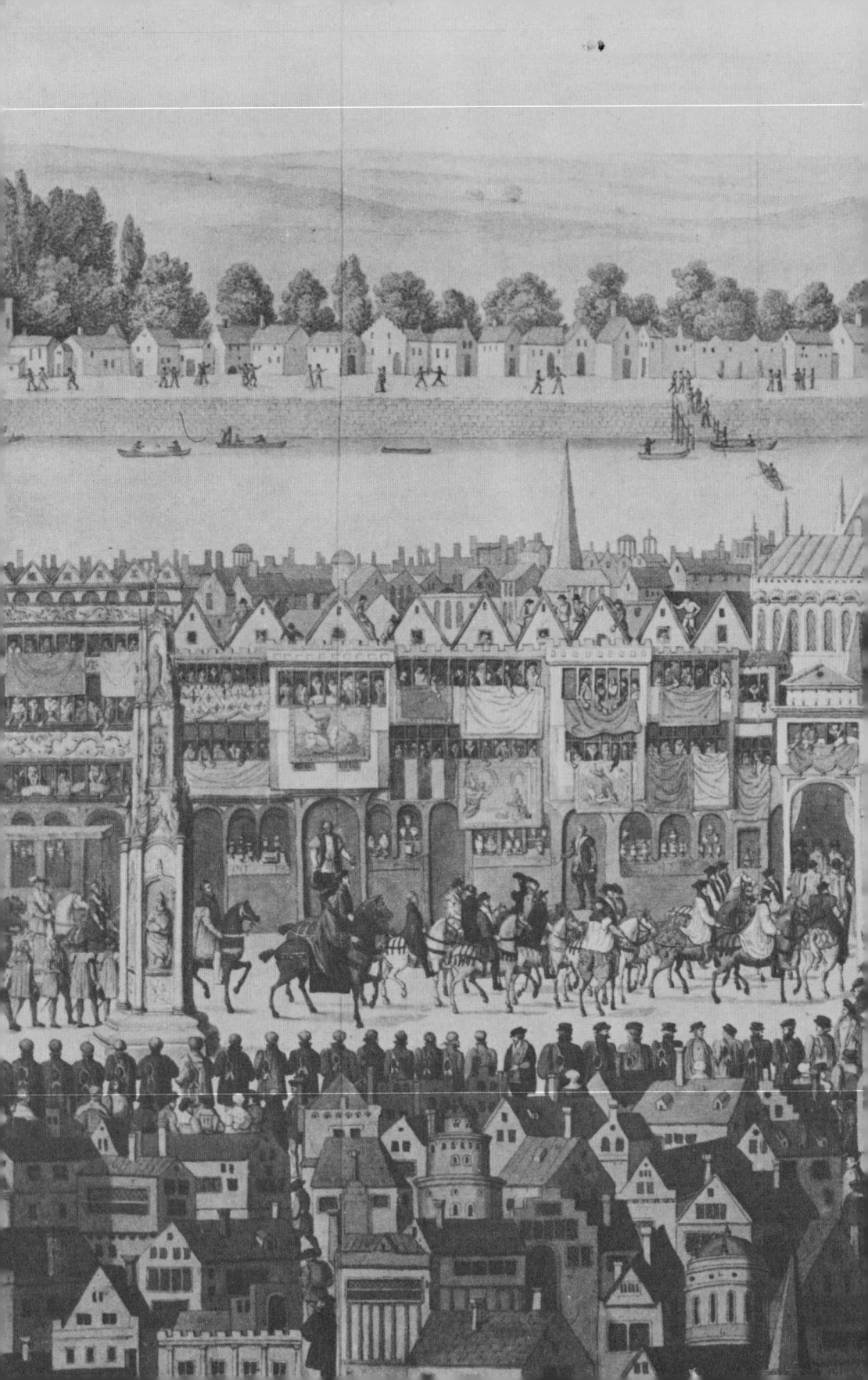